CORPORATE GOVERNANCE, DIGITALIZATION, AND ENERGY TRANSITION

CORPORATE GOVERNANCE, DIGITALIZATION, AND ENERGY TRANSITION

Imen Baccouche, PhD
Afef Khalil, PhD
Editors

AAP | APPLE ACADEMIC PRESS

First edition published 2026

Apple Academic Press Inc.
1265 Goldenrod Circle, NE,
Palm Bay, FL 32905 USA

760 Laurentian Drive, Unit 19,
Burlington, ON L7N 0A4, Canada

CRC Press
2385 NW Executive Center Drive,
Suite 320, Boca Raton FL 33431

4 Park Square, Milton Park,
Abingdon, Oxon, OX14 4RN, UK

Library and Archives Canada Cataloguing in Publication

CIP data on file with Canada Library and Archives

Library of Congress Cataloging-in-Publication Data

CIP data on file with US Library of Congress

ISBN: 978-1-77964-339-1 (hbk)
ISBN: 978-1-77964-340-7 (ebk)

DOI: 10.1201/9781779643407

Dedication

Dedicated to the tireless seekers of knowledge, whose curiosity and determination push back the boundaries of human understanding. Your dedication to unlocking the mysteries of the universe inspires us all to reach new heights of insight and innovation. May this compilation of wisdom and discovery be a testament to your relentless pursuit of truth.

—**Dr. Imen Baccouch**

Dedicates this book first and foremost to her mother "Najet" and her father "Kamel," who have always supported her through good times and bad. She also dedicates this book to her fellow researchers around the world. Research is about sharing insights and building community. Teaming up with others to create research knowledge has never been more crucial.

—**Dr. Afef Khalil**

About the Editors

Imen Baccouche, PhD
Researcher and Assistant Professor of Quantitative Methods, Tunis Higher School of Commerce (ESC), Tunisia

Imen Baccouch, PhD, is a Researcher and an Assistant Professor of Quantitative Methods at the Tunis Higher School of Commerce (ESC), Tunisia. She is the author of a book and several publications in international journals. Dr. Imen Baccouch is a member of the Economics and Industrial Management Laboratory (LEGI) at the Tunisia Polytechnic School, Tunisia. Her research interests include sustainable development, employability, energy transition and climate change.

Afef Khalil, PhD
Researcher and Assistant Professor, Higher Institute of Accounting and Business Administration (ISCAE), Tunisia

Afef Khalil, PhD, is a Researcher and an Assistant Professor at the Higher Institute of Accounting and Business Administration (ISCAE), Tunisia. She is a member of the "PRESTIGE" laboratory at the Institute of Higher Commercial Studies of Carthage (IHEC-Carthage), Tunisia. Dr. Khalil is the author of several books and publications in international journals. She is a referee and member of the editorial board of several journals.

Contents

Contributors

Mohammed El Amine Abdelli
IAE of Bretagne Occidentale-Laboratory of LEGO/ University of Western Brittany-UBO, France

Wissem Ajili
University of ESLSCA, France

Habiba Ben Ameur
Faculty of Economics and Management of Tunis, University of Tunis El Manar, Business and Research in Marketing (ERMA), Tunisia

Imen Baccouche
University of Manouba-ESC, Tunisia

Nizar Baklouti
Faculty of Economics and Management Sciences of Sfax, University of Sfax, Sfax, Tunisia

Naima Bentouir
Ain Temouchent University, Economics department, LMELSPM laboratory, Ain Temouchent, Algeria

Kaizar Chaimae
National School of Commerce and Management, University Chouaib Doukkali, El Jadida, Morocco

Luigi Pio Leonardo Cavaliere
Università di Foggia, Foggia, Italy

Fatine Fatima Ezzahra
National School of Commerce and Management, University Chouaib Doukkali, El Jadida, Morocco

Alessio Faccia
School of Business, University of Birmingham Dubai, Dubai, United Arab Emirates

Nadia Farjla
Department of Quantitative Methods, FSEG Sousse, Tunisia

Arsalan Hussain
College of Business Management, Institute of Business Management, Pakistan

Bincy Baburaj Kaluvilla
Emirates Academy of Hospitality Management, UAE

Afef Khalil
University of Manouba-ISCAE, Tunisia

Mourad Kertous
University of Brest, France

Mohamed Ali Khemiri
VPNC Lab, Faculty of Law, Economics and Management of Jendouba, University of Jendouba, Tunisia

Salma Mahouachi
ENVIE Laboratory, South Mediterranean University, Mediterranean School of Business, Tunis, Tunisia

Samir Maliki
University of Tlemecen, Algeria

Kaouther Saied Ben Rached
Faculty of Economics and Management of Tunis, University of Tunis El Manar, Tunisia

Manjeet Ridon
De Montfort University, Leicester, United Kingdom

Asma Sghaier
University of Toulon, France

Imen Ben Slimene
University of UHA, France

Rania Makni
Esprit School of Business, and Laboratory of Economics and Applied Finance (LEFA, LR05ES07), IHEC, Carthage University, Tunisia

Ritu Pareek
Birla Institute of Technology-Mesra, Jaipur Campus, India

Hilmi Yassine
National School of Commerce and Management, University Chouaib Doukkali, El Jadida, Morocco

Imed Zaiem
Faculty of Economics and Management Sciences, Nabeul, Tunisia

Preface

In recent years, the global landscape of corporate governance, digitalization, and energy transition has undergone radical transformations due to rapid advances in technology. These changes are having considerable impact on various sectors, including energy, economics, and governance. This book, entitled *Corporate Governance, Digitalization, and Energy Transition*, explores these interrelated areas and their implications for society today. It is a valuable resource for academics, practitioners, and policymakers seeking to master and understand the profound changes that lie ahead.

Coverage and Content of the Book

The book consists of 3 parts and 13 chapters. The book chapters highlight how technological innovations are reshaping corporate governance structures, facilitating the transition to sustainable energy systems and driving the digitalization of numerous facets of our lives.

Part I. Corporate Governance and Technological Transformations

The first part of the book explores the interaction between corporate governance and technology, and includes six chapters. The first chapter investigates the effect of the application of blockchain technology on corporate governance by presenting previous studies, company cases and the European Blockchain Service Infrastructure (EBSI) initiative. By applying blockchain technology to the evaluation of corporate governance, transactions carried out by companies in real time can be recorded and stored, enabling a large amount of information to be shared simultaneously. In Chapter 2, the authors analyze the impact of political stability on GDP from some Middle East and North Africa (MENA) countries (Egypt, Libya, Tunisia, and Algeria) during the period 1980–2020. Results show that indicators of corruption control and the rule of law have the highest impact on economic growth, while regulatory quality has the lowest. The third chapter aims to study the contribution of the implementation of a procedure manual for the international accounting standards IAS/IFRS's application, to the improvement of the internal control system within companies. Chapter 4 empirically investigates the effect of firms' practices on employment during the COVID-19 crisis. It further explores practices with which enterprises managed the lay-off effect during the COVID-19 crisis. The research paper highlights the importance of additional support measures that target the most vulnerable companies. In Chapter 5, the authors examine the impact of government support on the employment of small- and medium-sized enterprises (SMEs) during the COVID-19 crisis. A questionnaire survey was conducted based on 95 Tunisian SMEs used in this study. The main results indicate that during the COVID-19 pandemic, government support measures have had a positive impact on employment. This means that companies with higher employment rates need more financial relief and sales through credit. The authors of Chapter 6 highlight the difficulties that children experience when learning to eat healthily. It also covers the roles of parents, schools, and policymakers in promoting healthy eating among children. The authors conclude that it is essential to teach children to eat healthily and to create an environment that encourages good eating habits.

Part II. Digitalization

Besides completely altering our daily lives, digitalization has also modified the framework of business, research, and education. The second part of the book contains four chapters. In Chapter 7, the authors investigate the effect of attitude toward ChatGPT use on behavioral intention, highlighting the role of familiarity. An empirical study of 221 ChatGPT users shows that there is a significant relationship between attitude toward adopting this technology and behavioral intention. Moreover, familiarity positively moderates the link between these two variables. Chapter 8 discusses benefits and challenges of using Artificial Intelligence (AI) in education and explores its potential to improve student engagement, academic performance and institutional efficiency. Chapter 9 provides an overview of how digital platforms have become an integral part of education, with a focus on the Indian context. Results show that policymakers can develop targeted policies and initiatives to bridge the digital divide, ensuring that students in rural areas have equal access to digital education resources and opportunities. The authors of Chapter 10 focus on Malaysian SMEs' usage of fintech toward sustainable organizational performance with an international mindset as a moderating role. Results introduce the international mindset into current literature. This affects Malaysian SMEs' approach to risk in the context of their worldwide openness.

Part III. Energy Transition and Environmental Dynamics

The need for a sustainable energy transition has never been more pressing, even as the planet faces urgent environmental issues. The third part of this book explores the mechanisms of this transformation and provides pertinent information on its opportunities, challenges, and governance frameworks. This part comprises three chapters. Chapter 11 presents a review of blockchain technology's use for peer-to-peer exchanges between different stakeholders in the energy sector. They highlight the benefits of blockchain for the governance challenges associated with low-carbon energy and decentralized transitions. In Chapter 12, the authors examine the interaction between climate risk and liquidity risk in the MENA region. An empirical study of 68 MENA banks shows that any improvement in the climate risk index increases liquidity risk for Middle Eastern banks. However, there is no significant effect on North African banks. Finally, Chapter 13 emphasizes the effect of Environmental, Social, and Governance (ESG) criteria on the energy sector. This chapter invites investors to prioritize ESG components in their decision-making process, highlighting the benefits of socially responsible investment.

—***Editors***

Acknowledgments

The authors of the chapters and editors are equal partners in the production of this volume. The editors are very grateful to the authors for their valuable input. Our special thanks go to the reviewers for their precious comments and recommendations for improving the chapters in this book. The editors would also like to gratefully acknowledge the great support of the Apple Academic Press team for this project.

Abbreviations

ADF	Augmented Dickey–Fuller
AGFI	adjusted goodness-of-fit index
AI	artificial intelligence
AIC	Akaike Information Criteria
ARDL	Auto-Regressive Disseminated Slacks
BIC	Bayesian information criterion
BS	bank size
CAIC	Consistent Akaike Information Criterion
CAR	capital adequacy ratio
CEE	Central and Eastern European
CEF	Connecting Europe Facility
CRI	climate risk index
CSR	Corporate Social Responsibility
DAOs	decentralized autonomous organizations
DCT	dynamic capability theory
EBSI	European Blockchain Services Infrastructure
ESG	Environmental, Social, and Governance
GAFA	Google, Apple, Facebook, and Amazon
GMM	Generalized System of Moments
GPT	Generative Pretrained Transformer (GPT)
IAS	International Accounting Standards
ICRG	International Country Risk Guide Methodology
ICT	Information and Communication Technologies
IFRS	International Financial Reporting Standards
ILO	International Labor Organization
INF	inflation rate
ISO	International Organization for Standardization
ITS	Intelligent Tutoring Systems
LCOE	Levelized Cost of Energy
LMS	learning management system
LTD	loan-to-deposit
LTD	liquidity risk
MENA	Middle East and North Africa
NEP	National Education Policy
NGOs	nongovernment organizations
NLP	natural language processing

NPLs	nonperforming loans
PLS	partial least squares
POW	Proof of Work
PP	Phillips-Perron
RES	renewable energy sources
ROA	return on assets
ROI	return on investment
RPA	robotic process automation
SEM	structural equation model
SGMM	system-generalized method of moment's
SMEs	small- and medium-enterprises
SRI	Socially Responsible Investment
TOE	technological, organizational, and environmental

PART I

Corporate Governance and Technological Transformations

DOI: 10.1201/9781779643407-1

CHAPTER 1

Sustainable Corporate Governance Using Blockchain Technology

NIZAR BAKLOUTI

Faculty of Economics and Management Sciences of Sfax, University of Sfax, Sfax, Tunisia

ABSTRACT

This chapter investigates the potential impact of applying blockchain technology to corporate governance by presenting previous studies, corporate cases, and the European Blockchain Service Infrastructure initiative. The adaptation of blockchain technology to corporate governance can help decentralize the concentration of information by large Information and Communications Technologies global companies such as Google, Apple, Facebook, and Amazon (GAFA), and bring it back to the original internet. This also affects the corporate governance of GAFA. By applying blockchain technology to evaluate corporate governance, the transaction logs conducted by companies in real time can be recorded and preserved on this distributed ledger, enabling all participants to simultaneously share a large amount of information. This transaction history is difficult to tamper with using blockchain technology and enables real-time control and auditing of companies by stakeholders. This chapter proposes the application of blockchain technology to stakeholder management based on the fundamental concept of corporate governance and presents the possibility of solving environmental problems on a global scale and centralized concentration in the corporate world.

Corporate Governance, Digitalization, and Energy Transition: Imen Baccouche and Afef Khalil. (Eds.)

DOI: 10.1201/9781779643407-2

1.1 INTRODUCTION

The Coronavirus disease 2019 (COVID-19) pandemic has significantly disrupted the supply network encompassing individuals, goods, currency, and information. This novel condition of constrained mobility propels Information and Communication Technologies (ICT) to a level where they revolutionize how people interact, both virtually and in person. This facilitates fresh connections and spurred innovation. The deepening integration of ICT encourages novel concepts and inventive strategies in addressing COVID-19, recognized as a global challenge. These innovative approaches leverage a diverse array of ICT tools and reshape the conventional roles in orchestrating the movement and stockpiling of goods within supply chains, as well as price determination. This shift is in favor of embracing Industry 4.0 and blockchain technology, including the utilization of Bitcoin (BTC). This example can be interpreted according to contingency theory, moving from a static to a dynamic interpretation based on real-time data. COVID-19 is also a catalyst for innovation, making ambitious use of data, such as the dynamic analysis of the genome by Google's DeepMind. This approach to coupling ICT and pandemic management has a significant impact across all industry sectors.

In parallel with the societal evolution due to ICT, there is also growing interest in blockchain technology, often referred to as the "Internet of Value." The ecosystem around blockchain focuses on how the real world is represented in virtual space through network devices, as well as how information published in this ever-expanding virtual space is efficiently stored and used. Blockchain technology, initially associated with terms such as "virtual currency" or "crypto-currency" because of its use, is now considered a "crypto-asset" because of its potential for application in areas such as copyright, personal information, real estate, and supply chains. This is due to its ability to organize and store transaction history, which has earned it the nickname "Internet of Value." Blockchain technology is under development. It uses a system of mutual authentication of data between multiple computers, called peer-to-peer (P2P), to organize transaction history. This system creates a "distributed ledger" where information is shared equally among approximately 11,000 computers.

Although this revolutionary method of organizing, storing, and using information is promising, its use raises concerns because of its high energy consumption. The process of competing for the 6.25 BTC (approximately \$50,000 × 6.25 BTC = \$312,500) issued every 10 min in 2022 is challenging in terms of energy consumption. Competition in the mining operation was introduced by Wright (2008), allowing the P2P system to operate in an autonomous and decentralized manner. This competition, which is provided by the mining operation, is the basis of BTC's autonomy. Currently, the mining method evolves from Proof of Work (POW), which involves perfect competition, to Proof of Stake (POS), which resembles a monopoly or oligopoly in economic markets. The POW and POS protocols also use renewable energy sources to reduce their environmental impact. For example, high energy consumption is mitigated by decentralizing energy sources and using renewable sources in the POW and POS protocols. BTC, which uses blockchain technology, attracts speculative interest due to its volatility in terms of conversion to United States (US) dollars. However, the advent of portable network devices, such as smartphones, creates expectations of this technology, which is increasingly being adopted for various value exchanges, embodying the original idea of the "Internet of Value." Blockchain technology is also used in areas such as FinTech, which manages the history of cashless transactions.

Networks and the use of data become key drivers of social progress and are closely linked to social trust. To ensure the reliability of data, it is necessary to store it securely and to know exactly how it is used. This chapter proposes to adopt blockchain technology as a specific method of assessing corporate governance. Conceptually, corporate governance is about "controlling" the speed up and slow down (e.g., improving the competitiveness of the company and ensuring compliance with laws and regulations). By recording companies' instantaneous transaction logs in distributed ledgers based on blockchain technology, it becomes possible for all participants to share this information holistically and simultaneously. The immutable nature of transaction history in the blockchain allows stakeholders to monitor and audit businesses in real time. In addition, transaction history, cocreated with stakeholders, is stored on the network using blockchain technology, and its use can be organized instantly using machine learning. Information can be provided in a format that is tailored to the interests of each stakeholder. Therefore, we believe that blockchain technology can be extended to stakeholder management, which is an underlying concept of corporate governance and is of particular importance to companies and other stakeholders, especially on the ground.

However, due to being in its early stages of research, empirical studies on blockchain are currently limited. The adoption of blockchain technology by businesses is still relatively low, with only a small number of academics conducting empirical studies using data from China, India, and the United States. A study by Jain and Jain (2019) reveals that incorporating blockchain in a business's name leads to exceptional stock returns, although these gains diminish after two months and decline after five. According to Sheel and Nath (2019) using survey data from Indian businesses, blockchain enhances the adaptability, consistency, and agility of the supply chain, fosters trust among businesses, and improves overall corporate performance. Similarly, Hoxha and Sadiku (2019) examine the readiness to implement blockchain technology in real estate trading systems based on survey results obtained in Kosovo. They find that transparency, pricing, and transaction security have the most significant impact. According to Pan et al. (2020), blockchain improves operational effectiveness, increases asset turnover, and reduces the ratio of sales expenses within an organization. This technology is often adopted as a response to the expansion of business assets. The literature, using theoretical analysis and model-building techniques, suggests that blockchain can mitigate information asymmetry, reduce friction, and lower transaction costs. Furthermore, it enhances the effectiveness and accuracy of accounting processes. The potential benefits of blockchain extend beyond these aspects. It facilitates value creation, contributes to the achievement of sustainable development goals, and enables predictive capabilities, all of which are expected to enhance company performance (Al-Htaybat et al., 2019; Shahab and Allam, 2020).

In recent years, the concept of corporate governance has evolved to encompass stakeholders beyond just management and shareholders. This shift led to a convergence between corporate governance theory and the principles of Corporate Social Responsibility (CSR). Stakeholder management, which integrates theories from the new institutionalist economics and dynamic capabilities, emerged as a framework to explain and enhance corporate governance practices. Furthermore, this stakeholder management approach holds promise in addressing societal challenges, particularly in the realm of global environmental sustainability. One notable initiative is the European Blockchain Services Infrastructure (EBSI) in the European Union (EU). Aligned with EU values and legal frameworks, EBSI aims to establish an environmentally conscious, pan-European blockchain-based infrastructure. Currently, it is developed, deployed, and implemented. Therefore, the overarching question is as follows: How does the development of ICT, specifically blockchain, impact supply chains and corporate governance? How can the utilization of blockchain enhance transparency, traceability, and trust in transactions, while simultaneously contributing to the resolution of social issues such as environmental sustainability?

This chapter is structured into two main sections. In Section 1.2, we will conduct a literature review examining existing research and exploring the application of blockchain technology. This section will provide a solid foundation for understanding the key concepts and principles associated with blockchain. Section 1.3 will focus on case studies that showcase the practical implementation of blockchain technology. These case studies include BTC and Environmental, Social, and Governance (ESG) investment, which explores how blockchain can enhance sustainable investment practices. Additionally, we will examine the role of blockchain in stakeholder management, highlighting its ability to foster transparent and accountable relationships between organizations and their stakeholders. Lastly, we will discuss the EBSI, an important initiative that utilizes blockchain to establish a secure and efficient infrastructure in the EU. Finally, the chapter will conclude by summarizing the key findings from the literature review and case studies, providing insights into the potential benefits and challenges of implementing blockchain technology in various contexts.

1.2 LITERATURE REVIEW AND HYPOTHESES

According to the International Organization for Standardization (ISO), blockchain is defined as "a distributed ledger whose verified blocks are organized into a continuous chain of information for the exclusive use of postscripts, using linked cryptographic links. Blockchains are designed to create an unforgeable, definitive, and immutable record" (ISO/Transaction Cost (TC) 307, 2021). There are two ways to acquire BTCs, which are a form of cryptographic asset using blockchain technology. The first is to buy and sell BTCs on the market based on the exchange rate of each currency, while the second method is explained in Section 1.2.3 "Mining." In general, the first method is an easy way to obtain BTCs. According to Okada et al. (2017), the best way to quickly understand blockchain technology is to know how BTC works, which can be explained in six steps: (1) payment, (2) registration, (3) mining, (4) reward, (5) approval, and (6) circulation (Wright, 2008). By lowering costs, removing middlemen, and enabling new business models, blockchain and BTC technology can upend entire industries. However, these technologies also face trust and regulatory issues. Blockchain offers appealing benefits like transparency, immutability, and resistance to censorship, but problems like price volatility and money laundering call for extra care. Initial Coin Offerings are a promising investment strategy, but they come with hazards of fraud and excessive speculation. Widespread acceptance will depend on resolving technological, regulatory, and trust difficulties as well as increasing public awareness. Regulation is vital to stability and confidence (Okada et al., 2017). The problem is that digital technology is invisible to those who cannot see it, but it is visible to those who can. This issue of recognition will then be explained in Weber's concept of "authority." The six steps described above are therefore the following.

1.2.1 PAYMENT

For instance, a record is created in the blockchain ledger indicating that a unit of Bitcoin (1 BTC) has been transferred from A to B. This record is timestamped and stored across 11,000 distributed nodes worldwide. Cryptography serves as a method to prevent information leakage and internal fraud within a network involving numerous participants. It ensures the security of transactions in a virtual space by encrypting transaction information in a manner that only a third party possessing the corresponding public and private keys (held by the transaction initiator) can decipher. Moreover, Jack Dorsey, founder and Chief Executive Officer of Block (formerly Square), announced plans to develop an open-source, dedicated semiconductor chip-based system for BTC mining, accessible to individuals and businesses globally. This system aims to tackle the intricacies of both POW and POS mining methods, as well as the high entry barriers that hinder widespread participation. Intel also announced the development of their dedicated mining chip called the Bonanza Mine chip. The transaction records are stored across multiple computers, or nodes, in the network rather than a single computer.

1.2.2 REGISTRATION

When a transaction from A to B involving 1 BTC occurs, it is broadcast to at least eight nodes within the network. This broadcast is then relayed to the next set of eight nodes, continuing in a grid network that encompasses all 11,000 nodes. The term "distributed ledger" is used to describe this blockchain recording method because the data are not recorded and stored in a single centralized location but rather in multiple storage locations throughout the network.

1.2.3 MINING

The transfer transactions of 1 BTC from A to B are recorded as a set of information in a node at a specific time. Wright (2008) designed a program that combines incentives and competition to aggregate these records, approximately 2000 transactions, into a single block. This block consists of three components: (1) the compilation of hundreds or thousands of BTC transactions, (2) the consolidated information before this block, and (3) the compilation and final encryption of the block, known as mining. In the mining process, the SHA-256 hash function is calculated on the block of data until 16 zeros appear simultaneously. This requires a computer to perform approximately 850,000 calculations, taking about 10 min to complete.

1.2.4 REWARD

The mining process involves a competitive race between nodes, where the participant succeeding in encrypting the block first is rewarded. Mining enables each participant to include their transactions in the block of transactions. As of 2022, the mining reward is 6.25 BTC (with 1 BTC valued at approximately $50,000), in addition to transaction fees for each block. These two rewards represent the incentives generated by each block of transactions. The first reward is the newly created BTC from mining, known as the "base reward." The second reward is the commission income earned from each transaction, which will become the sole reward for miners once the mining process is exhausted around the year 2140.

1.2.5 APPROVAL

Following the mining process, a group of BTC transactions is recorded and stored as a single block on approximately 11,000 nodes worldwide, with each block being finalized every 10 min. This finalization represents the consensus approval of the transaction information on the distributed ledger. The approval method employed is known as POW, which involves a competitive race among participants to discover the block number (nonce), an encrypted hash value with around 16 leading zeros. As this discovery competition occurs globally and includes all participants, concerns are raised regarding the energy expended in the process. One potential solution to this issue is POS, which introduces the concept of "coin age" equal to the "amount of coins held" multiplied by the "coin holding period" for mining. In POS, a higher coin age leads to lower nonce difficulty and proportional authentication work. Consequently, POS requires less energy compared to POW. This solution allows for faster mining with reduced energy consumption, effectively addressing the problem.

1.2.6 CIRCULATION

The issuance of newly minted coins, known as the coinbase, is programmed to be halved approximately every 210,000 blocks. By January 2022, the total number of blocks reached approximately 718,000. The maximum limit for BTC transactions is set at 2,100,000 BTC. With a block created approximately every 10 min, this maximum coin limit is projected to be reached around the year 2140. Currently, approximately 17.5 million BTC have been issued, with 80% of the total already in circulation. This decreasing coin supply acts as a mechanism of scarcity, akin to the gold standard, enhancing BTC's role as a transactional medium. Why do digital technology and legal tender have value? How to interpret the perception of their value? In this chapter, we adapt C.I. Barnard's concept of the "zone of indifference." Barnard uses the concept of acceptance of "authority" to explain the sphere of indifference. His theory is strongly influenced by Max Weber's theory of organization. Why does the paper money of legal tender create the trust needed for transactions? If we think about the function of money and traditional currencies, we can see that they serve as a conduit for transactional data. Weber contributed to organizational theory in several ways. At a time when the economy was king, his sociological research on "bureaucratic control" in the late nineteenth century made a fundamental addition to our knowledge of contemporary nations, businesses, and large organizations in Europe.

Many types of crypto assets are developed and traded. According to the Bank of Japan, crypto-assets have three characteristics: (1) they can be used to pay unspecified third parties and exchanged for legal tenders such as the euro or the US dollar (USD), (2) they can be recorded and transferred electronically, and (3) they are not legal tender and are not assets denominated in legal tender (Fujiki, 2023). What is the difference between this transaction intermediary function supported by state authority, such as the Bank of Japan, and BTC? BTC does not require a third-party intermediary such as a financial institution (alternative to the Internet). The ownership value of BTC is mutually authenticated by a decentralized and autonomous P2P system (distributed ledger). This mutual authentication is carried out by 11,000 nodes (registration locations) around the world and differs from centralized authentication such as that of a central bank (see Figure 1.1). Weber's work had a significant impact on Stiegler, who accepted the notion of "acceptance of authority" previously described and examined bureaucracy as the most rational method of control over the tasks of large enterprises. This sort of dominance consists of (1) "traditional support," (2) "charismatic control," and (3) "legitimate control," which is the most functional form of control in modern times. One important type of dominance is when people follow the rules instead of a leader. The rules that apply to the subordinate and the supervisor in a supervisory relationship are identical. Being governed by rules and pursuing legitimacy about those norms are conceptually characteristics of legal rule (the idea of legitimacy), which is the primary basis of bureaucratic control. Additionally, privatization makes this bureaucracy appealing to society.

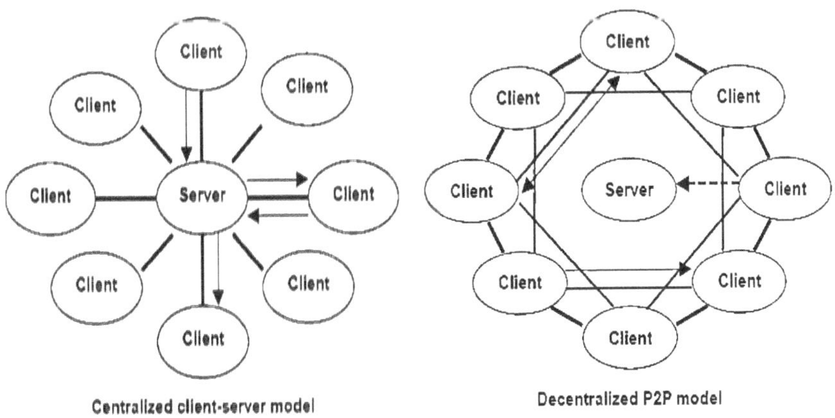

FIGURE 1.1 Centralized authentication (client–server model) and decentralized authentication (P2P model).

Source: Adapted from Ausland 2002

Weber et al. (1998) developed a cognitive theory of "authority" from the organizational concept. What is authority? If an organization depends on the conscious willingness of its participants to collaborate, it will consider the human decision to follow orders as an indicator of "authority" (command authority). If a participant in the organization does not obey an order, no "authority" is attributed to that order. Authority is a "mental preparation" that guides the behavior of people within the organization. Authority is therefore legitimized by the recognition of the free will of the members of the organization. Thus, it introduces an element of democracy into the idea of legality (Stiegler, 1998). There are similarities between the concept of democracy and the concept of P2P in blockchain technology. Blockchain technology works like a distributed ledger, organized in P2P. It processes transactions in ICT, records them in chronological order, and forms an "irreversible chain" of data sets every 10 min, using network protocols and consensus, without relying on a centralized intermediary such as a government or bank. Blockchain technology is a distributed ledger that records transactions, digitized smart contracts and other information on a series of distributed computer storage media. These records, once fixed, constitute the "mining operation." Once fixed, the mining operation is almost impossible to reassemble, forming a networked database of about 11,000 nodes, which participants can trust and which is highly transparent.

The foundation of corporate governance is the notion that the controlling body of corporate governance is the centralized "authority" described in Weber's theory of power. However, as opposed to a client–server framework, blockchain technology functions on a decentralized system. Vending machines are cited as an example of smart contracts. Vending machines automate the procedures from the entry of money to the receipt of goods before they are offered to the buyer. Here, the mechanism for automatically executing the contractual process of proof and transfer of ownership and other rights is called a smart contract (contract automation). This chapter examines the theoretical and technological concept of membership when the system turns into a decentralized (e.g., democratic) autonomous system of the P2P type. In recent years, the debate on corporate governance has expanded from the narrow concept of the relationship between "management" and "shareholders" to include "stakeholders" other than "management" and shareholders as a broad concept. In this sense, corporate governance is now linked to the field of CSR. The following three new institutionalist economic theories, which explain corporate governance theory, are presented in Table 1.1 aspects of transaction costs, agency theory, and property rights theory. Property rights theory and blockchain technology both have a role to play (Parmentoloa, 2023).

TABLE 1.1 Structure of Governance Theory in Blockchain

Corporate Governance Theory	Blockchain Technology
Agency Theory	P2P Authentication, Stakeholder Management
Transaction Cost Theory	Marketplace vs. Organization, Visualization of Transactions, and Reduction of Transaction Costs
Ownership Theory	Improved Transparency, Decentralization of Rights

The agency theory of Jensen and Meckling (1976) focuses on the conflict of interest between agents (managers) and principals (shareholders) based on the "separation of ownership and management" and the "administrative man" model. Such a conflict of interest promotes self-preserving behavior on the part of management, which reduces shareholders' dividends through the use of capital by diversifying activities, while shareholders demand higher dividends through the concentration of activities. The problems here are "adverse selection," for example, higher premium rates due to unhealthy people in insurance policies, and "moral hazard." In this theory, the "firm" is assumed to be a "contract nexus" composed of management-centric agency relationships. Blockchain technology allows instantaneous corporate transactions to be managed in a decentralized ledger and can increase the efficiency of the "audit system" to solve the two abovementioned problems and prevent falsification (Karpoff, 2021).

The theory of transaction costs developed by Ronald H. Coase in 1937 compares the costs associated with market exchanges with those of exchanges within organizations for the efficient allocation of resources. It aims to minimize monitoring costs and to determine which form of transaction is the most cost-effective. This theory highlights the importance of contracts in reducing these costs, and smart contracts offer the possibility of further simplifying these contracts. In addition, the theory of transaction costs takes into account the bounded rationality of economic actors and the presence of a "managerial person." The human figure of neo-institutional economics is founded on the assumption of all participant's "opportunistic" behavior. The use of blockchain technology in transaction cost theory allows for the lowering of contractual costs via blockchain-based smart contracts, raising the topic of the boundary between markets and organizations. In other words, transactions can be P2P or mined to eliminate information leakage and internal fraud using modern cryptography, which dramatically reduces monitoring expenses (Williamson, 1985).

The theory of ownership is based on bounded rationality as developed by Simon (managerial model) and influenced by Stiegler (1998). This model differs from that of the "economic man" who has perfect rationality and makes satisfactory decisions according to bounded rationality. In this model, the "manager" is not able to recognize all the characteristics of the goods, and it is difficult to attribute ownership to these characteristics. Therefore, both the positive and negative impacts of a commodity are viewed as externalities affecting third parties, primarily in the context of adverse effects. The concept here is that if a commodity suffers from pollution, establishing clear ownership rights beforehand (internalizing externalities) can optimize the overall economy's utility. Through the implementation of blockchain technology, which hinges on efficient transaction handling, the distinct utilities of a given commodity for each stakeholder can be more comprehensively discerned, leading to enhanced transparency. This, in turn, lays the groundwork for effective stakeholder management (Yermack, 2017). Consequently, the following hypothesis is proposed:

H1. The utilization of blockchain enhances corporate governance by augmenting traceability and transparency.

Freeman et al. (2001) believe that capitalism needs to be reconstructed by stakeholder theory, which sees enterprises as providing value for their stakeholders. It should be noted that classic conceptions of organizational theory, such as Weber's bureaucracy, continue to dominate the corporate environment since corporations are typically shareholder-owned and do not take into consideration effects other than those of shareholders (Freeman et al., 2001). This approach challenges the predominance of bureaucracy and the legitimacy that comes with it, where the government ensures shareholder ownership of companies through laws and regulations democratically passed by parliament. Stakeholder theory criticizes this dominant idea by asking whether such a purely economic model is applicable in the actual management of companies.

In 1999, however, Friedman considered internet money as a liberal concept that allows for the liberation of state power. He pointed out that the government's tax base would no longer consist of fixed assets such as real estate, but would become more liquid. He did not envisage any means of controlling electronic transactions in virtual space. Although democratic ideas such as P2P were lacking, he envisaged electronic currencies as a means of mediating between business and government. In a decentralized market economy, decision-making is left to businesses and households. Decentralized planning and direction by the government, as in socialist societies, is not considered feasible. Instead, the balance of economic activity is achieved through prices, which are set by the demand and supply of goods in the market (Friedman, 1993). The market and the price system construct an interest compensation mechanism based on personal preferences in a purely theoretical model. In this mechanism, all participants cooperate voluntarily, and no one can coerce the others. However, an underlying concept closely links stakeholder theory and Weber's discussion of bureaucracy: legitimacy.

The concept of "legitimacy" is similar to that of centralized authentication (client–server model) and decentralized authentication (P2P system). This mutual authentication is used to establish "legitimacy" in the field of ICT and partially represents the relationship between corporate governance and blockchain technology. The centralized authentication model, where information is concentrated in global ICT giants such as Google, Apple, Facebook, and Amazon (GAFA), can be replaced by a decentralized authentication model through blockchain technology. This allows a return to the original decentralized Internet. Milton Friedman, who views companies as serving the price function akin to suppliers in economics, contends that "management bears the duty of maximizing economic profit for shareholders and should not shoulder additional responsibilities." Management must operate the business efficiently for the benefit of shareholders, all while adhering to the law and societal norms. Therefore, actions such as donations run counter to the interests of shareholders. Furthermore, "if management assumes social responsibility without maximizing profits for shareholders, it will undermine the foundations of a free society" (Friedman, 1962), and critiques the behavior of companies that prioritize social responsibility over price adjustment. This leads to the following hypothesis:

H2. Blockchain enhances stakeholder management effectiveness.

1.3 METHODOLOGY

1.3.1 CASE STUDIES

The use of blockchain technology in BTC has grown exponentially. The USD conversion rate rose from over $40,000 per 1 BTC in 2020 to over

$60,000 in the spring of 2021. Transaction volume reached between $40,000 and $50,000 in 2022. The exchange of securities via smartphones and FinTech helps to expand the potential for deployment of this technology, as uses crypto-assets as a means of cashless transactions.

Blockchain technology offers a new mechanism for recording corporate financial records in a decentralized ledger using cryptography and ICT. This opens up new research perspectives in the study of corporate governance, which focuses on the ownership structure of companies. In the financial sector, large institutional investors and key players invest in blockchain technology, especially in stock exchanges, offering new methods to settle share transactions and track corporate ownership. Blockchain is used here to track the settlement of stock transactions and ownership of companies (Gajo, 2021).

It is essential to assess the impact of blockchain technology on stakeholders such as management, shareholders, employees, consumers, and traders. The potential benefits of blockchain technology, such as reduced costs, increased liquidity, more accurate record-keeping, and transparency of ownership, could significantly alter the balance of power between these stakeholders (Yermack, 2017). "Smart contracts"—algorithms that enable a more functional use of blockchain technology—could enable the design of securities such as stocks and bonds in structures that are more closely related to the management of the business. This change will require management to acquire new skills and qualifications and may require the use of external professional consultants. In addition, stock option schemes that motivate managers will have to evolve to take account of the changing structure and nature of these securities (Marcel and Edward, 2008).

1.3.2 BTC AND ESG INVESTMENT

When considering BTC and ESG investment, we consider a model in which the main issue is the "global environment" as well as other aspects such as "human social networks" and "industry network analysis (governance)." These elements provide new solutions for addressing the "global environment" problem. An important aspect is the relationship with renewable energy. The research of the Cambridge Centre for Alternative Finance (CCAF) at the University of Cambridge focuses on three main areas: First, the FinTech ecosystem; second, the "financial sustainability index"; and finally, the "Cambridge Bitcoin Electricity Consumption Index (CBECI)." The "CBECI" is a method to check whether BTC mining methods (POW and POS) use renewable energy sources to promote the aforementioned sustainability without burdening the environment.

A regression between the quarterly dollar price of BTC and the CCAF electricity consumption index reveals a positive coefficient of 0.8, indicating a positive benefit of 1% (0.8 × 1%). The context is that many BTCs are used for overseas remittances due to restrictions that prevent the Chinese currency (yuan) from circulating overseas. At the same time, BTC mining uses cheap and environmentally friendly electricity produced from coal in China. However, this energy activity, particularly by Sinopec and other companies in Inner Mongolia, also leads to human rights problems. Tensions between the United States and China have increased due to these human rights issues, including Sinopec's activities.

A regression analysis of the E3V data was conducted for the explained variables: Bitcoin price (X_1), US interest rate (X_2), gold price (X_3), and NASDAQ (X_4). The results show a strong correlation between the BTC price and the NASDAQ (0.844**). The explained variables of the e-commerce data and the BTC price (X_1) have a significant negative correlation at 10%, while the correlation with the NASDAQ (X_4) is positive and significant at 1%. The regression equation is as follows:

$$Y = -6.59 \times 10^{(-16)} - 0.211\, X_1 + 0.068\, X_2 - 0.233\, X_3 + 0.863\, X_4$$

This regression analysis suggests that if the price of BTC continues to rise and fluctuate, it will not be able to become the main payment method in e-commerce. However, if other companies such as Tesla or Visa adopt BTC as a payment method, this will lead to an increase in price due to the trust placed in these well-known companies. This shows that blockchain technology has the potential to be a promising proxy for the NASDAQ index (Gajo, 2021).

1.4 RESULTS AND DISCUSSION

An example of the application of blockchain technology in the securities market is securities settlement, which offers three key benefits: increased transparency, faster settlement times, and improved transaction capacity with reduced transaction costs. First, the use of blockchain ensures increased transparency as all transactions are publicly recorded, thereby preventing short selling, malicious trading, and transaction tampering. Second, blockchain technology enables shorter settlement times, with transactions being verified in less than a minute and ownership transferred more quickly compared to traditional settlement processes that can take several business days. Finally, the adoption of blockchain allows for improved transaction capacity by leveraging P2P authentication, resulting in significant cost reductions. By eliminating intermediaries like brokerage firms, transactions can be executed directly with the exchange, leading to lower brokerage fees. However, the adoption of blockchain technology will not mean the disappearance of all old systems. For example, email has coexisted with postal services for over 20 years. Similarly, the regulation of the cryptocurrency market is likely to retain the traditional framework for securities transactions. Blockchain technology will automate and simplify many processes related to securities transactions, such as issuance, distribution, and custody, which will impact related activities and industry. Efforts to apply blockchain technology to securities settlement will provide the benefits mentioned above, which will significantly change the assumptions of the three corporate governance theories: transaction cost theory, agency theory, and ownership theory. These changes will lead to a better understanding of shareholders as owners of companies and to more advanced and effective stakeholder management. In Japan, an organization is conducting demonstrations, surveys, and studies on the applicability of Distributed Ledger Technology, also known as blockchain, to financial infrastructure. This initiative is carried out in collaboration with a wide range of stakeholders, including financial institutions and information technology providers.

The application of blockchain technology to stakeholder management is illustrated in conceptual Figure 1.2, showing how blockchain technology can be used to manage owners, workforce, customers, and suppliers. The mutual sharing of information between stakeholders, such as customers, competitors, suppliers, and the government, is also illustrated. Blockchain technology allows for greater control of businesses through greater transparency, faster settlement times, and increased transaction capacity with lower transaction costs than before. The conceptual scheme integrates the environmental dimension with the economic, technological, environmental, and social platforms. It is based on the new St. Gallen business model developed by Urlich in 1978.

TOP APPLICATIONS	KEY ASSESSMENT CRITERIA
• Certificates of origin • Utility billing • Demand response • Electric vehicles • Transactive energy	• Technical architecture • Governance • Features • Data collection and reliability • Throughput • Development process • Ecosystem • Innovation • Regulatory alignment

FIGURE 1.2 Top Applications and Key Assessment Criteria for Blockchains in the Energy Sector.

Source: Adapted from Miller & Mockel, 2018.

The President of the European Commission, Ursula Gertrud von der Leyen, has emphasized the significance of a "digital transition" within the "European Green Deal" for reaching sustainability targets. EBSI has been unveiled as the European Commission's flagship project as part of this shift. EBSI aims to develop, deploy, and operate a secure blockchain infrastructure that aligns with the EU values and legal frameworks, while also prioritizing environmental sustainability. To support the Digital Single Market, the EU provides investment funds through the Connecting Europe Facility (CEF) platform. CEF serves as a cross-sector, cross-border platform that leverages existing EU platforms to facilitate digital public services and business activities. The European Commission, consisting of the heads of state and government of the EU, holds executive functions within the EU governance structures, complementing the EU Council's ministerial-level competencies. The European Parliament functions as a general assembly of shareholders, with 751 members until 2019. These three institutions collectively form the main policymaking bodies within the EU.

EBSI is part of a broader list of initiatives, which includes the following: (1) Big Data Test Infrastructure, (2) Context Broker, (3) eArchiving,

(4) eDelivery, (5) eID, (6) eInvoicing, and (7) eSignature. These initiatives aim to address various challenges related to information access, interoperability, and cross-border communication. While the expansion of computer networks and the Internet has brought about a decentralized information environment worldwide, there are still obstacles to achieving full interoperability and seamless cross-border communication. The EU encounters challenges in using cross-border online tools and services, such as compliance with the General Data Protection Regulation (GDPR). To ensure the success of digital networks and services, the EU's Digital Single Market must overcome these obstacles and effectively address the cross-border use of data (European Commission, 2021).

Similarly, the European Commission is trying to use blockchain technology to achieve a low-carbon society, such as COVID-19. Blockchain is a technology that can significantly improve transparency, accountability, and traceability of greenhouse gas emissions. It can provide companies with accurate, reliable, standardized, and versatile data on their carbon emissions. Smart contracts are a variant of blockchain technology. The energy consumption of mining operations such as POW in BTC has become an issue, and the information classification methods of blockchain technology also make it possible to better calculate, track, and report on the reduction of carbon dioxide emissions in economic activities (European Commission, 2021). The CBECI at Cambridge University, UK, estimated that the total energy consumed by the POW mining process was about 128 terawatts in 2001. CBECI calculates that the total energy consumed by the extraction process was about 128 terawatts in 2001. Alex noted that in 2018, the BTC network consumed 2.55 Gigawatts (GW) of electricity and will consume 7.67 GW shortly, which is more than the electricity consumed in Ireland (3.1 GW) and Austria (3.2 GW). It has been noted that this consumption is comparable to countries such as Ireland (3.1 GW) and Austria (8.2 GW) (European Commission, 2021).

However, the EU believes that blockchain technology can network low-carbon initiatives organized by companies. It also points out that the contribution of each company's efforts to a low-carbon society can be measured. To do this, it would be ideal for the EU to become home to a significant number of innovative environmental technology start-ups. All parties, including corporations, governments, and individuals, will be connected by platforms built on the blockchain that will be developed by the CEF and EBSI previously mentioned. The EU GDPR is a regulation to protect personal data within the EU, especially since 2015, as personal data and a wide range of other data around the world have important implications for the competitive advantage of businesses. This regulation is the first of its kind in the EU. It also aims to regulate the export of personal data outside the EU by ICT giant GAFA Microsoft.

Blockchain technology allows for the tracking and reporting of greenhouse gas emission reductions throughout the supply chain, including manufacturers, suppliers, distributors, and consumers. Measures to promote environmental technologies with blockchain technology will encourage environmental start-ups to fight climate change. Public and institutional investors are focusing on ESG investments, supporting low-carbon start-ups. This supports sustainable finance initiatives and climate change action through green bonds, FinTech, and alternative financing mechanisms. BTC can be seen as an investment vehicle, but it can also help invest in or promote projects using blockchain technology for a low-carbon society, such as sustainable energy control systems. In this way, EU countries and national government agencies can work together to support the introduction, development, and adaptation of blockchain-based solutions to help combat climate change and reduce greenhouse gas emissions. In addition, partnerships are planned with United Nations agencies and international financial institutions such as the World Bank, the European Investment Bank, and the European Bank for Reconstruction and Development, to support the strengthening of the environmental innovation technology ecosystem in the EU and to improve access to finance for start-ups and Small and Medium Enterprises active in sustainable energy technologies (Alex, 2018).

1.5 CONCLUSION

This chapter explores the impact of applying blockchain technology on corporate governance. It highlights the transition from information concentration to decentralization, thus promoting democracy on the internet. Current business models in ICT are divided into "blue" and "red," with implications for data privacy. Blockchain technology enables decentralized storage of personal data and contributes to addressing social issues, particularly environmental sustainability.

Corporate governance is evolving toward a stakeholder-oriented approach and corporate social responsibility. Institutional economic theories are adapting to democracy and decentralized data sharing. The presented case studies demonstrate the use of smart contracts and blockchain technology for securities settlement, offering benefits such as transparency and reduced transaction costs.

The EU's EBSI initiative focuses on reducing greenhouse gas emissions and safeguarding human rights and personal data. It criticizes the current monopoly system and promotes the use of blockchain technology for sustainable supply chains. The EU has embraced blockchain technology as an environmental tool.

Despite progress, challenges remain, particularly in understanding the trends of new companies and startups applying blockchain technology to corporate governance. However, blockchain technology holds promising prospects for the future industry. Future research could delve into analyzing new companies and startups through empirical studies. It is also important to continue exploring the implications of blockchain technology for corporate governance, with a focus on addressing social and environmental issues.

KEYWORDS

- **blockchain technology**
- **corporate governance**
- **decentralization (democratization)**
- **stakeholder management**
- **sustainability**

REFERENCES

Al-Htaybat, K., Hutaibat, K. & von Alberti-Alhtaybat, L. (2019). Global brain-reflective accounting practices: Forms of intellectual capital contributing to value creation and sustainable development. *Journal of Intellectual Capital*, 20(6), 733–762. https://doi.org/10.1108/jic-01-2019-0016.

Alex, V. D. (2018). Bitcoin's growing energy problem. *Joule*. https://doi.org/10.1016/j.joule.2018.04.016.

Åslund, J. (2002) Authentication in peer-to-peer systems. Master's Thesis, Linköping University, Department of Computer and Information Science.

European Commission. (2021). Blockchain for Climate Action. https://digital-strategy.ec.europa.eu/en/policies/blockchain-climate-action.

Freedman, M. (1962). Capitalism and Freedom. University of Chicago Press, Chicago, IL.

Freeman, E. R., Harrison, J., Wick, A., Parmar, B. & Colle, S. (2001). A Stakeholder Approach to Strategic Management. Blackwell, Malden, MA, USA.

Friedman, M. (1993). Do we need central banks? [Transcript of speech]. https://miltonfriedman.hoover.org/internal/media/dispatcher/215005/full.

Fujiki, H. (2023). Attributes needed for Japan's central bank digital currency. *Japanese Economic Review (Oxford, England)*, 74(1), 117–175. https://doi.org/10.1007/s42973-021-00106-7.

Gajo, M. (2021). Nasdaq startet technologie platform Nasdaq data link. *Die Aktiengesellschaft*, 66(20), 299–300. https://doi.org/10.9785/ag-2021-662010.

Hoxha, V. & Sadiku, S. (2019). Study of factors influencing the decision to adopt blockchain technology in real estate transactions in Kosovo. *Property Management*, 37(5), 684–700, https://doi.org/10.1108/pm-01-2019-0002.

Jain, A. & Jain, C. (2019). Blockchain hysteria: Adding "blockchain" to company's name. *Economics Letters*, 181, 178–181. https://doi.org/10.1016/j.econlet.2019.05.011.

Jensen, M. C. & Meckling, W. H. (1976). Theory of the firm: Managerial behavior, agency costs, and ownership structure. *Journal of Financial Economics*, 3, 305–360.

Karpoff, J. M. (2021). The future of financial fraud. *Journal of Corporate Finance*, 69, 10–16. https://doi.org/10.1016/j.jcorpfin.2020.101694.

Marcel, K. & Edward, R. (2008). The hanging chads of corporate voting. *Georgetown Law Journal*, 96(4), 1227–1281.

Miller, D., & Moekel, P. (2018). Using Blockchain to Enable Cleaner, Modern Energy Systems in Emerging Markets (EM Compass Note 61). International Finance Corporation. Retrieved from https://documents.worldbank.org/curated/en/276911547847581837/pdf/133881-EMCompass-Note-61-Blockchain.pdf

Okada, H., Yamasaki, S. & Bracamonte, V. (2017). Proposed classification of blockchains based on authority and incentive dimensions. *19th International Conference on Advanced Communication Technology (ICACT)*. ICACT-TACT, Phoenix Park, 593–597.

Pan, X., Pan, X., Song, M., Ai, B. & Ming, Y. (2020). Blockchain technology and enterprise operational capabilities: An empirical test. *International Journal of Information Management*, 52(101946), 10–19. https://doi.org/10.1016/j.ijinfomgt.2019.05.002.

Parmentola, A., Petrillo, A., Tutore, I. & De Felice, F. (2022). Is blockchain able to enhance environmental sustainability? A systematic review and research agenda from the perspective of Sustainable Development Goals (SDGs). *Business Strategy and the Environment*, 31, 194–217.

Shahab, S. & Allam, Z. (2020). Reducing transaction costs of tradable permit schemes using Blockchain smart contracts. *Growth and Change*, 51(1), 302–308. https://doi.org/10.1111/grow.12342.

Sheel, A. & Nath, V. (2019). Effect of blockchain technology adoption on supply chain adaptability, agility, alignment and performance. *Management Research Review,* 42(12), 1353–1374. https://doi.org/10.1108/mrr-12-2018-0490.

Stiegler, B. (1998). Technics and Time, 1: The Fault of Epimetheus (R. Beardsworth & G. Collins, Trans.). Stanford University Press, Stanford, CA, USA.

Weber, E. U., Blais, A. R., & Betz, N. E. (1998). A domain-specific risk-attitude scale: Measuring risk perceptions and risk behaviors. *Journal of Behavioral Decision Making*, 12(4), 263–290.

Williamson, O. E. (1985). Employee ownership and internal governance. *Journal of Economic Behavior & Organization,* 6(3), 243–245. https://doi.org/10.1016/0167-2681(85)90033-2.

Wright, C. S. (2008). Bitcoin: A peer-to-peer electronic cash system. *SSRN Electronic Journal.* https://doi.org/10.2139/ssrn.3440802.

Yermack, D. (2017). Corporate governance and blockchains. *Review of Finance,* 21(1), 39–78. https://doi.org/10.1093/rof/rfw074.

CHAPTER 2

Impact of Political Instability on Economic Growth in the Middle East and North Africa (MENA) Countries: An Application of the Auto-Regressive Distributive Lags (ARDL) Bound Testing Approach

NEDIE FARJALAH[1*] and ASMA SGHAIER[2*]

[1]*Department of Quantitative Methods, FSEG Sousse, Tunisia*

[2]*University of Toulon, France*

*Corresponding authors

ABSTRACT

This chapter points to analyze the effects of political steadiness on Net Residential Item (GDP) (2010 steady US $) on a few Middle East North Africa nations (Egypt, Libya, Tunisia, and Algeria) during the period 1980–2020. This analysis is based on the Auto-Regressive Distributive Slacks approach proposed by Pesaranc et al. The empirical estimate yields interesting results. The relationship between financial development and soundness is emphatically long and short for each nation (Egypt, Libya, Tunisia, and Algeria). The consideration explores the presence of the long-run relationship between the distinctive political pointers and the development of the economy. The study utilized board information investigation, utilizing yearly information covering the period of 1980–2020, for the four chosen Middle Eastern nations. The observational discoveries of the

Corporate Governance, Digitalization, and Energy Transition: Imen Baccouche and Afef Khalil, (Eds.)

DOI: 10.1201/9781779643407-3

analysis, utilizing the Vector Blunder Redress Demonstrate, highlight the effects of different political insecurity markers on financial development. Besides, these results show that there is a solid long-run relationship between a few political markers and financial development. More specifically, it appears that the control of corruption and the rule of law indicators have the most significant impact on economic development, while regulatory quality has the least effect.

2.1 INTRODUCTION

Political soundness plays a vital role in the productive development of a nation. Political instability is characterized as the tendency to implement change through "inherent" or "unconstitutional" means. In addition, there are various sources of political uncertainty, likely to be implanted in fear-based oppression and social and ethnic strife. This study takes into consideration two viewpoints of political uncertainty, videlicet, authoritative insecurity, and social uneasiness and political violence. The primary perspective is measured by using a variable that gauges the number of times the key leader has been in office, while the political stability indicator measures the opposite factor. This indicator is a private measure of political query and violence motivated by the terrain including terrorism. This indicator assesses the liability of political insecurity and politically motivated violence.

Terrorism is defined as political violence against civilian populations whose objective is to maximize the external and internal disruption of countries. Bounan (2003) defines terrorism as "the set of criminal operations, of a nature and importance, variable intended to intimidate a population to obtain special privileged outcomes." It is possible to distinguish between two forms of terrorism. State terrorism manifests itself when the state seeks to control the resistance of what it considers to be a rival for the control of power. Social groups to achieve a political goal that affects some people use individual terrorism. In addition, international terrorism refers to dangerous or violent actions affecting the internal stability of people, such as the violation of state criminal law. These activities destabilize respectful life and government arrangements. For a long time, the world has seen a rise in worldwide fear mongering proven by the collaboration of psychologically militant bunches or ethnic and devout bunches. The use of terrorism is linked to both social and economic imbalances and their political consequences can lead to dangerous assessments that globalize risk.

Other studies are studying ethnic and social conflicts, which can be social, manifested in civil wars that affect a country and deteriorates human development and economic growth rates. Social conflicts arise from the social organization itself, when it shows economic, social, and political disparities. Lipset (1960) described the concept of political instability as follows: "A country is considered as stable if it is a democracy or a liberal dictatorship and consistent for 25 years." However, recent political and economic scholars shifted the concept from traditional political instability to political stability. The main concept is that the effectiveness of a government depends primarily on the coherence of a strong political government. A government is considered inefficient if the policy goals vary over a short period. An unstable political system could hinder economic growth, the relationship between economic growth and political volatility can be approached from two perspectives. First, a politically unstable environment creates uncertainty and volatility, which reduces private investment and slows down growth. Second, political uncertainty changes the nature of investments and changes the pattern of spending. This has a direct impact on economic growth rather than on investment (Asteriou and Price, 2001). The possibility of a change of government threatens future policies and encourages investment elsewhere in a safe place than in a risky environment (Gupta, 1990; Barro, 1991; Alesina et al., 1996; Perotti, 1996; Ades and Chua, 1997). Since 2011, mass protests across nearly all Arab countries have shattered the notion of Arab exceptionalism, leading to the surprising fall of four dictators (in Tunisia, Egypt, Libya, and Yemen) and significant political changes in many other nations in the region. The most frequently asked question will be how political instability influences financial development.

Political insecurity is likely to dock policymakers' midairs leading to suboptimal short-term macroeconomic programs. It may also lead to an advance visit switch of programs, creating instability and thus, adversely influencing macroeconomic execution. Unlike the theoretical analysis by Khemraj (2020), this study goes further by assessing the impact of political uncertainty, including ethnopolitical conflict, on economic growth In fact, although the country's history has been marked by serious events of political instability over the past six decades, no previous study has examined the emprirical relationship or impact of political instability on economic peformance. This study aims to addres this gap in the literature by utilizing econometric tools. It will moreover include the beachfront within the writing that utilizes information from a single nation that is brief in the drive. Moreover, it will donate new substantiation with respect to the relationship between beneficial development and political uncertainty in a destitute resource-rich nation.

The remaining part of the chapter is organized as follows; Section 2.2 looks at the previous generally hypothetical writing almost the relationship between political uncertainty and beneficial development within the Middle East and North Africa (MENA) nations; whereas Section 2.3 traces the technique and information utilizing an observational demonstrate. Section 2.4 analyzes discoveries and Section 2.5 gives conclusions and approaches counteraccusations.

2.2 LITERATURE REVIEW

The drop in political frameworks has stimulated the intrigue of analysts and has provoked a closer examination of the impact of political instability on financial development and the Net Residential Item (GDP) development rate. Over the last few decades, the address of whether political insecurity influences financial development rates has been a critical inquiry among financial specialists and policymakers. Such intrigue stems essentially from the imperative arrangement suggestions for the required activities that can quicken financial development and thriving. Experimental studies on this issue have given blended comes about. There is no agreement among financial specialists and policymakers approximately the nature of the relationship between political flimsiness and financial development. Various econometric techniques have been utilized to examine the subject. In the following subsections, we provide a brief review of studies that have addressed the nexus between political instability and economic growth

Various studies have argued for the presence of an inverse relationship between political volatility and economic performance. Alesina and Perotti (1996) indicated that, concerning private investment, political instability leads to low growth, creating risk and uncertainty, and reducing investment volumes. When the size of investment decreases, the output level also decreases, reducing employment and income, increasing prices, and stimulating inflation of capital markets and goods. Due to this decrease in national productivity, pressure has shifted more toward imports, which could reduce currency reserves. The empirical literature on the relationship between political instability and economic growth is relatively recent due to missing data. Political turmoil may be responsible for low economic growth (Kuznets, 1966), especially in times of government change. North (1990) said that institutional quality plays an important role in the long-run economic performance. Similar studies found a theoretical link between political instability and economic growth (Benhabib and Rustichini, 1996; BrockBlomberg, 1996; Devereux and Wen, 1998; Svensson, 1998; Ghate et al., 2003; Darby et al., 2004).

Jong-A-Pin (2009) examined the multidimensional nature of political instability (an exploratory factor analysis on a set of 25 indicators of political instability). The author states that political insecurity has four dimensions: politically motivated violence, mass civil kick, insecurity in the political governance, and insecurity of the political governance. Using a Generalized System of Moments (GMM) system, the author determined the unproductive impact of political insecurity on profitable growth and proved that the four confines have a negative effect on profitable growth. The instability of the political regime has a robust and significant negative effect on economic growth. The empirical results also indicated that the first two dimensions are the challenges to the political regime, while the last two represent real changes to the government and the political system (Sanders, 1981). The instability of the political regime (and not instability within the political regime) refers to the uncertainty that investors express toward the security of property rights (Svensson, 1998). The prediction of Darby et al. (2004) shows that political instability within governments reduces the likelihood of re-election, which leads to lower public investment and, hence lower economic growth.

Financial development invigorates insecurity within the political framework, so the need of development triggers politically motivated violence. At that point, we are able to claim that popular government (or political competition) triggers financial development, but it has input impacts. According to Kuznets (1966, 1973), technological progress is essential for economic growth; however, it must be accompanied by robust democratic institutions that provide citizens with political freedom and allow them to participate in political processes. In fact, the interaction between political precariousness and financial development can be classified into four bunches:

To begin with, the financial literature argues that political instability incorporates a negative effect on financial development, but there is no causality within the inverse course (Alesina et al., 1996). Other proof demonstrates that financial development leads to political solidness, but not bad habit versa (Borner and Paldam, 1998). Another drift within the writing claims that the causal relationship between political flimsiness and financial development works both ways (Zablotsky, 1996; Gyimah-Brempong and Traynor, 1999). Other studies have examined the absence of a causal relationship between the factors (Campos and Nugent, 2002).

There is a large literature that examined the effects of political instability on economic growth. It has pointed to several reasons why higher degrees of political instability can cause lower economic growth rates. Political instability has a damaging impact on key macroeconomic variables, such as investment, unemployment, and inflation (Rodrik, 1991). The link is straightforward, as political instability would imply future risk, which lowers investments and hence affects the growth of an economy both contemporaneously and over a longer horizon. Furthermore, a politically unstable economy is likely to cause corruption and other distorting activities. Therefore, political instability is likely to have a negative impact on economic growth.

Examining panel data from around 100 countries, Aisen and Veiga (2008) found that higher inflation volatility is associated with higher degrees of political instability, ideologically polarized action and fragmentation of the political system, and lower economic freedom. They further argued that economic policies in politically unstable countries tend to be discontinued more frequently compared to countries that are more politically stable. Such discontinuity of economic policies will then result in more volatile inflation rates. Recognizing the high costs on economic growth and welfare caused by inflation volatility, they urged policymakers in developing countries to improve institutions and create practical mechanisms favorable to long-run price stability. Such discontinuity of economic policies will also negatively influence investment, which thrives on stability and therefore will further lower employment and growth. Alesina and Drazen (1991) and Castro and Veiga (2004) have shown that delay in the implementation of inflation stabilization programs is associated with greater political instability. This finding suggests that even higher and more volatile inflation rates would be common in the presence of political instability.

Numerous observational studies have recorded that political instability encompasses a negative effect on major macroeconomic factors, such as

GDP, expansion, and private speculation. For this case, Jong-A-Pin (2009) inspected the causal impact of political insecurity on financial development employing an energetic board system GMM and demonstrates and detailed that the insecurity of the political administration encompasses a critical negative impact on financial development. Alesina et al. (1996), looking at information on 113 nations watched from 1950 to 1982, appeared that GDP development is impressively lower in nations and periods with a tall affinity for government collapse. Özler and Rodrik (1992), Mauro (1995), and Alesina and Perotti (1996), among others, have reported similar results. In a later paper, Aisen and Veiga (2013) experimentally inspected the issue utilizing the system-GMM estimator for straight energetic board information models covering 169 nations watched from 1960 to 2004. Their consideration affirmed the prior discoveries that political instability unfavorably influences financial development by bringing down physical and human capital aggregation and it moreover found that political instability brings down efficiency development rates to a larger extent. Therefore, the previous literature appears to concur on the significance of political soundness to financial development. Political solidness is accepted to form the required structure and pull in private financial specialists and multilateral businesses that can set the organization for development and will too lead to the usage of ideal long-term macroeconomic approaches. This suggests that frequent changes in economic policies, which typically lead to greater instability that negatively affects a nation's macroeconomic performance, will be less observed. Over the last few decades, a large number of cross-country empirical studies have examined the relationship between political institutions and development (Nawaz, 2015; Heshmati and Kim, 2017).

These studies concluded that political institutions have a positive affect on beneficial development. Other considers set up a negative relationship between well-known teaching and productive development (Tavares and Wacziarg, 2001 Kurzman et al., 2002; Abeyasinghe, 2004; Iqbal and Daly, 2014). Additionally, a growing number of studies have highlighted the weaker and ineffective aspects of institutions affecting economic performance in Africa (Rachdi and Rachdi and Saidi, 2015), especially in Sub-Saharan African. Territorial organization environments are influenced by destitute authorization of the run the show of law, debasement, fumble, nonattendance of solid respectful society, and political obstacle. Still, such cross-sectional studies did not determine the extent to which political institutions affect economic development over time.

Hence, investigation that is more distant is required to get it how republic, political viciousness, and well-known duty affect productive execution. Based on the following discussions and the limited literature regarding the relationship between political stability and economic development in Central and Eastern European (CEE) countries, we look at whether such a relationship exists, as well as the reasons behind it. Harfst in his study concludes that these nations are not that unsteady, as they can have administration steadiness. Employing a retrogression investigation for Western Balkan nations, Hysa uncovered that the relationship between debasement and mortal improvement is solid for these bunches of nations. Thus, advanced corruption levels in this region are associated with low economic development. This connection is set up to be more grounded for Western Balkans compared to the European Union nations. These tall circumstances of debasement, for case, in Albania, are still show since of the being issues with the run the show of law, which ever, we may relate with political frailty and destitute government execution. Most extreme of the underneath substantiation built up that teach matter for beneficial development and advancement, in spite of the fact that the conclusion made is conflicting.

2.3 ANALYTICAL FRAMEWORK DATA AND METHODOLOGY

2.3.1 DATA SOURCES

The data used for the empirical analysis are extracted from the World Bank database of World Development Indicators, World Government Indicators, the Database of Political Institutions, and the International Monetary Fund (IMF). For the empirical analysis, we examined the period stretching from 1980 to 2022 for four African countries: Tunisia, Algeria, Egypt, and Libya.

In this study, economic growth is seen as dependent on the World Bank's World Development Indicators. In the literature on measuring economic growth, GDP has been widely used. Political instability comes from the International Country Risk Guide Methodology (ICRG). The GDP variable is communicated in logarithms and millions of US dollars. Political steadiness is an evaluation of both the government's capacity to carry out its announced program(s) and its capacity to remain in office. The hazard rating relegated is the entirety of three subcomponents, each with an extreme score of four focuses and a least score of focuses. A score of 4 focuses speaks to Exceptionally Moo Hazard and a score of focuses to

Exceptionally Tall Hazard (The subcomponents are: *Government Unity *Legislative Strength* Popular Support). The study period is from 1980 to 2022.

The description of all our variables is summarized in Table 2.1.

TABLE 2.1 Descriptive Statistics

Variables	Mean	Min	Max	Obs
	Tunisia			
Political stability	8.300794	4.166667	11.00000	35
GDP (2010 constant US $)	3.14E+10	1.50E+10	5.09E+10	35
	Algeria			
Political stability	7.996825	4.250000	10.50000	35
GDP (2010 constant US $)	1.28E+11	8.54E+10	2.03E+11	35
	Egypt			
Political stability	8.194048	3.916667	11.00000	35
GDP (2010 constant US $)	1.53E+11	2.86E+11	6.50E+10	35
	Libya			
Political stability	7.790238	4.750000	11.00000	35
GDP (2010 constant US $)	5.35E+10	2.84E+10	7.48E+10	20

Sources: Political Stability Indicators, ICRG (2022) and Economic Growth, World Bank (2022).

Notes: The descriptive study is based on the availability of data from Tunisia, Libya, Algeria, and Egypt for the 1984–2022 period.

2.3.1 METHODS

In this chapter, we utilize the Auto-Regressive Disseminated Slacks (ARDL) cointegration approach to look at the brief- and long-term cointegration relationship between financial development and political steadiness for each nation. The ARDL cointegration strategy was presented by Pesaran and Shin (1999) and amplified by Pesaran et al, (2001). Compared to other cointegration strategies (Engle-Granger test, 1987; Johansen test, 1988; Johansen and Juseluis test, 1990) the ARDL cointegration approach has preferences. This cointegration strategy does not require the suspicion that all factors come from the same integration arrange. This approach can be connected indeed in case the factors are $I(0)$ or $I(1)$. We chose this method for two fundamental reasons:

To begin with, it is successful in executing brief and long-term connections between diverse factors that do not have the same integration arrange, given that these factors are stationary and the integration arrange is $I(0)$ or $I(1)$. Moment, the ARDL approach can expel issues related with overlooked and auto-correlated factors. Third, it can be valuable for a little application Pesaran M, Shin Y, Smith R. Bounds testing approaches to the examination of level connections.

The simple model equation is as follows:

$$\ln(GDP)_t = a_0 + \beta_1 PS_t + \varepsilon_t \quad (2.1)$$

$\varepsilon(t)$ is white noise, ln(GDP) is the logarithm of economic growth, and PS is the factor that determines political stability.

The ARDL model used in this study is expressed as follows:

$$\ln(GDP)_t = \beta_0 + + \beta_1 \ln GDP_{t-1} + \beta_2 + (PS)_{t-1} + \Sigma^n_{k=1} \beta_{1k} \Delta \ln(GDP)_{t-k} + \Sigma^n_{k=1} \beta_{2k} \Delta PS_{t-k} + \varepsilon_t \quad (2.2)$$

where Δ ln is the log operator; β_0 is the constant; β_1 and β_2 are mean short-term dynamics; while β_{1k} and β_{2k} are the long-term coefficients and ε is the error term of the white noise. The ARDL approach considers $\beta_1 \neq \beta_2, (p+1)^k$ number of regressions to obtain the optimal lag length for each variable, where p is the maximum number of lags to use, and k is the number of variables in the equation. The selection of appropriate offset is based on a criterion, in our study the appropriate offset is based on Akaike Information Criteria (AIC). The bounds test is based on the Wald statistic (F-statistic) that tested the null hypothesis of no cointegration. The first step of the ARDL approach consists of estimating Equation 2.2 by an Ordinary Least Square.

2.3.1 RESULTS

2.3.1.1 UNIT ROOTS TESTS

To detect stationarity and integration order of the variables, we use the tests of Phillips-Perron (PP) and Dickey-Fuller Generalized Least Squares (DF-GLS), whose critical threshold is 5%, and with a null hypothesis ($H0$) of nonstationarity of the variable. The results in Table 2.2 indicate that all the variables are stationary at the level and first difference. In this case, we can use the ARDL approach for our empirical estimation. Table 2.2

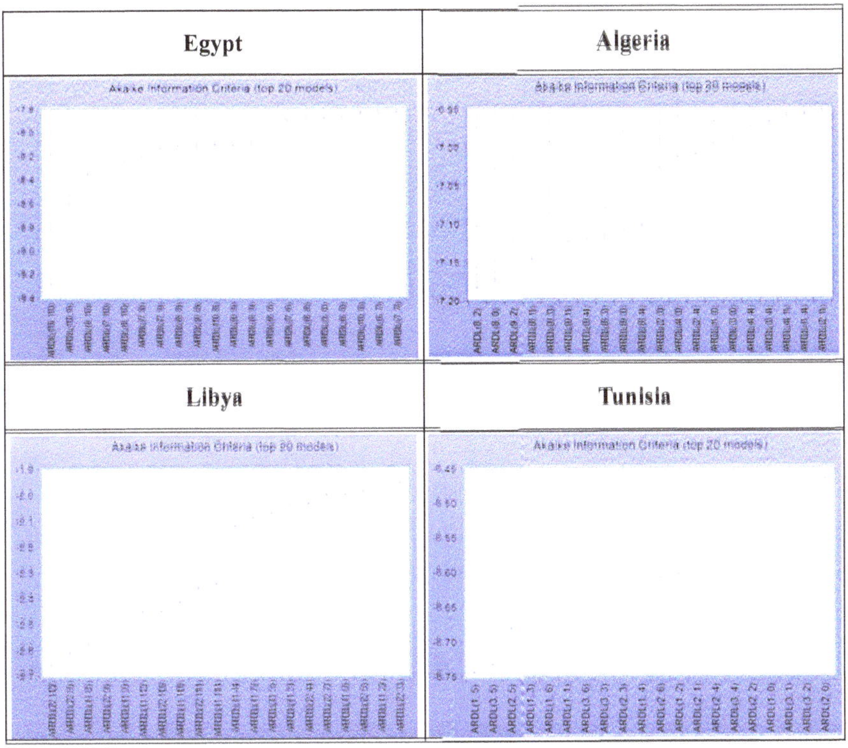

FIGURE 2.1 Akaike information criteria (AIC).

Source: Authors.

reports the results of the Augmented Dickey–Fuller (ADF) test and PP unit root tests for the study variables. For Algeria, Tunisia, Libya, and Egypt, LnGDP seems to be stationary in the ADF and PP test at the 5% level. Moreover, PS is stationary of order 1 ($I(1)$) for Tunisia and Libya at the 5% threshold. For Algeria, PS is stationary at levels $I(0)$ for the ADF at the 10% level ($I(1)$ for PP at the 5% level). For Egypt, the ADF test shows that PS is stationary of order 1 ($I(1)$) at the 5% threshold ($I(1)$ for the PP test). The two ADF and PP tests show that the series is stationary at $I(0)$ or $I(1)$. The unit root test confirms that none of the series is integrated into $I(2)$. Therefore, we may apply the ARDL bounds testing procedures to determine the long-run relationship between economic growth and political stability.

TABLE 2.2 Stationarity Test

Country		ADF		Order of Integration	PP		Order of Integration
		At the Level	**In First Difference**		**At the Level**	**In First Difference**	
Tunisia	LnGDP	−1.363 (0.588)	−5.992 (0.000*)	I(1)	−1.382 (0.579)	−6.007 (0.000*)	*I*(1)
	PS	−1.885 (0.335)	−5.441 (0.001*)	*I*(1)	−1.835 (0.357)	−5.407 (0.001*)	*I*(1)
Algeria	LnGDP	1.103 (0.996)	−3.737 (0.008*)	*I*(1)	1.180 (0.997)	−3.853 (0.005*)	*I*(1)
	PS	−2.830 (0.064**)		*I*(0)	−1.899 (0.328)	−4.221 (0.002*)	*I*(1)
Libya	LnGDP	−3.135 (0.040*)		*I*(0)	−3.109 (0.042)		*I*(0)
	PS	−1.770 (0.387)	−6.026 (0.000*)	*I*(1)	−1.826 (0.362)	−6.026 (0.000*)	*I*(1)
Egypt	LnGDP	−0.456 (0.886)	−3.522 (0.014*)	*I*(1)	−1.943 (0.309)	−4.806 (0.000*)	*I*(1)
	PS	−1.943 (0.309)	−4.806 (0.000*)	*I*(1)	−2.117 (0.239)	−4.747 (0.000*)	*I*(0)

Source: Authors.

Notes: *and ** denote significance at the 5% and 10% levels, respectively.

2.3.3.1 ARDL BOUNDS TESTS FOR COINTEGRATION

The ARDL estimate examines the relationship between the variables in terms of their past values as well as the current and past values of LnGDP and PS. The "Eviews 9" software has the option to run the ARDL modeling automatically. To determine the lag number, we adopt the Hannan-Quinn criterion. The number of lags for Tunisia, Egypt, Algeria, and Libya are (1, 5), (10, 10), (8, 2), and (2, 12), respectively; these results are reported in Table 2.3.

Figure 2.1 shows the best 20 models according to the AIC, which confirms our results. The results of the Autocorrelation of Residuals test shown in Table 2.4 indicate that there is no autocorrelation in the residuals of our model, which is essential to continue our estimation. If there is an autocorrelation of errors, the evaluation of the parameters will not be homogeneous. This is because of the shifted values of the dependent variable, which are represented as independent variables in the model. The Wald test was used to determine a long-term cointegration relationship

TABLE 2.3 ARDL Estimation

Variables	Tunisia: ARDL (1,5)				Alegria: ARDL (8,2)				Libya: ARDL (2,12)				Egypt: ARDL (10,10)			
	Coef.	Std. Error	t-Stat.	Probability	Coef.	Std. Error	t-Stat.	Probability	Coef.	Std. Error	t-Stat.	Probability	Coef.	Std. error	t-Stat.	Prob
D(LnGPDT(-1))	1.000994	0.000656	1526.143	0.0000*	0.652598	0.208931	3.123504	0.0075*	−0.286057	0.187137	−1.528600	0.1702	0.480657	0.386381	1.240000	0.3018
D(LnGPDT(-2))					0.258952	0.268479	0.964513	0.3512					0.515063	0.565050	0.911535	0.4292
D(LnGPDT(-3))					−0.103606	0.305344	−0.339310	0.7394					−0.950731	0.557028	−1.706791	0.1864
D(LnGPDT(-4))					−0.221371	0.287205	−0.770779	0.4537					0.265498	0.455606	0.609492	0.5853
D(LnGPDT(-5))					−0.116432	0.252665	−0.460815	0.6520					0.036684	0.445339	0.082744	0.9383
D(LnGPDT(-6))					0.135255	0.225119	0.600816	0.5576					0.023132	0.304447	0.075981	0.9442
D(LnGPDT(-7))					0.362207	0.226823	1.596867	0.1326					0.453654	0.344146	1.260029	0.2968
D(LnGPDT(-8))					−0.520735	0.160685	−3.240721	0.0059*					−0.524889	0.352746	−1.488021	0.2535
D(LnGPDT(-9))													−0.026367	0.333209	−0.079130	0.9419
D(PST)	0.005775	0.001339	2.819456	0.0097*	−0.002591	0.001871	−1.385354	0.1876	0.098880	0.014713	6.720796	0.0005*	0.708046	0.312512	2.265663	0.1084
D(PST(-1))	−0.004051	0.001777	−2.280218	0.0322*	0.002147	0.002395	0.896359	0.3852	−0.038554	0.020236	−1.905225	0.0984***	0.001657	0.001458	1.152727	0.3325
D(PST(-2))	0.005364	0.001711	2.130151	0.0441*	−0.002211	0.001702	−1.299024	0.2149	−0.061262	0.017209	−3.559858	0.0092*	−0.001487	0.001392	−1.068081	0.3638
D(PST(-3))	−0.001767	0.001704	−1.036705	0.3107					−0.029463	0.014544	−2.025793	0.0824***	0.001036	0.001311	0.790627	0.4869
D(PST(-4))	0.001237	0.001718	0.720365	0.4786					−0.021569	0.015126	−1.425976	0.1969	0.000668	0.001317	0.507075	0.6470
D(PST(-5))	−0.002235	0.001253	−1.881209	0.0830***					−0.014482	0.014124	−1.025367	0.3393	−0.000998	0.001774	−0.562430	0.6131
D(PST(-6))									−0.036305	0.013945	−2.603440	0.0352*	0.004763	0.001831	2.601410	0.0805
D(PST(-7))									−0.042970	0.014288	−3.007524	0.0197*	−0.001980	0.001839	−1.076502	0.3606
D(PST(-8))									−0.013902	0.025835	−0.538114	0.6072	0.001190	0.002008	0.592492	0.5952
D(PST(-9))									−0.012253	0.024788	−0.494288	0.6362	0.001383	0.001546	0.894926	0.4368
D(PST(-10))									−0.001054	0.023948	−0.043996	0.9661	0.001835	0.000998	1.838632	0.1633
D(PST(-11))									−0.038079	0.021246	−1.792502	0.1162				
D(PST(-12))									0.038079	0.021246	1.792502	0.1162				
C	0.233005	0.112317	2.074542	0.0473*	6.005505	1.395268	4.310571	0.0007*	6.762545	2.810899	2.405830	0.0471*	0.477848	0.185546	2.575369	0.0821**
Trend					0.007409	0.001758	4.263558	0.0008*								
R-squared	0.997914				0.998727				0.922407				0.976355			
Adjusted	0.997370				0.997636				0.761792				0.810840			
R-squared	2971.144				915.3369				5.690420				2971.144			
F-statistic	5441.396				0.000000				0.013551				0.000009			
Prob (F-statistic)																

Notes: *and ** denote significance at the 5% and 10% levels, respectively.

Source: *Authors.*

between the endogenous variable and the set of independent variables. In our case, this test aims to check whether LnGDP per capita has long-term cointegration links with PS for Tunisia, Algeria, Libya, and Egypt. The null hypothesis ($H0$) and the alternative hypothesis ($H1$) are as follows:

$$H0 : \beta_1 = \beta_2$$

$$H1 : \beta_1 \neq \beta_2$$

TABLE 2.4 Autocorrelation of Residuals

Tunisia			
AC	**PAC**	**Q-Stat**	**Prob**
1 −0.16	−0.16	0.8601	0.354
2 −0.27	−0.31	3.2591	0.196
3 −0.11	−0.25	3.6557	0.301
4 0.136	−0.05	4.2862	0.369
5 0.129	0.054	4.8759	0.431
6 −0.35...	−0.35	9.4546	0.150
7 0.037	−0.08	9.5092	0.218
8 0.216	0.046	11.432	0.178
9 −0.02...	−0.11	11.461	0.245
10 −0.15...	−0.13	12.515	0.252
11 −0.03...	−0.04	12.571	0.322
12 0.312	0.152	17.661	0.126

Algeria			
AC	**PAC**	**Q-Stat**	**Prob**
1 0.066	0.066	0.1457	0.703
2 −0.12...	−0.213	0.7167	0.699
3 0.11...	−0.09	1.1939	0.754
4 0.28...	−0.209	4.1712	0.383
5 0.14...	−0.16	4.9969	0.416
6 0.183	0.106	6.3296	0.387
7 0.068	0.04	6.5201	0.48
8 0.114	0.062	7.0675	0.682
9 0.033	−0.022	7.1397	0.623
10 0.08...	−0.086	8.2574	0.69
11 0.12...	−0.000	11.927	0.534
12−0.169	0.039	13.637	0.477
13 0.005	−0.014	13.639	0.553
14 0.263	0.191	18.371	0.303

TABLE 2.4 *(Continued)*

Egypt			
AC	**PAC**	**Q-Stat**	**Prob**
1 −0.23...	−0.23...	1.5733	0.21
2 −0.15..	−0.22...	2.2957	0.317
3 −0.33...	−0.48	5.7212	0.126
4 0.287	0.02....	2.367	0.079
5 0.004	−0.12...	8.3674	0.137
6 0.127	0.045	0.045	0.177
7 −0.17...	0.001	0.001	0.183
8 −0.04...	−0.09	10.154	0.254
9 −0.03...	−0.05...	0.192	0.335
10 −0.36	−0.18...	10.154	0.284
11 −0.03...	−0.19...	10.295	0.504
12 0.003	−0.18...	10.296	0.509

Libya			
AC	**PAC**	**Q-Stat**	**Prob**
1 −0.00	−0.00	0.0011	0.974
2 −0.09	−0.09	0.3099	0.856
3 −0.05	−0.06	0.4406	0.932
4 −0.08	−0.09	0.7545	0.944
4 −0.08	−0.09	0.7545	0.944
5 −0.00	−0.02	0.7573	0.980
6 −0.08	−0.10	1.0386	0.984
7 −0.08	−0.11	1.3922	0.986
9 −0.03	−0.08	1.7151	0.995
10 0.120	0.061	2.4368	0.992
11 0.090	0.048	2.8631	0.992
12 −0.08	−0.10	3.2188	0.994
13 −0.08	−0.10	3.5863	0.995
14 −0.07	−0.12	3.9658	0.996
15 0.148	0.105	5.3625	0.989
16 0.036	−0.00	5.4493	0.993

Source: *Authors*.

Table 2.5 shows the results of the bounds-testing approach. We found a long-run relationship between the variables in Tunisia and Egypt, Libya, and Algeria. This conclusion is based on *F*-values of

61.98163 for Tunisia, 9.752624 for Algeria, 11.17129 for Egypt, and 9.438124 for Libya, exceeding the upper bound values at the 1%, 2.5%, 5%, and 10% levels. In this case, we reject the null hypothesis of no cointegration and we accept the alternative hypothesis, which assumes the presence of long-run relationships between different variables of our econometric model.

TABLE 2.5 ARDL Bounds Test. Null Hypothesis (*H0*): No Long-Run Relationships

Test statistic	Tunisia	Algeria	Egypt	Libya
F-statistic	Value K 61.98163 1	Value K 9.752624 1	Value K 11.17129 1	Value K 9.438124 1
Critical value bounds Significance	|0 Bound | 1 Bound	|0 Bound | 1 Bound	|0 Bound | 1 Bound	|0 Bound | 1 Bound
10%	2.44 3.28	5.59 6.26	4.04 4.78	4.04 4.78
5%	3.15 4.1	6.56 7.3	4.94 5.73	4.94 5.73
2.5%	3.88 4.92	7.46 8.27	5.77 6.68	5.77 6.68
1%	4.81 6.02	8.74 9.63	6.84 7.84	6.84 7.84

Source: Authors.

The results of short- and long-run estimations are presented in Tables 2.6 and 2.7. In the long term, a 1% increase in political stability leads to an increase in economic growth of 0.092% (Tunisia), 0.024% (Algeria), 0.009% (Egypt), and 0.102% (Libya). This finding confirms the hypothesis that political stability influences long-term economic growth. Several studies have shown that the causal relationship between political instability and economic growth works both ways (Zablotsky, 1996; Gyimah-Brempong and Traynor, 1999). Other studies have found no causal relationship between the variables (Campos and Nugent, 2003). Other studies have reported direct and indirect effects of political instability on economic growth (Schneider and Frey, 1985; Barro, 1991; Levine and Renelt, 1992). Thus, the negative impact of political instability has indirect consequences on growth factors such as savings and investment. Other studies have highlighted the indirect effect of the "brain drain" (Adebayo, 1985; Kwasi, 1992), which is the process of human capital depletion caused mainly by political unrest. The Error Correction Model regressions on the relationship level must be estimated. The results indicate that economic growth converges to a

TABLE 2.6 Short-Run Estimation

Variables	Tunisia: ARDL (1,5)				Alegria : ARDL (8,2)				Libya: ARDL (2,12)				Egypt: ARDL (10,10)			
	Coef.	Std. Error	t-Stat.	Probability	Coef.	Std. Error	t-Stat.	Probability	Coef.	Std. Error	t-Stat.	Probability	Coef.	Std. Error	t-Stat.	Prob
D(LnGPDT(-1))					0.192408	0.164226	1.171607	0.2585	0.229323	0.302909	0.757070	0.5040	−0.480070	0.374261	−1.282716	0.2897
D(LnGPDT(-2))					0.360195	0.187241	1.923688	0.0724**					0.034995	0.366753	0.095421	0.9302
D(LnGPDT(-3))					0.363452	0.158936	2.286783	0.0362*					−0.915738	0.345946	−2.647055	0.0772**
D(LnGPDT(-4))					−0.026247	0.152239	−0.172407	0.8653					−0.650239	0.332159	−1.957618	0.1452
D(LnGPDT(-5))					0.014126	0.147321	0.095886	0.9248					−0.613556	0.204925	−2.994053	0.0579**
D(LnGPDT(-6))					0.161293	0.145735	1.106757	0.2848					−0.590424	0.233360	−2.530097	0.0854**
D(LnGPDT(-7))					0.441455	0.148641	2.969942	0.0090*					−0.156790	0.229094	−0.684392	0.5429
D(LnGPDT(-8))													−0.681679	0.319620	−2.132782	0.1227
D(LnGPDT(-9))													−0.708046	0.312512	−2.265663	0.1084
D(PST)	0.003775	0.001339	2.819456	0.0097*	−0.001254	0.001020	−1.230091	0.2364	0.120494	0.012882	9.353650	0.0026*	0.000445	0.001048	0.425054	0.7008
D(PST(-1))	−0.003644	0.001711	−2.130151	0.0441*					−0.086567	0.049164	−1.760787	0.1765	0.001487	0.001392	1.068081	0.3638
D(PST(-2))	0.001767	0.001704	1.036705	0.3107					−0.003027	0.021537	−0.140541	0.8971	−0.001036	0.001311	−0.790627	0.4869
D(PST(-3))	−0.001237	0.001718	−0.720365	0.4786					0.002231	0.013211	0.168882	0.8766	−0.000668	0.001317	−0.507075	0.6470
D(PST(-4))	0.002235	0.001233	1.812092	0.0830**					−0.004990	0.012954	−0.385197	0.7258	0.000998	0.001774	0.562430	0.6131
D(PST(-5))									0.044161	0.013053	3.383299	0.0430*	−0.004763	0.001831	−2.601410	0.0803
D(PST(-6))									−0.028985	0.018208	−1.591862	0.2097	0.001980	0.001839	1.076502	0.3606
D(PST(-7))									−0.013365	0.029160	−0.458320	0.6779	−0.001190	0.002008	−0.592492	0.5952
D(PST(-8))									0.038842	0.031389	1.237417	0.3040	−0.001383	0.001546	−0.894926	0.4368
D(PST(-9))									−0.033402	0.028935	−1.154447	0.3319	−0.001835	0.000998	−1.838632	0.1633
D(PST(-10))									0.055058	0.026905	2.046348	0.1332	−0.039273	0.017008	−2.309025	0.1041
D(PST(-11))									−0.064853	0.020683	−3.135615	0.0518**				
D(PST(-12))																
Trend					0.006817	0.001673	4.074457	0.0009*								
CointEq (-1)	−0.022481	0.010948	−2.053442	0.0495*	−0.501345	0.121825	−4.115278	0.0008*	−0.722303	0.382590	−4.503617	0.0108*	−0.372098	0.102993	−3.612853	0.0013*

Notes: *and ** denote significance at the 5% and 10% levels, respectively.

Source: Authors.

long-run equilibrium level with an adjustment speed of 2.24% (Tunisia), 50.13% (Algeria), 72.30% (Libya), and 37.20% (Egypt) through the political stability channel. To check the robustness of the different results, we use the Breusch-Godfrey tests (Serial Correlation LM), the Breusch-Pagan-Godfrey test (Heterosedasticity), and the Jarque-Bera test (normality). The results presented in Table 2.8 prove the success of the test of normality of residuals, the test of the absence of serial autocorrelation of order 1 (LM-test), and that of homoscedasticity.

TABLE 2.7 Long-Term Estimate

Variables	Tunisia	Alegria	Egypt	Libya
	Coefficient	**Coefficient**	**Coefficient**	**Coefficient**
PS	0.092 (0.05**)	0.024 (0.063**)	0.009 (0.013*)	0.102 (0.016*)
Constant	10.364 (0.000*)	10.686 (0.000*)	10.743 (0.000*)	9.812 (0.000*)
Trend		0.014 (0.000*)		

Source: Authors.

Notes: *and ** denote significance at the 5% and 10% levels, respectively.

2.3.1 ROBUSTNESS CHECK

As a final step, we use diagnostic tests to assess the robustness of our empirical model. The Cumulative Sum of Recursive Risiduals (CUSUMSQ) and the Cumulative Sum of Recursive Risiduals (CUSUM) are used to determine the stability of the model over time estimated by the ARDL approach. These two tests come in figures. If both the CUSUM and CUSUMSQ curves are within two critical terminals at the 5% threshold, we therefore accept the null hypothesis, which assumes the stability of the coefficients of the regression, and subsequently, the model is stable over time. Figures 2.2 and 2.3 indicate that the four Tunisian, Algeria, Egypt, and Libya curves of CUSUM and CUSUMSQ are within two bounds of the 5% confidence interval. These results confirm that our econometric model is stable over time for the four studied countries.

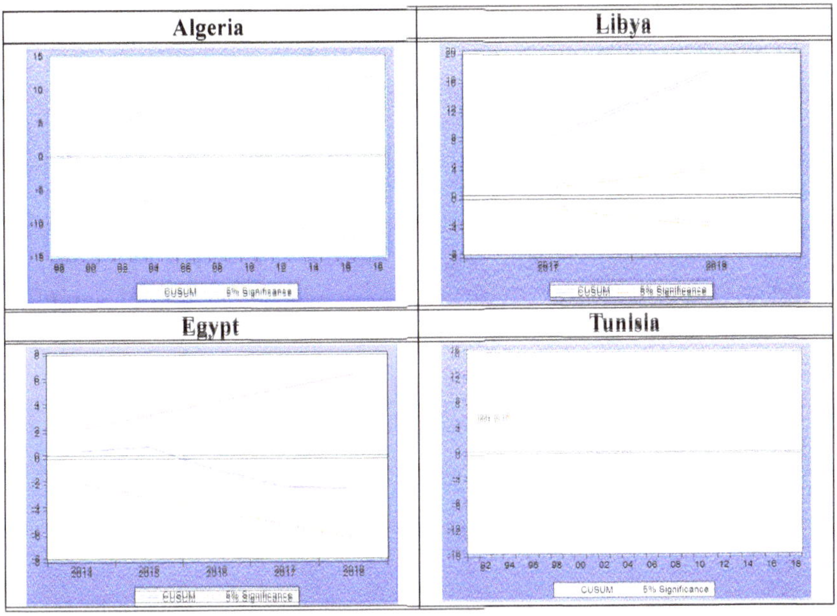

FIGURE 2.2 CUSUM test.

Source: Authors

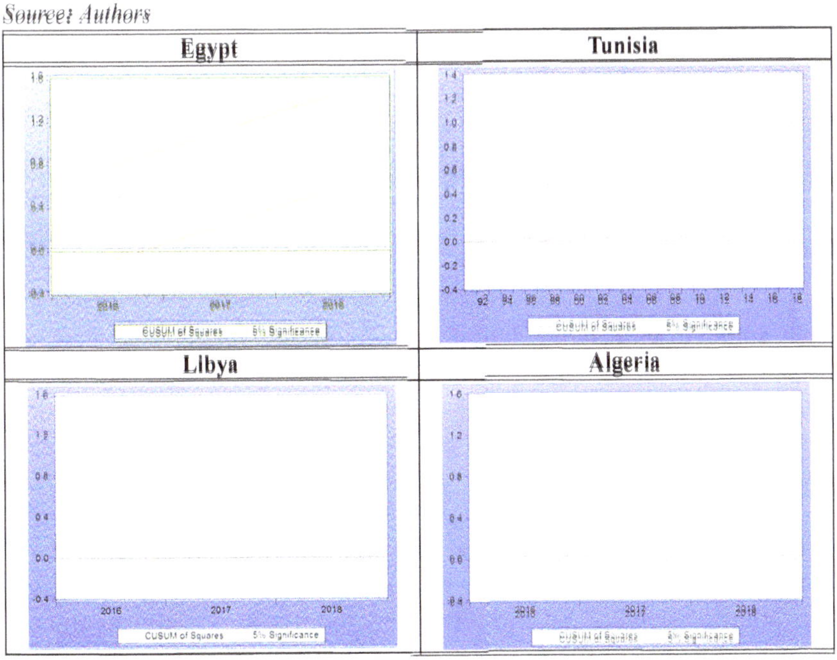

FIGURE 2.3 CUSUMSQ test.

Source: Authors.

The value of the statistic must then be verified under the null hypothesis that indicates the stability of the relationship curve in an interval (Bresson and Pirotte, 1995) fixed by two straight lines. In the case of a time series, the stability tests, also called structural change tests, examine the stability of the estimated coefficients of the equation while showing the presence of a structural change in the correlation. The CUSUM test is then adapted to test the hypothesis of stability of the long-run relations between economic growth and political stability. For the four countries, the CUSUM and CUSUMQ test curves are within the 5% confidence interval. This implies that the models chosen to estimate the relations between economic growth and political stability.

TABLE 2.8 Robustness Test

Tunisia	Algeria	Egypt	Libya
	Breusch-Godfrey Serial Correlation LM Test		
0.281 (0.757)	2.217 (0.145)	1.051 (0.567)	0.294 (0.747)
	Heteroskedasticity Test: Breusch-Pagan-Godfrey		
0.401 (0.919)	1.106 (0.413)	2.722 (0.222)	0.343 (0.924)
	Jarque-Bera (test de normalité)		
1.728 (0.094)	1.811 (0.404)	0.437 (0.803)	0.114 (0.944)

Source: Authors.

2.4 CONCLUSION AND POLITICAL IMPLICATIONS

This study examined the long-term equilibrium relationship between economic growth and political stability in Tunisia, Libya, Egypt, and Algeria over the 1984 to 2022 period. Our analysis proves that the political stability influences economic growth in the four countries but at different levels. We constructed a model to determine the relationship between economic growth as a dependent variable explained by political stability. After checking that the integration order is strictly less than two, the cointegration test proves the presence of cointegration relationships, implying that political stability has a positive and significant effect on economic growth for the future of the Tunisian economy, Egypt, Algeria, and Libya.

With these results, we can recommend more policy effects. A high propensity for executive change is associated with political uncertainty and in some cases threats to property rights, which negatively affects economic growth. In addition, international terrorism designates dangerous or violent actions affecting the internal stability of people such as the violation of the penal rights of the State. These actions destabilize civil life and government policy. Conflicts can be social conflicts and civil wars that affect a country and deteriorate its human development and economic growth. Social conflicts stem from the social organization itself, which is based on a differentiation of economic, social, and political rights.

In the MENA region, we can conclude that the institutional failures of these countries end up disrupting long-term economic growth. At the same time, the significance of the political stability index could not be confirmed, although its impact was found to be positive. For future studies, a longer period of observation would bring new insights into this area of research for the African region in general. The question then arises: What are the main channels of the transmission of political instability to economic growth?

The objective of this chapter is to consider the effect of political solidness on financial development within the case of Tunisia, Egypt, Libya, and Algeria. This study gives an examination of the relationship between political precariousness and financial development for the period from 1984 to 2022 in African nations utilizing the settled impacts demonstrate. The study aimed to examine the effect of political instability on financial development in transition countries of the African region.

Political stability is a crucial factor in driving economic and social transitions. Political stability has a positive impact on economic growth for some MENA countries. This result is expected because political instability negatively affects economic growth and leads to poor governance. Similarly, the instability of the regime refers to the uncertainty that investors face regarding the security of property rights (Svensson, 1998). It has a negative effect on trade, the increase of military expenditures, and the decrease in the share of government expenditures. Keefer and Knack (1997) have shown, moreover, that political instability has negative effects on investment and growth, and that the subjective indices of corruption and the quality of administration are negatively associated with Economic Growth.

This finding helps us understand that, unlike what Aisen and Veiga (2013) revealed, frequent changes in legislative control have a positive impact on productive development, contributing to the literature in this field.

Consistent with the study by Hysa and Çela (2019), these findings appear to be highly significant as they provide new directions and perspectives regarding political stability and the necessity of cycles of change in legislative powers. In addition, other factors are considered as control factors in our model, particularly trade openness, insincerity, and net capital flows are found to be critical in explaining the development of GDP per capita.

To conclude, this chapter inspected wrangles about and writing discoveries on the portion of political steadiness in productive development. The investigation discoveries stay urgent for the CEE regions since they honored and emphasized a few issues, videlicet, the long-term remain of authoritative pioneers within the same overseeing position, which adversely affects the cheapness of this locale. Contemporaneously, the centrality of the political soundness marker might not be confirmed, undoubtedly, in spite of the fact that its affect was set up to be positive. For future studies, a longer period of observation could provide new insights into this area of investigation for the African region. Tabassam et al. (2016) have shown that political instability has a negative impact on economic development. The question that then arises is: what are the main channels through which political instability affects economic development?

KEYWORDS

- **Arab countries**
- **Auto-Regressive Distributive Lags**
- **economic growth**
- **political instability**

REFERENCES

Abeyasinghe, R. (2004). Democracy, political stability, and developing country growth: Theory and evidence. Economics Research Honors, Spring 2004.

Adebayo, A. (1985). Brain drain within the Ecowas region. Issue. *Journal of Opinion*, 14, 37–38.

Ades, A. & Chua, H. B. (1997). Thy neighbor's curse: Regional instability and economic growth. *Journal of Economic Growth*, 2(3), 279–304.

Aisen, A. & Veiga, F. J. (2013). How does political instability affect economic growth? *European Journal of Political Economy*, 29, 151–167.

Aisen, A. & Veiga, F. J. (2008).The political economy of seigniorage. *Journal of Development Economics*, 87, 29–50.

Alesina, A. & Drazen, A. (1991). Why are stabilizations delayed? *American Economic Review*, 81, 1170–1188.

Alesina, A., Ozler, S., Roubini, N. & Swagel, P. (1996). Political instability and economic growth. *Journal of Economic Growth*, 1(2), 189–212.

Alesina, A. & Perotti, R. (1996). Income distribution, political instability and investment. *European Economic Review*, 40, 1203–1228.

Asteriou, D. S. & Price S. (2001). Political instability and economic growth: UK Time Series Evidence Scottish. *Journal of Political Economy*, 48(4), 12–26.

Barro, R. (1991). Economic growth in a cross section of countries. *Quarterly Journal of Economics*, 106, 407–443.

Benhabib, J. & Rustichini, R. (1996). Social conflict and growth. *Journal of Economic Growth*, 1, 125–142.

Besley, T., Persson, T. & Sturm, D. (2005). Political Competition and Economic Performance: Theory and Evidence from the United States. NBER Working Paper, 11484.

Borner, S. & Paldam, M. (1998). The Political Dimension of Economic Growth. Palgrave Macmillan, New York.

Bounan, M. (2003). Logique de Terrorisme. Allia Edition, France.

Bresson, G. & Pirotte, A. (1995). Econométrie des séries temporelles: Théorie et application. PUF.

BrockBlomberg, S. (1996). Growth, political instability and the defense burden. *Economica*, 63, 649–672.

Campos, N. F. & Nugent, J. B. (2003). Aggregate investment and political instability: An econometric investigation. *Economica*, 70(279), 533–549.

Campos, N. & Nugent, J. (2002). Who is afraid of political instability? *Journal of Development Economics*, 67, 157–172.

Castro, V. & Veiga, F. J. (2004). Political business cycles and inflation stabilization. *Economic Letter*, 83(1), 1–6.

Darby, J., Li, C. & Muscatelli, A. (2004). Political uncertainty, public expenditure and growth. *European Journal of Political Economy*, 20, 153–179.

Devereux, M. & Wen, J. F. (1998). Political instability, capital taxation, and growth. *European Economic Review*, 42, 1635–1651.

Engle, R. F. & Granger, C. W. J. (1987).Co-integration and error correction: Representation, estimation, and testing. *Econometrica*, 55(2), 251–276.

Ghate, C., Le, Q. & Zak, P. (2003). Optimal fiscal policy in an economy facing sociopolitical instability. *Review of Development Economics*, 7, 583–598.

Gupta, D. (1990).The Economics of Political Violence. Praeger, New York.

Gyimah-Brempong, K. & Traynor, T. L. (1999). Political instability, investment and economic growth in Sub-Saharan Africa. *Journal of African Economies*, 8(1), 52–86.

Heshmati, A. & Kim, N. (2017). The Relationship between economic growth and democracy: Alternative representations of technological change. IZA Discussion Papers 10880, Institute of Labor Economics (IZA).

Hysa, E. & Çela, A. (2019). Relationship between Governance and Human Development in European Countries: Panel Regression Analysis. The 2019 IAI Academic Conference Proceedings, Rome, Italy.

Iqbal, N. & Daly, S. (2014). Rent-seeking opportunities and economic growth in transitional economies. *Economic Modelling*, 37, 16–22.

Johansen, S. (1988). Statistical analysis of cointegration vectors. *Journal of Economic Dynamics and Control*, 2(2–3), 231–254.

Johansen, S. & Juselius, K. (1990). Maximum likelihood estimation and inference on cointegration-with applications to the demand for money. *Oxford Bulletin of Economics and Statistics*, 52(2), 169–210.

Jong-A-Pin, R. (2009). On the measurement of political instability and its impact on economic growth. *European Journal of Political Economy*, 25, 15–29.

Keefer, P. & Knack, S. (1997). Why don't poor countries catch up? A cross-national test of an institutional explanation. *Economic Inquiry*, 35, 590–602.

Khemraj, T. (2020). Two ethnic security dilemmas and their economic origin. Special Edition Working Paper, Faculty of Social Sciences, University of West Indies, Cave Hill Campus.

Kurzman, C., Werum, R. & Burkhart, R. E. (2002). Democracy's effect on economic growth: A pooled time-series analysis, 1951–1980. *Studies in Comparative International Development*, 37(1), 3–33.

Kuznets, S. (1966). Modern Economic Growth.Yale University Press, New Haven, CT.

Kuznets, S. (1973). Modern economic growth: Findings and reflections. *American Economic Review*, 63(3), 247–258.

Kwasi, F. A. (1992). Political instability and economic growth: Evidence from Sub-Saharan Africa. *Economic Development and Cultural Change*, 40, 829–841.

Levine, R. & Renelt, D. (1992). A sensitivity analysis of cross-country growth regressions. *American Economic Review*, 82, 942–963.

Lipset, S. M. (1960). Political Man Social Bases of Politics. Doubleday Company, Garden City.

Mauro, P. (1995). Corruption and growth. *Quarterly Journal of Economics*, 110, 681–712.

Nawaz, S. (2015). Growth effects of institutions: A disaggregated analysis. *Economic Modelling*, 45, 118–126.

North, D. C. (1990). Institutions, institutional change and economic. Cambridge University Press, New York.

Özler, S. & Rodrik, D. (1992). External shocks, politics and private investment: some theory and empirical evidence. *Journal of Development Economics*, 39(1), 141–162.

Perotti, R. (1996). Growth, income distribution, and democracy: What the data say. *Journal of Economic Growth*, 1(2), 149–187.

Pesaran, M. H., Shin, Y. & Smith, R. J. (2001). Bounds testing approaches to the analysis of level relationships. *Journal of Applied Econometrics*, 16, 289–326.

Pesaran, M. H & Shin, Y., (1999). An autoregressive distributed lag modeling approach to cointegration analysis, In Strom, S., Holly, A., Diamond, P. (Eds.), Centennial Volume of Rangar, University Press, Cambridge.

Rachdi, H. & Saidi, H. (2015). Democracy and economic growth: Evidence in MENA countries. *Procedia-Social and Behavioral Sciences*, 191, 616–621.

Rodrik, D. (1991). Policy uncertainty and private investment in developing countries. *Journal of Development Economics*, 36(2), 229–242.

Sanders, D. (1981). Patterns of Political Instability. The MacMillan Press, London, UK.

Schneider, F. & Frey, B. S. (1985). Economic and political determinants of foreign direct investment. *World Development*, 13, 161–175.

Svensson, J. (1998). Investment, property rights and political instability: Theory and evidence. *European Economic Review*, 42, 1317–1341.

Tabassam, A. H., Hashmi, S. H. & Rehman, F. (2016). Nexus between political instability and economic growth in Pakistan. *Procedia—Social and Behavioral Sciences*, 230, 325–334.

Tavares, J. & Wacziarg, R. (2001). How democracy affects growth. *European Economic Review*, 45(8), 1341–1378.

Zablotsky, E. E. (1996). Political stability and economic growth. A Two Way Relation. Universidad del CEMA. CEMA Working Papers.

CHAPTER 3

A Procedure Manual for the Application of International Accounting Standards (IAS)/International Financial Reporting Standards (IFRS) as an Internal Control Tool

FATINE FATIMA EZZAHRA*, HILMI YASSINE, and KAIZAR CHAIMAE

National School of Commerce and Management, University Chouaib Doukkali, El Jadida, Morocco

*Corresponding author

ABSTRACT

The function of internal control has made significant strides in both theoretical and practical aspects. This progress aligns with the introduction of International Accounting Standards (IAS)/International Financial Reporting Standards (IFRS), particularly in response to financial scandals that mandated the strengthening of transparency and reliability in communicated financial information. Focusing on the manual of accounting procedures as a tool for precision and accuracy, our study explores the theoretical framework associating it with the internal control function. The primary objective of this chapter is to examine how the implementation of a procedure manual, aligned with IAS/IFRS, contributes to enhancing the internal control system within companies. Upon analyzing the document, it is evident that the creation of a procedure manual based on the international accounting framework facilitates a smoother transition to IAS/IFRS.

Corporate Governance, Digitalization, and Energy Transition: Imen Baccouche and Afef Khalil. (Eds.)

DOI: 10.1201/9781779643407-4

3.1 INTRODUCTION

In a globalized context, the International Accounting Standards (IAS)/International Financial Reporting Standards (IFRS) have emerged to establish a unified accounting language, aimed at enhancing the comparability of performances of companies worldwide. Thus, the opening up of the national economic fabric to foreign investors and stakeholders has revealed the significance of transitioning to IFRS standards, which represents a true change and challenge for Moroccan companies. In this regard, to incorporate it within a sound standardization vision and make it effective, the transition of a major Moroccan company named Alpha (fictitious name due to confidentiality) to IAS/IFRS standards involves the creation of a manual of accounting procedures that facilitate familiarity with these standards, mitigating any risks arising from confusion during their implementation (Eustache Akpane, 2008; Bragg, 2016).

It is within this perspective that the focus of our study lies, namely: How could the implementation of an accounting procedure manual for IAS/IFRS application effectively contributes to the enhancement of internal control in Moroccan companies? We will attempt to address this primary question through the following research questions:

- What challenges does the company face regarding the use of IFRS?
- What advantages does an IFRS Application Procedure Manual hold in terms of internal control?
- What would be the impact of applying IFRS reclassifications and adjustments on the company's financial statements? Consequently, in its financial ratios?

To tackle the research problem and achieve the objective of designing and implementing an IFRS manual, we will conduct a study using various qualitative and quantitative methods, including document analysis, semi-structured interviews, and questionnaires. These tools will form a robust basis for deriving our findings. To this end, our study will start with a literature review, establishing the link between the manual, the transition to IAS/IFRS standards, and internal control. We will then proceed to present the research objectives and methodology, highlighting the hypotheses and the relevance of the topic. Subsequently, the empirical framework, constituting the third section, will encompass the development of an IFRS

Application Procedure Manual designed to overcome challenges encountered during the implementation of these standards within the designated company. This section will deduce the impact of applying the manual's instructions on the entity's financial ratios and the practice of its internal control.

3.2 LITERATURE REVIEW AND HYPOTHESIS

The procedure manual: "is a written document describing procedures, in whole or in part, of various processes within an organization, whether public or private. It explains, in readily understandable language, who does what, about whom, when (timeframe), where, how, and for what purpose" (Eustache Akpane, 2008). The accounting procedure manual is a document drafted by the principles, standards, and rules of account management. It outlines the successive stages of executing an accounting operation and encompasses the financial aspect of an organization, featuring instructions related to establishing its accounting practices. In other words, it is a document drafted by the principles, standards, and rules of account management. It outlines the successive stages of executing an accounting operation and encompasses the financial aspect of an organization, featuring instructions related to establishing its accounting practices. The primary objective of implementing a procedure manual is to formalize work practices within the company. More specifically, it aims to:

- Describe, in accessible language, who does what, where, when, how, and for what purpose.
- Provide a form of reference to consult in the event of an error or omission.
- Serve as a point of reference for controls.
- Strengthen the internal control framework and address the need for ongoing control, even self-control.
- Address reliability and security requirements.

Thus, the development of a procedure manual falls under the responsibility of the Chief Executive Officer (CEO), and its implementation involves distinguishing between five essential phases.

Therefore, the development of any manual must take into consideration precise formalization (format, style, quality) and well-defined basic rules (clarity, conciseness, reliability, coherence). In his renowned book "Accounting Best Practice," Bragg (2016) addresses executives who are called to work in a seemingly magical manner: handling transactions, drafting reports, enhancing efficiency, and devising new processes all within optimal timeframes and costs. The aim is to significantly bolster the performance of their accounting and financial departments. The procedure manual is defined as "An accounting procedure manual which is more than just a document; it is a tool for maintaining control, ensuring accuracy, and minimizing risks in financial processes. It safeguards the integrity of financial data and guides employees through the proper steps, fostering a culture of accountability" (Bragg, 2016). He asserts then, that an accounting procedure manual transcends being a mere document; it functions as an instrument to uphold control, ensure precision, and mitigate risks in financial procedures. It protects the accuracy of financial information and directs employees through appropriate steps, thereby nurturing a sense of responsibility. Drawing from his extensive experience as a former CEO and controller of multiple firms, the author also advocates for the use of an accounting procedure manual containing methods and procedures adapted to the complexity and uniqueness of each entity. As a result, its impact on the accounting management of an organization elucidates the interest in establishing a connection between the Procedure Manual and IAS. As the world of finance continues its rapid globalization, the IAS / IFRS standards stand as beacons of convergence, bridging the gap between disparate accounting practices. These internationally recognized standards serve as a unifying framework, ensuring consistency and comparability in financial reporting across diverse industries and geographies. Underpinned by the principles of transparency, accuracy, and relevance, IAS/IFRS standards not only enhance the quality of presented financial information but also foster trust among stakeholders. By establishing a common language for financial reporting, these standards empower businesses to adeptly navigate the complexities of our interconnected global marketplace. The transition to IAS/IFRS standards signifies a strategic stride toward coherent and dependable financial communication, consequently facilitating informed decision-making, bolstering investor confidence, and fortifying the bedrock of a resilient financial ecosystem (Barbu and Piot, 2012). These standards were developed by the International Accounting Standards Board in the aftermath of financial scandals (such as Enron, Worldcom, Hauspie, Vivendi, Lernout, etc.) and are designed to standardize the presentation of accounting data exchanged on an international scale. Overall, their emergence can be explained by several factors.

Furthermore, the main challenge in implementing these standards is to facilitate the functioning of the financial market while strengthening the circulation of capital and achieving a better company evaluation through more transparent and comparable information (Disle and Noël, 2007). In addition, the initial studies consider the international accounting differences as a consequence of distinct choices made by various countries in handling identical transactions. In comparison to the Moroccan accounting framework, the international framework presents several points of divergence, which are outlined in Table 3.1.

TABLE 3.1 Comparison Between the Moroccan Accounting Framework and the IAS/IFRS Standards

Divergences	Gross Cash Accruals	IAS/IFRS Standards
Vision	Legal vision of the company: Accounting serves as a tool for management and control, of social organization (regulation, control, state, notion of prudence).	Economic vision of the company: Accounting becomes a relevant tool that allows on the one hand to inform the stakeholders in the financial framework, and on the other hand to measure the added value created for the investors.
The idea of presenting a true and fair view	Accurate and impartial representation of the accounts, reflecting the legal status of the company's assets and liabilities = Evaluation of the assets.	Ensuring an equitable display of an organization's financial position, performance, and cash flows = Measurement of Profitability.
The legal aspect	Precedence of law over facts: Only the assets owned by the company are recorded in the assets.	Precedence of economic reality over form (substance over form): The presence of leased/financed assets in the company's assets of the company.
Valuation of assets	Book value of assets: Assets valued at historical cost.	Market value of assets: Assets valued according to the concept of fair value (fair value).
Relation to taxation	The intimate connection between accounting and taxation.	Independence of accounting from taxation, strategic management, and results.
Summary statements	Financial statements by the Plan General Accounting Plan.	Financial statements by IAS/IFRS standards.

Source: Authors

However, differences in principles and financial statement presentation between the two frameworks are also evident, which will have a direct impact on the financial ratios calculated from the financial statements. This impact can encompass fair value impact and the impact of revaluation of financial instruments, tangible and intangible assets, potentially affecting both the asset and liability sides, as well as equity (Raffournier, 2017). Thus, the main financial ratios that can be used to calculate and evaluate the financial situation of companies are shown in Figure 3.1.

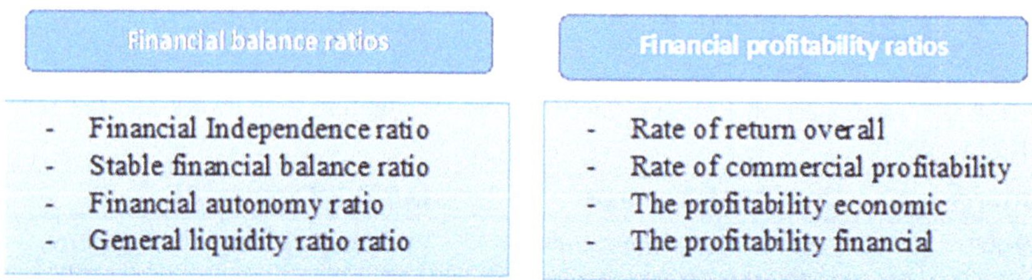

FIGURE 3.1 Main ratios for the evaluation of the financial situation.

Source: Authors.

Despite this, many scholars argue that IFRS standards have the effect of reducing result manipulation and enhancing the efficiency of stock markets (Kasznik, 1999; Leuz, 2003). It is crucial to recognize that the reception of IAS involves diverse interpretations that go beyond these perspectives. These differing stances reflect the dynamic nature of financial reporting practices and underscore the multifaceted impact that the implementation of IFRS standards can have on various facets of corporate functioning and financial ecosystems. As such, a comprehensive analysis of the implications and outcomes of IFRS adoption remains a critical area for scholarly exploration and empirical investigation. In this context, numerous studies have been undertaken across various countries to explore the favorable influence of IFRS on equity, as exemplified in the subsequent table (Table 3.2).

On the other hand, internal control, a fundamental cornerstone of effective organizational governance, encompasses the systematic processes, policies, and practices that safeguard assets, ensure accurate financial reporting, and promote compliance with regulations. It acts as a shield against risks, both operational and financial, enhancing the reliability and integrity of financial information. Internal control, as per the definition by the Committee of Sponsoring Organizations of the Treadway Commission (COSO), is "a process, implemented by an entity's board of directors, management, and other personnel, with the aim of providing reasonable assurance concerning the achievement of objectives in the following areas: effectiveness and efficiency of operations, reliability of financial reporting, and compliance with applicable laws and regulations" (COSO, 2013). Scholars have extensively examined the intricate relationship between internal control and organizational performance. Notably, Raghunandan and Wright (2009) emphasize the vital role of internal control in minimizing fraudulent activities and errors that could otherwise undermine financial data credibility. Moreover, Al-Matari et al. (2014) underscore the link between effective internal control mechanisms and enhanced operational efficiency, citing how a well-designed control environment can lead to streamlined processes and improved resource allocation. The establishment of an accounting procedure manual aligns seamlessly with the principles of internal control. Such a manual, often accompanied by an internal control framework, serves as a blueprint to standardize operations, enhance transparency, and streamline accountability. According to Begum and Chou (2018), a structured manual of procedures contributes to minimizing risks, providing a clear structure that guides employees through predefined steps, thereby reducing the likelihood of errors and inconsistencies. Similarly, Serdarusic and Horvat (2018) stress that a well-documented manual not only clarifies roles and responsibilities but also augments the effectiveness of internal control mechanisms, leading to a more efficient and controlled environment. Thus, we hypothesize that:

H1. The various accounting departments of the entity encounter several difficulties in practicing the IAS of IFRS.

H2. The accounting procedure manual for the application of IFRS would promote standardized, effective, and efficient transaction processing.

H3. The IFRS-driven reclassifications and adjustments outlined in the new manual would result in a more favorable depiction of financial statements and ratios for Company X.

H4. An IFRS-based accounting procedure manual would serve as an asset for internal accounting control, enhancing the quality of financial reporting.

TABLE 3.2 Study of the Positive Impact of IFRS Between Different Countries

References	Sample	Country	Period	Measures	Results
Bartov et al. (2005)	417 companies	Germany	1998–2000	Value relevance	The outcomes disclosed under the United States Generally Accepted Accounting Principles (US GAAP) and IFRS are deemed more pertinent than the results published under local German standards.
Boumediene (2013)	150 companies	France	2003–2004 2006–2007	Value relevance	The application of IFRS increases the information content of accounting figures.
	208 companies	Turkey	2002–2007	Management of results	The quality of accounting information has improved and the financial market has become more active.
Boumediene et al. (2014)	96 companies	France	2003–2004 2006–2007	Management of results (discretionary discretionary)	The extent of earning management decreases.
Bouchareb et al. (2014)	146 companies	France	2003–2006	Earnings management (discretionary accruals)	The level of discretionary accruals decreases significantly after the application of IFRS.

Source: Adapted from Hassine (2018)

3.3 METHODOLOGY

To formalize our analysis, we deemed it necessary to establish a research objective, followed by specific objectives that collectively contribute to the realization of the overarching goal. The primary objective of our research is to propose an IFRS Procedure Manual aimed at concretizing the transition to IAS within Company X, addressing accounting, organizational, and legal requisites. To comprehend the ultimate goal of our study, we have decomposed it into specific objectives, namely:

- Identify shortcomings related to the application of IAS/IFRS standards within the group.

- Implement the transition to the international accounting framework by updating adopted accounting methods and valuation rules, while mastering various IFRS reclassifications.
- Design a manual for IFRS application procedures.
- Assess the impact of implementing the instructions from this manual on the group's financial statements and select ratios.
- Demonstrate the utility of an IFRS Procedure Manual in terms of internal accounting control.

Thus, having pinpointed our study's objectives, selecting an appropriate research methodology becomes crucial. Our study adheres to the positivist paradigm, wherein we seek to establish causal relationships among three aspects:

- The transition into IAS/IFRS standards: Raised issues
- Significance of conceiving an IFRS Procedure Manual: For organizing their application
- The contribution of the accounting procedure manual under IFRS, in the internal control and financial ratio evaluation.

To address our research questions, our study adopts a qualitative and quantitative approach. This choice is driven by the desire to gain an in-depth understanding of the importance of implementing an IFRS Procedure Manual and to explore the perceptions of various stakeholders regarding its impact on the internal control framework. This dual approach allows us to explore and apply different dimensions of our research problem, offering the opportunity for innovation and the pursuit of new ideas.

The chosen epistemological methodology dictates the use of a research method grounded in a set of investigative techniques and data collection methods. In this regard, we utilized various data collection techniques, including the following.

3.3.1 OBSERVATION

During our internship, we engaged in both nonparticipant observation, acquainting ourselves with our study's context, particularly the company referred to as Company X for confidentiality reasons, situated in the Casablanca-Settat region and operating in the industrial sector. Additionally, we employed participant observation in certain actions (missions, training, reporting) concerning accounting management and centralization efforts.

3.3.2 INTERVIEWS

This technique aims to gather reliable and meaningful information, favoring our qualitative study. Questions related to specific themes were posed to interviewees using an interview guide, allowing them to express their thoughts freely without being confined to specific parameters. The main elements of the conducted interviews are as follows.

Interview Type	Semistructured
Number of Interviewees	18
	5 accounting managers
	3 internal auditors
	10 accounting agents
Duration	Up to 20 min maximum
Analysis Type	Horizontal: by theme Vertical: by target

By employing these methods, we intend to obtain a comprehensive understanding of the interplay between the implementation of IFRS, the creation of an IFRS Procedure Manual, and their influence on internal control and financial ratios within the organizational context of the company.

3.3.3 THE DOCUMENTATION REVIEW

The documentation review involves the exploration of internal documents from the company, such as the existing procedures manual and archived/ ongoing financial statements (primarily the Balance Sheet, Income Statement, and Cash Flow Statement). It also encompasses external documents from sources outside the company, including books, articles, studies, and theses relevant to our research theme.

3.3.4 THE SURVEY

A poststudy survey is used as part of a quantitative study, yielding quantifiable numerical data. Administered internally, the questionnaire is directly aimed at a limited number of individuals (20 respondents). These individuals are key stakeholders within the company center, specifically Accounting Managers, Internal Auditors, and Chief Accountants. To streamline our research process, we have compiled this summary table of the research methodology adopted (Figure 3.2).

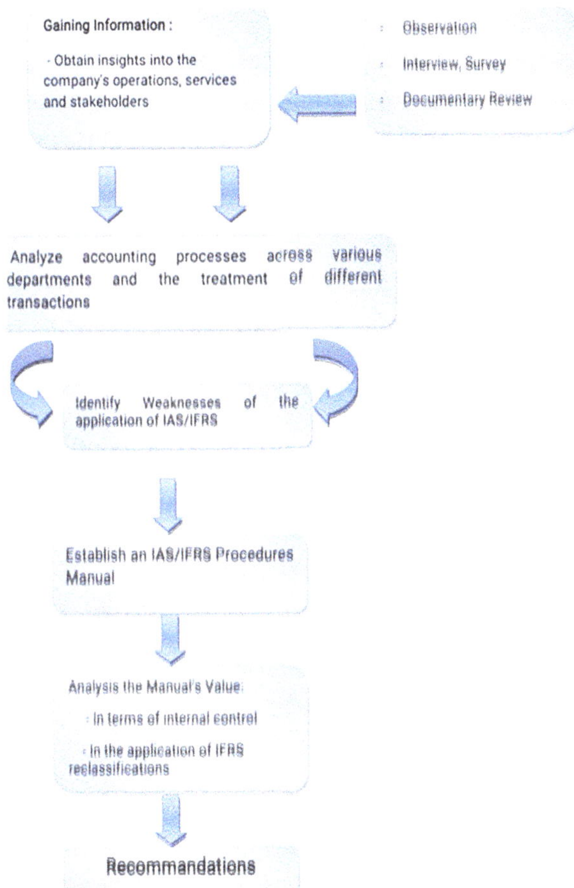

FIGURE 3.2 Summary of the research methodology.

Source: Authors

Overall, the articulated methodology serves as an intricate roadmap, guiding us through the exploration of our research inquiries and objectives. As we step into the realm of our study's outcomes, we anticipate uncovering insights that illuminate the efficacy of the proposed IFRS Procedure Manual within our specific organizational context. By leveraging a blend of quantitative and qualitative data analysis, we aspire to contribute noteworthy insights to the realms of accounting and organizational governance. This forthcoming presentation of empirical findings strives to forge a tangible bridge between theoretical constructs and practical implementation, unveiling practical implications that hold relevance for both the academic domain and real-world corporate practices. As we embark on the discussion of results, we unveil the empirical tapestry that sheds light on the intricacies of our study, offering a comprehensive perspective that bridges theory and practice.

3.4 RESULTS AND DISCUSSION

With our research methodology detailed, we move to the next vital phase: discussing the results. The methodology serves as the foundation for presenting our findings and insights, enabling a thorough exploration of theoretical ideas in real-world contexts. As we shift our focus to the results, we will unravel the practical side of our study, showcasing how theory aligns with real outcomes.

3.4.1 ANALYSIS OF ISSUES RAISED BY THE COMPANY REGARDING THE PRACTICE OF IAS/IFRS STANDARDS

We proceed to analyze the challenges faced by the company regarding the application of IAS/IFRS standards, as presented in Table 3.3.

Observation: All these difficulties hindering the use of IAS/IFRS standards within the Company X group lead to the risk of errors and internal control issues. Hence, there is a need for an organized support system that dictates the application modalities of various IFRS reclassifications and adjustments while ensuring effective internal control.

Solution: Create an IFRS Application Procedure Manual. Following the key steps in developing any manual, the IFRS Application Procedure Manual went through: a preparation phase (scope, information collection), an execution phase (procedure description and review), and a final phase (structure definition, manual writing). It was then subject to verification by managers and financial executives before being disseminated within the department, pending future updates.

Manual Structure: The IFRS Application Procedure Manual implemented within Company X consists of two main parts (Refer to the manual):

1st Part: Encompasses accounting processes related to various departments within the Accounting Department, depicted by flow diagrams.

2nd Part: Devoted to methods for applying IAS adopted within the company X, notably the standards: IAS1, IAS 16, IAS 17, IAS 21, and IAS 37.

3.4.2 THE CONTRIBUTION OF THE IAS PROCEDURE MANUAL TO THE INTERNAL CONTROL OF COMPANY X

After being implemented within the "Finance Accounting" department, the IFRS Application Manual has been instrumental in shaping the internal control system. Its significance is apparent in its capacity to tackle issues arising from the lack of a framework (as mentioned earlier), thereby enabling the effective implementation of these standards and ensuring precision in financial records. Consequently, the checklist provided at the manual's end serves as evidence of specific controls established for areas identified as sensitive in terms of accounting aspects, including lease reclassification, equity calculation, fair value determination, period specialization, and more.

3.4.3 IMPACT OF IAS/FRS ADOPTION ON VARIOUS FINANCIAL RATIOS OF COMPANY X

A static analysis of the results obtained through the calculation of financial stability ratios for Company X reveals that, based on IFRS financial statements, the balances of equity, income, and permanent funds appreciate. This enhancement contributes to the subsidiary's autonomy, independence, and financial equilibrium in comparison to local standards. Nevertheless, the subsidiary continues to grapple with liquidity issues unrelated to financial statement presentation. This challenge is linked to its developmental

TABLE 3.3 Challenges of Implementing IAS/IFRS Standards within the Company

Problem	Weaknesses	Risks
Problem-related to Fixed Assets	• Predominant use of historical cost instead of fair value. • Difficulty in fair value estimation.	• Distortion of accounting information. • Erosion of faithful representation of accounts.
Problem-related to Accounting Framework	• The use of a procedure manual is based on the National General Chart of Accounts, whereas the IAS/IFRS application requires certain reclassifications and adjustments.	• Nonalignment with principles of the international framework.
Accounting Allocation Problem	• Inconsistent accounting allocation of various operations across different departments.	• Poor interaction among departments. • Risk of errors and inaccuracy in accounts.
Lack of IFRS Reclassification Proficiency	• Inability of different departments to execute necessary IFRS reclassifications and adjustments, especially those related to leasing, exchange differences, provisions, depreciation, and others.	• Impairment to the consolidation process. • Need for successive rectifications.
Issue related to Future Anticipations	• Difficulty in establishing reliable long-term forecasts concerning the useful life of tangible assets.	• Incapability to estimate depreciation rates.
Problem with Financial Statement Presentation	• Lack of information in accounting books and presentation of accounts and various financial statements.	• Inaccuracy in statutory accounts. • Diminished informational quality.

Source: Authors

phase, as it was launched at the end of 2016 and began its export activities a year later. Consequently, its short-term debts have surged, resulting in insolvency vis-à-vis various creditors.

In terms of profitability, IAS/IFRS standards enable the subsidiary to generate more returns on its funds compared to adherence to the GAAP. These standards place a greater emphasis on shareholders since their inherent purpose is to create value for investors, catering to the demands of financial markets.

However, our study encountered several limitations, including data confidentiality and the partial utilization of IFRS by the entity, with certain standards left unapplied. Additionally, challenges related to Enterprise Resource Planning automation were noted due to inadequate training for accounting agents and managers to effectively use the system.

In light of these challenges, our recommendations include the following:

- Implementing a more robust information system to manage accounting difficulties.
- Providing training for administrative personnel in international accounting, to align them with challenges faced by management concerning the application of IAS/IFRS standards.
- Fully adopting IAS/IFRS standards within the group to ensure comprehensive and effective conversion.
- Automating the manual and integrating it into the information system with modules for various services: Accounts Payable, Accounts Receivable, General Ledger, etc.
- Training all stakeholders involved in the various procedures established within the accounting department to equip them with the necessary knowledge to execute their tasks proficiently.
- Regularly updating the manual to assume the existence of an effective internal control system, thereby ensuring the reliability of the contained procedures.

3.5 CONCLUSION

In conclusion, the development of the procedure manual becomes imperative for Company X, aiming for a smooth and efficient transition to IAS. This document stands as a contribution to the description and adjustment of procedures in line with evolving international accounting norms, thereby enhancing the internal control system (Henry and Monkam-Daverat, 2001). Moreover, our primary objectives set out initially have been achieved. Our study, conducted through various investigative and data collection techniques, enabled us to identify weaknesses within the existing system and uncover numerous obstacles that hinder the proper use of IAS/IFRS standards. These challenges largely stem from the absence of a framework directing IFRS reclassifications and adjustments to be carried out by each accounting unit within the department. Therefore, the establishment of an IFRS application procedure manual serves as an opportunity for the group's accounting system and its subsidiaries. On one hand, it facilitates the assessment of financial ratios for the subsidiary through the precision and transparency of provided financial statements, governed by the manual's directives. On the other hand, it bolsters the efficiency of internal control, which will be rooted in standards promoting information quality dissemination. However, the creation of this accounting procedure manual does not signify an easy triumph, as it still confronts several limitations highlighted in the last section of the last chapter. To counter these, a set of recommendations has been proposed in that very chapter. It is important to note that this procedure manual remains adaptable and dynamic. Regular updates, through appended notes or modifications, are necessary in response to the evolution of IAS on one hand, and changes in the group's structure and activities on the other. Furthermore, the company's new strategic directions, considering its subsidiaries, for global expansion demand a redoubling of efforts concerning the presentation of financial statements under IFRS, ultimately bolstering its international standing. Thus, the involvement of all staff members in this vision becomes essential for enhanced accounting operations across the group's activities and instilling complete trust among stakeholders.

NOTES

1. https://www.institut-numerique.org
2. https://www.compta-facile.com
3. https://www.performance-publique.budget.gouv.fr
4. https://rfcomptable.grouperf.com/

KEYWORDS

- **accounting procedure manual**
- **document analysis**
- **IAS/IFRS**
- **internal control**
- **theoretical framework**

REFERENCES

Al-Matari, E. M., Al-Swidi, A. K., Fadzil, F. H. & Al-Matari, Y. A. (2014). The impact of corporate governance on corporate performance: Evidence from Bahrain Bourse. *Asian Social Science*, 10(14), 74–87.

Barbu, E. & Piot, C. (2012). Adoption of IAS/IFRS by listed French groups. A will or a constraint?. *French Review of Management*, 2(3), 53–74.

Bartov, E., Givoly, D., & Hayn, C. (2002). The rewards to meeting or beating earnings expectations. *Journal of Accounting and Economics*, 33(2), 173–204.

Begum, D. & Chou, P. I. (2018). Internal control weaknesses and financial reporting quality: Evidence from the Sarbanes-Oxley Act. *Review of Quantitative Finance and Accounting*, 50(4), 1093–1127.

Bouchareb, M., Ajina, A., & Souid, S. (2014). Does the adoption of IFRS influence earnings management towards small positive earnings? Evidence from France. *International Journal of Academic Research in Accounting, Finance and Management Sciences*, 4(1), 143–155.

Boumediene, S. L. (2013). Impact of adopting IAS-IFRS on the handling of accounting data: The case of France. *Journal of Applied Business Research*, 29(5), 1313–1322.

Bragg, S. (2016). Accounting Best Practices. Edition no. 7, USA.

Disle, C. & Noël, C. (2007). The revolution of IFRS standards: A convergence of accounting towards finance? *Sciences and Management Review*, 224(2), 17–27.

Eustache Akpane, M. (2008). Manual of procedures's redaction. International Institute of Management, Abidjan.

Hassine, M. (2018). The adoption of IFRS and the quality of accounting information. *CCA Review*, 2(16), 263–270.

Henry, T. & Monkam-Daverat, I. (2001). Write the company procedures: Practical. Edition no. 3, Organisation Editiond, France.

Kasznik, R. (1999). On the association between voluntary disclosure and earnings management. *Journal of Accounting Research*, 37, 57–81.

Leuz, L. (2003). Earnings management and institutional factors: An international comparison. *Journal of Financial Economics*, 3, 505–527.

Raffournier, B. (2017). The role and current status of IFRS in the completion of national accounting rules—Evidence from Switzerland. *Journal of the European Accounting Association*, 2(4), 5–16.

Raghunandan, M. S. & Wright, A. M. (2009). The impact of corporate governance mechanisms on the relationship between insider ownership and audit fees. *Journal of Accounting and Public Policy*, 28(5), 384–406.

Serdarusic, H. & Horvat, J. (2018). Internal control and efficiency of business operations. *Procedia Computer Science*, 147, 358–363

CHAPTER 4

Firms' Short-Term Employment Management during the COVID-19 Crisis

AFEF KHALIL[1], WISSEM AJILI[2], MOURAD KERTOUS[3], MOHAMMED EL AMINE ABDELLI[4], IMEN BEN SLIMENE[5], and SAMIR MALIKI[6]

[1]*University of Manouba-ISCAE, Manouba, Tunisia*

[2]*University of ESLSCA, Paris, France*

[3]*University of Brest, Brest, France*

[4]*IAE of Bretagne Occidentale-Laboratory of LEGO, Vannes Cedex, France/University of Western Brittany-UBO, Brest, France*

[5]*University of UHA, Mulhouse, France*

[6]*University of Tlemecen, Tlemecen, Algeria*

*Corresponding author

ABSTRACT

The study empirically investigates the effect of firms' practices on employment during the COVID-19 crisis. Furthermore, how and by which enterprises manage the lay-off effect during the COVID-19 crisis. A survey was used on 1008 companies covering 10 European and Mediterranean countries in 2020. The main results prove that firms' practices and government support measures positively affect employment during the COVID-19 crisis. In addition, companies with a high proportion of female employees have better employment levels. The study highlights

Corporate Governance, Digitalization, and Energy Transition: Imen Baccouche and Afef Khalil. (Eds.)

DOI: 10.1201/9781779643407-5

the importance of additional support measures that target the most vulnerable companies.

4.1 INTRODUCTION

Since 1918, the pandemics have posed health, political, and social challenges, as well as situations of economic instability for humanity (Bakour and Ouassou, 2020; Oudda et al., 2020). Several years later, precisely in December 2019, the world was again confronted with a health crisis, COVID-19. The recent crisis has had a significant impact on vital sectors of the global economy, namely, tourism, textiles, industry, transportation, cross-border trade, international trade, etc. (Kamaruddin et al., 2020; Kraus et al., 2020). The COVID-19 crisis paralyzed many economic activities and even led to the partial or total closure of some businesses (Fitriasari, 2020; Lutfi and Kornelius, 2020; Brodeur, et al., 2020; Wei et al., 2021). As a result of barrier measures issued by national authorities, borders have been closed. Ntererwa and Lukundji (2020) and Jedwab et al. (2021) argue that the economic impact of the health crisis in COVID-19 is likely to be more severe than expected. Several studies suggest that the global economy will continue to suffer for years to come. The world will take longer than expected to recover from the economic downturn caused by the COVID-19 pandemic (Brodeur et al., 2020; Katherine et al., 2020; Nghiem and Wilson, 2021).

Furthermore, the Organization for Economic Cooperation and Development estimates that containment measures would have reduced global gross domestic product (GDP) by 2% per month, or an annual rate of 24% (Bakour and Ouassou, 2020). These estimates are in line with the level of economic collapse not seen since the Great Depression of the 1930s. The International Monetary Fund estimates that global GDP will be −3% in 2020.[1] Studies indicate that the COVID-19 crisis has had serious socioeconomic consequences. The population became impoverished during the crisis, having lost their jobs and housing. This resulted in a higher overall mortality rate. The individual difficulties in households became a social issue as well (Kalenkoski and Pabilonia, 2020). Carranza et al. (2020) estimate that the rate of extreme poverty in the world is expected to increase

1.www.imf.org

from 8% in 2019 to over 9% in 2020. Global poverty has increased for the first time in over two decades.

Many studies suggest that thousands of jobs could be lost as companies around the world reduce supply as a result of the decline in demand and due to the COVID-19 crisis. Kraus et al. (2020) report that 22 million people in the United States lost their jobs in just one month, that the unemployment rate in Austria increased more than doubled, and that the recession forced 29% of all Swiss workers. In addition, Kalenkoski and Pabilonia (2020) found that the number of active business owners decreased by 22% between February and April 2020. From April to June 2020, Carranza et al. (2020) argue that the total hours worked were 20% below the average for the last quarter of 2019. According to the International Labor Organization (ILO), lost work hours have had a significant impact on jobs in the first half of 2020. ILO estimates suggest a decline in working hours of about 10.7% in the second quarter of 2020 compared to the last quarter of 2019, which translates to 305 million full-time workers. There will be more people losing their jobs as a result. Getting a job for those who are already unemployed is becoming increasingly difficult (Webb et al., 2020). Consequently, businesses could face a shortage of skilled labor (Cepel et al., 2020). Wall (2020) adds that job losses have led to significant reductions in workers' income. It is vital to consider the impact of the COVID-19 crisis on the labor market (Brodeur et al., 2020; Carranza et al., 2020; Gupta et al., 2020).

To mitigate the effects of the COVID-19 crisis on employment, firms adopted new practices such as credit purchases and sales. Many governments have implemented support measures, such as direct financing, tax benefits, and deferrals in tax payments (Levashenko and Koval, 2020). To help businesses avoid temporary layoffs, some governments have adopted measures such as laminating work hours, providing new workplaces, and taking safety measures for self-employed workers. Wall (2020) states that governments in advanced countries of the world have allocated funds to companies in different forms and are subject to various conditions to avoid the negative impact of the COVID-19 pandemic on employment. Lu et al. (2020) add that many support measures have been intensively adopted by countries, such as direct financing, wage subsidies, tax breaks, tax reductions, and other measures. Bakour and Ouassou (2020) argue that states are called upon to review their employment policies and implement innovative approaches to job creation.

The purpose of this study is to examine how firms are implementing new practices and using government support measures to manage the short-term employment impacts of the COVID-19 crisis. In other words, this chapter seeks to identify good practices that helped firms preserve employment during crises. To the best of our knowledge, few studies examine firms' practices and government support measures during the COVID-19 crisis. Thus, this chapter fills the gaps in this literature by exploring the impact of business practices and support measures (e.g., tax exemptions/reductions, wage subsidies, credit sales, credit purchases, tax deferrals) on employment during the COVID-19 crisis. Our chapter provides an analytical framework for stakeholders and policymakers on the impact of business practices and public support measures on employment. Private and public decision-makers can adopt new practices deduced from the current crisis to anticipate and limit the effects of future crises.

The chapter is organized into the following sections. Section 4.2 presents the literature review and the hypotheses. The next section presents the sample and the variables used. Section 4.4 discusses the results of the empirical study. Section 4.5 concludes by discussing the theoretical and managerial implications.

4.2 LITERATURE REVIEW AND HYPOTHESES

4.2.1 FIRMS PRACTICES AND EMPLOYMENT

Firms are critical to job preservation, wealth creation, and income security, especially for those affected by the economic and financial crisis (Fitriasari, 2020) Since the COVID-19 crisis, activities in companies have declined, and the number of workers has decreased (Didier et al., 2020; Bui et al., 2022). Ferrando and Ganoulis (2020) argue that firms become financially fragile during times of crisis. Indeed, operating revenues do not cover personnel costs. This is the reason why companies have had to put staff on technical leave or early retirement. It appears, therefore, that the COVID-19 crisis is a new challenge for companies. Companies have taken measures to respond to the crisis in the short term and come out stronger in the long term (Kraus et al., 2020). According to Dvoulet and Luke (2016), financial measures are "policy measures" that include debts, government equity, nonrepayable grants, interest rate grants, and late tax payments. Levashenko and Koval (2020) argue that many firms used financial instruments such as buying on credit and selling on credit to reduce the negative effects of the COVID-19 crisis on employment. Financial policies stimulate employment, create new jobs, and promote economic growth. The firms may have intended to use trade credit as a substitute for other sources of financing during the crisis (Ferrando and Ganoulis, 2020). Furthermore, firms should sell on credit to retain customers and employees, and thus avoid the negative employment impacts of the COVID-19 crisis (Levashenko and Koval, 2020). Kraus et al. (2020) and Ntererwa and Lukundji (2020) argue that firms are suffering from a dramatic drop in demand for goods and services as consumers reduce their purchases of nonessential goods and services, leisure, and travel. Kraus et al. (2020) suggest that consumer demand and spending may decline further in 2020. In addition to credit sales, Fitriasari (2020) and Levashenko and Koval (2020) focus on firms' use and execution of other financial measures, such as late payment of taxes, to decrease default risk and retain employees. Baumgartner and Caliendo (2008) conducted a study of 775 German firms between 2003 and 2006. They indicate that firms that apply financial measures have a low unemployment rate and a high level of personal income. This result is also confirmed by Rodríguez-Planas (2010) for a sample of 437 Romanian firms from 2000 to 2002. We hypothesize the following:

H1. Proactive firm practices have a significant impact on the employment level during the COVID-19 crisis.

4.2.2 GOVERNMENT SUPPORT MEASURES AND EMPLOYMENT

Governments should play an important role in designing exit scenarios that ensure the economy grows, and reduce the negative impacts of the COVID-19 pandemic (Cepel et al., 2020). Indeed, government policies help firms and decrease the crisis economic effects (Cox, 2020; Wang et al., 2020). Lu et al. (2020) add that government support is essential for firms with little cash to survive and recover during a crisis. Additionally, Carranza et al. (2020) and Fitriasari (2020) argue that policies must help firms retain employees, provide insurance for those who lose their jobs, and facilitate alternative employment and employability support for those who are unemployed. Danquah et al. (2020) report that policymakers in Sub-Saharan Africa have responded to the negative impact of the pandemic on careers and incomes with a variety of measures, ranging from cash transfers to the poor to loans to small and medium enterprises. Direct financial assistance is becoming more common as a cost-effective way to support poor businesses, according to Blusteina et al. (2020). In addition, governments should introduce time-targeted tax incentives, such as tax exemptions or reductions. These incentives are designed to facilitate postcrisis recovery, support investment, and ease pressure on firms. Wang et al. (2020) argue that government support measures aim to help firms retain employees, assess their risks, and improve risk acceptance by financial institutions. In addition to providing loans and tax incentives, Gunn et al. (2021) argue that the introduction of a wage subsidy scheme helps employers retain employees, as well as doubling the regular unemployment insurance rate through a new coronavirus-related top-up payment. Wage subsidies are provided to employers or employees in the form of payments that fully or partially cover wages and other payroll-related expenses like social security contributions and income taxes (Eliana et al. 2020). Employment subsidies also affect employers' labor demand benefits and workers' labor supply incentives. Eliana et al. (2020) add that wage subsidies help increase employment when labor demand is low relative to supply. Wage subsidies decrease firms' effective wages and raise employee wages. Caliendo and Kühn (2015) conducted a study of 405 German firms between 2003 and 2008. The authors find that subsidies promote employment. However, Bauer (2018) surveyed 8000 Swiss and Dutch companies. The author demonstrates that government subsidies increase the unemployment rate. Feldmann (2016) conducted a study of 19 industrial countries from 1985 to 2002. The results indicate that long-term unemployment is likely to increase due to wage subsidies. Dvoulетý and Lukeš (2016) show that subsidized firms perform worse than unsubsidized firms. Thus, we state the following hypothesis:

H2. Government support measures have a significant impact on the employment level during the COVID-19 crisis.

4.3 METHODOLOGY

4.3.1 SAMPLE AND DATA COLLECTIONS

To assess the impact of the short-run COVID-19 crisis on the employment level, we used data from a World Bank survey conducted between February and October 2020. The decision to analyze the first wave was motivated by the large lockdown. Furthermore, this period has experienced the most severe effects of the crisis, considering its magnitude and its unpredictable nature. Our sample includes 1008 companies from 10 European and Mediterranean countries (Bulgaria, Czech Republic, Greece, Hungary, Italy, Malta, Morocco, Poland, Romania, and Russia).

The World Bank survey is designed to obtain information about:

- The profile of the company: its size, sector of activity, geographical location, and market (local or international);
- The impact of the pandemic on its activity level, sales, production chain, distribution networks, and suppliers;
- The policies and measures put in place internally to respond to the pandemic include remote sales, remote work, and other measures;
- The effects of the pandemic on the employment level such as job retention, partial unemployment, and dismissal;
- The effects of the crisis on access to short and medium-term financing: cash flow, customer deadlines, supplier deadlines, debt, etc.
- The effect of the crisis on risks (operating, liquidity, solvency, bankruptcy, etc.);
- The support measures used by the public authorities during the crisis: the government or local aid, tax exemptions or reductions, subsidies;
- Expectations regarding the pandemic evolution and the confidence level in the short and medium term.

We add other variables from the World Bank website,[2] such as the number of infections, population density, death rate, and gross national income. To address our research question, we chose a quantitative analysis approach.

4.3.2 *VARIABLE MEASUREMENT*

4.3.2.1 MEASUREMENT OF THE DEPENDENT VARIABLE

In this study, we analyze the firm's practices to preserve employment and avoid layoffs during the COVID-19 crisis. We note that unemployment

2. www.worldbank.org

was difficult to measure during the recent crisis. Some questions in the World Bank survey are unclear as to why a respondent is not at work, particularly whether the respondent is staying at home due to economic conditions or health reasons. These overlap in the COVID-19 pandemic, and there may be misreporting. Different measures are considered to create a complete view of unemployment in the second half of 2020. According to Phélinas (2014), Cohen (2020), and Green and Loualiche (2021), our two key measures are the following.

UNEMPL 1 = The logarithm of the workers' number laid off

UNEMPL 2 = The logarithm of the workers' number put on leave for COVID-19 reasons

4.3.2.2 MEASUREMENT OF THE INDEPENDENT VARIABLES

Through a review of various research literature, we identified five characteristics to analyze the empirical effect of firm practices and government support measures on employment during the COVID-19 crisis. Sales on credit (SALCRED) is a binary variable that is equal to 1 if the enterprise has increased its sales on credit and 0; otherwise, (PURSCRED) is a binary variable that is equal to 1 if the enterprise has increased its purchases on credit and 0; otherwise, Delays payment taxes (PAYDELTAX) is a binary variable that is equal to 1 if the enterprise has paid taxes with a delay and 0; otherwise, Fiscal exemptions/reductions (FISCALRED) is a binary variable that is equal to 1 if the enterprise has obtained fiscal exemptions/reductions from the State and 0; otherwise, Wage subsidies (SUBVENTION) is a binary variable that is equal to 1 if the enterprise has obtained wage subsidies from the State and 0; otherwise.

We introduce eight control variables to ameliorate our empirical findings. Size is the total number of workers in the enterprise, GENDER is the percentage of female workers, and ACTDECR is a binary variable that is equal to 1 if the activity of the enterprise decreases and 0; otherwise, POPDENS is the average population density in the country, COV1 is the total number of infections in the country, COV2 is the death rate, and MED is a binary variable that is equal to 1 if the country is Mediterranean and 0; otherwise, RNB is the logarithm of gross national income per capita of the country. The used variables are listed in Table 4.1.

TABLE 4.1 Definition of Variables

Variables	Name	Definition		Measure
Dependent variables	**UNEMP1**	Unemployment1		The logarithm of the workers' number laid off
	UNEMP2	Unemployment2		The logarithm of the workers' number put on leave for COVID-19 reasons
		Independent Variables		
Interest variables	**Firms' policies**	SALCRED	Sales on credit	A binary variable that is equal to 1 if the enterprise has increased its sales on credit and 0; otherwise
		PURSCRED	Purchases on credit	A binary variable that is equal to 1 if the enterprise has increased its purchases on credit and 0; otherwise
		PAYDELTAX	Delays payment taxes	A binary variable that is equal to 1 if the enterprise has paid taxes with a delay and 0; otherwise
	Government support measures	FISCALRED	Fiscal exemptions/ reductions	A binary variable that is equal to 1 if the enterprise has obtained fiscal exemptions/reductions from the State and 0; otherwise
		SUBVENTION	Wage subsidies	A binary variable that is equal to 1 if the enterprise has obtained wage subsidies from the State and 0; otherwise
Control variables	**GENDER**	Female workers		The percentage of female workers
	SIZE	Firm's size		The total number of workers in the enterprise
	ACTDECR	Decrease activity		A binary variable that is equal to 1 if the activity of the enterprise decreases and 0; otherwise
	POPDENS	Population density		The average population density in the country
	COV1	Infections' number		The total number of infections in the country
	COV2	Death rate		Number of deaths/Total number of infections
	MED	Mediterranean country		A binary variable that is equal to 1 if the country is Mediterranean and 0; otherwise
	RNB	Gross national income		The logarithm of gross national income per capita of the country

We propose the following two models to investigate the effect of firms' practices and government support measures on employment during the COVID-19 pandemic:

$$\begin{Bmatrix} In(UNEMPL1_i) = \alpha_1 + X_i\beta_1 + \varepsilon_{i1} \\ In(UNEMPL2_i) = \alpha_2 + X_i\beta_2 + \varepsilon_{i2} \end{Bmatrix}$$

With,

X_i: a vector of all independent variables; a: a constant, β_i: a marginal effect of each factor in both equations; and ε_{it}: the error term.

The regression models allow us to identify the employment factors (UNEMP1 and UNEMP2). To highlight nonlinear marginal effects, we used the log-linear form. The log transformation was also applied to the quantitative explanatory factors to measure the elasticities.

4.4 RESULTS AND DISCUSSION

4.4.1 DESCRIPTIVE STATISTICS

The descriptive statistics in Table 4.2 show that the UNEMPL1 and UNEMPL2 variables have a mean of 5.4 and 15.22, respectively. Additionally, enterprises report, on average, having laid off 15.22 workers. Regarding firms' practices, 23.6% of the sampled companies show that their sales on credit increased. In addition, 21.4% of the firms in our sample indicate an increase in their credit purchases, and 12.2% of enterprises report that they have benefited from additional delays in paying tax from their authorities. For the same period, 36.1% of the companies say they have benefited from fiscal exemptions/reductions, and 61.9% of firms have obtained wage subsidies from the State.

Furthermore, Table 4.2 shows that the average percentage of female workers (GENDER) is 37.8%. The mean for firm size (Size) is 86.08 employees, while the average population density in the country (POPDENS) variable ranges from 8.82 to 1.46. Table 4.2 also indicates that the mean for the number of infections in the country (COV1) variable is estimated at 4.17, while its minimum and maximum values are 0.422 and 11.87, respectively. The average death rate because of COVID (COV2) is 11.56. (RNB) variable ranges from 23.6 to 40.45 with an average of 38.31. We note that the company's activity decreases by about 65.7% during the COVID-19 crisis; 32.2% of countries are Mediterranean.

TABLE 4.2 Descriptive Statistics

Variables	Mean	Sd	Min	Max
UNEMPL 1	15.22	129.2	0	5 000
UNEMPL 2	5.424	26.10	0	600
SALCRED	0.236	0.425	0	1
PURSCRED	0.214	0.410	0	1
PAYDELTAX	0.122	0.327	0	1
FISCALRED	0.361	0.480	0	1
SUBVENTION	0.619	0.485	0	1
GENDER	0.378	0.272	0	100
SIZE	86.08	383.7	0	20 000
ACTDECR	0.657	0.475	0	1
POPDENS	130.9	242.6	8.820	1.463
COV1	4.178	2.932	0.422	11.87
COV2	11.56	1.458	9.023	15.25
MED	0.322	0.467	0	1
RNB	38.31	2.830	23.60	40.45

4.4.2 DISCUSSION AND POLICY IMPLICATIONS

Table 4.3 summarizes our results on the relationship between firms' practices and government support measures and their effect on employment during the COVID-19 crisis.[3] The variable (SALCRED) has a significant and positive impact on the variable (UNEMPL 2). This result suggests that if companies use sales on credit heavily, this will reduce the number of workers put on leave for COVID-19 reasons. Thus, *H*1 is confirmed, suggesting that proactive firms' practices have a significant impact on employment levels during the COVID-19 crisis. In other words, firms that had been selling on credit reduced the number of workers put on leave for COVID-19 reasons. The finding confirms previous research (Didier et al., 2020; Kraus et al., 2020; Lu et al., 2020; Ntererwa and Lukundji, 2020; Wall, 2020) and indicates that sales on credit allow the company to maintain their customers and, consequently, to keep their employees.

The coefficient of the (FISCALRED) variable is positive and significant on the (UNEMPL1) variable at the 5% level, which indicates that fiscal exemptions/reductions obtained from the government positively affected employment levels during the COVID-19 crisis. It appears that tax exemptions and reductions help enterprises reduce pressure on their employees and

3. We note that the results are interpreted according to the data analysis method used.

retain them. The result implies that fiscal exemptions/reductions encourage firms to reduce the number of workers laid off. We argue that the government should provide more fiscal exemptions/reductions to the companies and support them during crises. According to Blusteina et al. (2020), governments should start considering how to deal with the immediate and long-term effects of COVID-19's economic crisis, especially in the area of joblessness. This positive relationship confirms previous research findings (Cepel et al., 2020; Eliana et al., 2020; Lu et al., 2020; Suomi et al., 2020; Wang et al., 2020). Otherwise, results show that other dependent variables (SUBVENTION, PURSCRED, PAYDELTAX) do not significantly impact employment levels during the COVID-19 crisis. Even though the study period is short, the result could be significant in the long term, explaining the research result.

Regarding control variables, Table 4.3 indicates that the (GENDER) variable has a positive and significant effect on variables (UNEMPL1) and (UNEMPL2). In the COVID-19 pandemic, the presence of female workers positively influenced employment levels. This means that companies with a high proportion of female employees have better retention rates. The pertinent relationship is contradictory to several researchers' findings (Adams-Prassl et al., 2020; Alon et al., 2020; Eliana et al., 2020). Alon et al. (2020) show that the closure of schools and daycare centers has contributed to increased demand for childcare, which has a negative effect on working women. (SIZE) variable has a positive and significant impact on variables (UNEMPL1) and (UNEMPL2) at a 1% level. This means that the company's size decreases the number of workers laid off and employees put on leave for COVID-19 reasons. Plus, (ACTDECR) variable exhibits a positive coefficient and is statistically significant. This outcome indicates that if enterprises declare a decrease in their activities, this generates an increase in the workers' number laid off 47.9% and the number of workers put on leave for COVID-19 reasons 20.1%. In Table 4.3, we find that the (POPDENS) variable negatively affects employment levels during the crisis. Furthermore, the result indicates that the variables linked to the COVID-19 epidemic (COV1 and COV2) positively influence employment. Indeed, an increase of 1% in the death rate enhances the number of workers laid off by 56.2% and the number of workers put on leave for COVID-19 reasons to 29.4%. Results show that if the number of infections is more than 1%, it increases the number of leaves due to COVID-19 by 8.82%. An increase in gross national income per capita of 1% reduces unemployment. Finally, we note that the (MED) variable does not significantly impact unemployment. In other words, if the country is part of the Mediterranean, this does not significantly affect the number of people on leave for COVID-19 reasons and the number of workers laid off.

TABLE 4.3 Panel Regression Results

Variables	UNEMPL 1	UNEMPL 2
SALCRED	0.217	0.157**
	(0.138)	(0.031)
PURSCRED	0.068	0.060
	(0.643)	(0.413)
PAYDELTAX	0.130	0.059
	(0.356)	(0.370)
FISCALRED	0.289**	0.079
	(0.016)	(0.148)
SUBVENTION	0.124	0.046
	(0.298)	(0.457)
GENDER	0.392**	0.492***
	(0.033)	(9.66e-08)
SIZE	0.498***	0.799***
	(0.000)	(0.000)
ACTDECR	0.479***	0.201***
	(0.002)	(0.004)
POPDENS	−0.007***	−0.004***
	(6.06e−09)	(2.93e−09)
COV1	0.562***	0.294***
	(3.33e−05)	(1.98e−05)
COV2	0.020	0.088***
	(0.542)	(3.28e−10)
MED	−0.208	−0.011
	(0.382)	(0.862)
RNB	−0.848***	−0.460***
	(6.36e−09)	(1.00e−07)
Constant	26.19***	13.77***
	(5.24e−09)	(3.05e−07)
R^2	49.9%	68.4%
N	1008	

Notes: *** $p<0.01$, ** $p<0.05$, * $p<0.1$.

4.5 CONCLUSION

The COVID-19 crisis affected global economic growth and threatened businesses worldwide (Albitar et al., 2020; Brodeur et al., 2020; Goodell, 2020; Kalenkoski and Pabilonia, 2020; Kim et al., 2020). The disease impacted the working world, which intensified unemployment after job losses and the productive apparatus' shutdown (Al-Fadly, 2020; Kamaruddin et al., 2020; Lu et al., 2020). According to Cepel et al. (2020), unemployment statistics indicate strong growth on a global scale. Kalenkoski and Pabilonia (2020) report that the number of working company owners decreased by 22% between February and April 2020. Many countries have been working intensively on introducing various financial and nonfinancial support measures to avoid the negative impacts of the COVID-19 crisis and to minimize unemployment, such as direct financing, tax credits, tax relief, and financial incentives loans for operating services at lower interest rates (Bakour and Ouassou, 2020; Cepel et al., 2020).

We aim to discuss in this chapter how firms manage unemployment by their practices (e.g., sales on credit, purchases on credit, delays in paying taxes) and government support measures (e.g., tax exemptions/reductions, wage subsidies) during the COVID-19 pandemic, which provides suggestions for future researches following this exogenous shock. We have resorted to a methodology based on the quantitative approach to answer this question. Data were collected respectively using the questionnaire survey. The results indicate that fiscal exemptions/reductions obtained from the State and sales on credit positively affected employment during the COVID-19 crisis. This means that enterprises need to increase fiscal exemptions/deductions and sell on credit to maintain workers. On the other hand, purchases on credit, delays in payment taxes, and wage subsidies do not significantly impact employment levels during the COVID-19 crisis. To retain their employees, enterprises must maximize liquidity, lower costs, and use government support measures. Therefore, companies and states are required to review their practices and implement innovative approaches to reduce unemployment.

4.5.1 *THEORETICAL IMPLICATIONS*

This chapter gives a great insight into the current literature in various respects. First, the research chapter offers a new perspective on how enterprises manage unemployment using practices and government support measures during the COVID-19 pandemic. Previous studies have examined the effect of the COVID-19 pandemic, but only a few have related the firm's practices and government support measures and their impact on decreasing unemployment. Second, to the best of our knowledge, our research is the first to diagnose the effect of companies' practices and government support measures on unemployment during the crisis of COVID-19. Third, by presenting new empirical evidence, this study aims to fill the gaps in the literature.

4.5.2 PRACTICAL IMPLICATIONS

This chapter offers helpful and practical evidence for various professionals (academics, regulators, investors, etc.). During the COVID-19 pandemic, this research chapter provides useful information on how enterprises manage unemployment using practices and government support measures. Company authorities should therefore consider the research results and spend more effort implementing financial access measures, which will ensure business effectiveness. Additionally, supervisory authorities should strengthen their strategies and ensure strong corporate governance.

4.5.3 LIMITATIONS OF THE STUDY AND FUTURE RESEARCH

In this study, we examine the effect of firms' practices and government support measures on employment during the COVID-19 crisis. Despite the current gap in the literature, there are still several avenues that future studies can address. First, this research is restricted to 2020. Future researchers should add years because the more we advance, the more the impact of firms' practices and government support measures on employment during the COVID-19 crisis becomes clear. Second, more empirical analysis of companies' practices and government support measures is needed. Similarly, forthcoming studies should focus more on the impact of gender on employment during the COVID-19 crisis. Third, we recommend further study to discuss the policy concerns about how (and why) this epidemic impacts sales. The practical consequences of these questions must be explored in the future. Furthermore, for corporate social responsibility

(CSR) operations, COVID-19 faces significant challenges. The following issues could be solved with further research, regardless of whether businesses decide to exit, retain, or extend their CSR operations. After the pandemic, will CSR transparency increase in consistency and quantity? Which of the key drivers for CSR activities will be the most important during the crisis?

KEYWORDS

- **COVID-19 crisis**
- **employment**
- **firms' practices**
- **gender**
- **government support measures**
- **lay-off**

REFERENCES

Adams-Prassl, A., Boneva, T., Golin, M. & Rauh, C. (2020). Inequality in the impact of the coronavirus shock: evidence from real-time surveys. *Cambridge-INET Working Paper Series.*. https://www.inet.econ.cam.ac.uk/working-paper-pdfs/wp2018.pdf.

Albitar, K., Gerged, A. M., Kikhia, H. & Hussainey, K. (2020). Auditing in times of social distancing: the effect of COVID-19 on auditing quality. *International Journal of Accounting & Information Management*. https://doi.org/10.1108/IJAIM-08-2020-0128.

Al-Fadly, A. (2020). Impact of COVID-19 on SMEs and employment. *Entrepreneurship and Sustainability Issues*, 8(2), 629–648. https://doi.org/10.9770/jesi.2020.8.2(38).

Alon, T. M., Doepke, M., Olmstead-Rumsey, J. & Tertilt, M. (2020). The Impact of COVID-19 on Gender Equality. *Working Paper Serie-National Bureau of Economic Research*. https://doi.org/10.3386/w26947.

Bakour C. & Ouassou S. (2020). Les politiques sociales en contexte du COVID-19 : INDH Le programme d'amélioration du revenu et inclusion économique des jeunes. *Revue Internationale du Chercheur*, 1(2), 388–410.

Bauer, P. C. (2018). Socius: Sociological research for unemployment, trust in government, and satisfaction with democracy: An empirical investigation. *A Dynamic World*, 4, 1–14. https://doi.org/10.1177/2378023117750533.

Baumgartner, H. J., & Caliendo, M. (2008). Turning unemployment into self-employment: effectiveness of two start-up programs. *Oxford Bulletin of Economics and Statistics*, 70(3), 347–373. https://doi.org/10.1111/j.1468-0084.2008.00505.x.

Blusteina, D. L., Duffyb, R., Ferreirac, J. A., Cohen-Scalid, V., Cinamone, R. G. & Allanf, B. A. (2020). Unemployment in the time of COVID-19: A research agenda. *Journal of Vocational Behavior*, 119, 1–5.

Brodeur, A., Gray, D., Islam, A. & Bhuiyan, S. J. (2020). A Literature Review of the Economics of COVID-19. *Institute of Labor Economics-Discussion paper series*, 13411.

Bui, D., Dräger, L., Hayo, B. & Nghiem, G. (2022). The effects of fiscal policy on households during the COVID-19 pandemic: Evidence from Thailand and Vietnam. *World Development*. https://doi.org/10.1016/j.worlddev.2022.105828.

Caliendo, M. & Künn, S. (2015). Getting back into the labor market: The effects of start-up subsidies for unemployed females. *Journal of Population Economics*, 28(4), 1005–1043. http://hdl.handle.net/10.1007/s00148-015-0540-5.

Carranza, E., Farole, T., Gentilini, U., Morgandi, M., Packard, T., Santos, I. & Weber, M. (2020). Managing the employment impacts of the COVID-19 crisis: Policy options for relief and restructuring. *Jobs Working Paper*, 49, 1–33.

Cepel, M., Gavurova, B., Dvorsky, J. & Belas, J. (2020). The impact of the COVID-19 crisis on the perception of business risk in the SME segment. *Journal of International Studies*, 13(3), 248–263.

Cohen, G. D. (2020). Measuring employment during COVID-19: Challenges and opportunities. *Business Economics*, 55, 229–239.

Cox, N. (2020). New Zealand and Covid-19: A swift and firm response. *The Round Table*. 10.1080/00358533.2020.1757287.

Danquah, M., Schotte, S. & Sen, K. (2020). COVID-19 and employment: Insights from the Sub-Saharan African experience. *The Indian Journal of Labour Economics*, 63, 23–30. 10.14254/2071–8330.2020/13–3/16.

Didier, T., Huneeus, F., Larrain, M. & Schmukler, S. L. (2020). Financing firms in hibernation during the COVID-19 pandemic. World Bank. https://doi.org/10.1596/33611.

Dvouletý, O. & Lukeš, M. (2016). Review of empirical studies on self-employment out of unemployment: Do self-employment policies make a positive impact? *International Review of Entrepreneurship*, 14(3), 361–376. 10.1515/cejpp-2016–0032.

Eliana, C., Santos, I., Morgandi, M., Weber, M., Farole, T., Packard, T. & Gentilini, U. (2020). Managing the employment impacts of the COVID-19 crisis: Policy options for relief and restructuring. *World Bank*, 1–36.

Feldmann, H. (2016). Government size and unemployment: Evidence from industrial countries. *Public Choice*, 127, 451–467.

Ferrando, A. & Ganoulis, L. (2020). Firms' expectations on access to finance at the early stages of the Covid-19 pandemic. *Working Paper Series—The European Central Bank*, 2446, 1–46.

Fitriasari, F. (2020). How do small and medium enterprise (SMEs) survive the COVID-19 outbreak? *Journal of Economic Innovation*, 5(2), 53–62. https://doi.org/10.22219/jiko.v5i02.11838.

Goodell, W. J. (2020). COVID-19 and finance: Agendas for future research. *Finance Research Letters*, 35, 101512. 10.1016/j.frl.2020.101512.

Green, D. and Loualiche, E. (2021), State and local government employment in the COVID-19 crisis, *Journal of Public Economics*, 193, 1–11.

Gunn, F. N. M. V. G., O'Campo, P., Anagnostou, M., Muntaner, C., Wanigaratne, S., Perri, M. Carolyn Ziegler, C. & Angie, A. (2021). COVID-19 economic response and recovery: A rapid scoping review. *International Journal of Health Services*, 51(2), 247–260. 10.1177/00207314211002785.

Gupta, S., Montenovo, L., Nguyen, T. D., Rojas, F. L., Schmutte, I. M., Simon, K. I., & Wing, C. (2020). Effects of social distancing policy on labor market outcomes. *Working Paper* National Bureau of Economic Research. (No. w27280).

Jedwab, R., Khan, A. M., Russ, J. & Zaveri, E. D. (2021). Epidemics, pandemics, and social conflict: Lessons from the past and possible scenarios for COVID-19. *World Development*. https://doi.org/10.1016/j.worlddev.2021.105629.

Kalenkoski, C. M. & Pabilonia, S. W. (2020). Initial impact of the COVID-19 pandemic on the employment and hours of self-employed coupled and single workers by gender and parental status. *IZA Institue of Labor Economics*, 13443, 1–46.

Kamaruddin, M. I. H, Ahmad, A., Husain, M. H. & Abd Hamid, N. S. (2020). Graduate employability post-COVID-19: The case of a Malaysian public university. *Higher Education, Skills and Work-Based Learning*. 10.1108/HESWBL-05–2020-0114.

Katherine, B., Picchioni, F., Natarajan, N., Guermond, V., Parsons, L., Zanello, G., & Batemane, M. (2020). Compounding crises of social reproduction: Microfinance, over-indebtedness and the COVID-19 pandemic. *World Development*, 36, 1–4. 10.1016/j.worlddev.2020.105087.

Kim, J., Kim, J. & Wang, Y. (2020). Uncertainty risks and strategic reaction of restaurant firms amid COVID-19: Evidence from China. *International Journal of Hospitality Management*, 92(102752), 1–10. 10.1016/j.ijhm.2020.102752.

Kraus, S., Clauss, T., Breier, M., Gast, J., Zardini, A. & Tiberius, V. (2020). The economics of COVID-19: initial empirical evidence on how family firms in five European countries cope with the corona crisis. *International Journal of Entrepreneurial Behavior & Research*. 10.1108/IJEBR-04–2020-0214.

Levashenko, A. & Koval, A. (2020). Measures of Financial and Non-Financial Support to Small and Medium-sized Enterprises (SMEs) in the Wake of COVID-19 (May 17, 2020). *Monitoring of Russia's Economic Outlook-Trends and Challenges of Socio-economic Development-Moscow,* 7–10. https://ssrn.com/abstract=3629597.

Lu, Y., Wu, J., Peng, J. & Lu, L. (2020). The perceived impact of the Covid-19 epidemic: evidence from a sample of 4807 SMEs in Sichuan Province, China. *Environmental Hazards,* 19(4), 323–340. https://doi.org/10.1080/17477891.2020.1763902.

Lutfi, M. & Kornelius, Y. (2020). The impact of social distancing policy on small and medium-sized enterprises (SMEs) in Indonesia. *Problems and Perspectives in Management*, 18(3), 492–503. http://dx.doi.org/10.21511/ppm.18(3).2020.40.

Nghiem, N. & Wilson, N. (2021). The potential impact of COVID-19 related unemployment on increased cardiovascular disease in a high-income country: Modeling health loss, cost and equity. *PLoS One*, 16(5), 1–14. https://doi.org/10.1371/journal.pone.0246053.

Ntererwa, J. A. & Lukundji, V. K. (2020). Incidence de la crise sanitaire du COVID-19 sur l'endettement des Petites et Moyennes Entreprises de la ville de Bukavu. *International Journal of Accounting, Finance, Auditing, Management and Economics*, 1(2), 230–247. 10.5281/zenodo.4027483.

Oudda, Y., Assaad, I. M. & Bennis, L. (2020). Les retombées de la crise sanitaire Covid-19 sur l'Economie Marocaine. *Revue du contrôle, de la comptabilité et de l'audit*, 4(2), 452–475. https://www.revuecca.com/index.php/home/article/view/581.

Phélinas, P. (2014). Comment mesurer l'emploi dans les pays en développement? *Revue Tiers Monde*, 2(218), 15–33. https://www.cairn.info/revue-tiers-monde-2014–2-page-15.htm.

Rodríguez-Planas, N. (2010). Channels through which public employment services and small business assistance programs work. *Oxford Bulletin of Economics and Statistics*, 72(4), 458–485. https://doi.org/10.1111/j.1468–0084.2010.00593.x.

Suomi A., Schofield T. P. & Butterworth P. (2020). Unemployment, Employability and COVID-19: How the global socioeconomic shock challenged negative perceptions toward the less fortunate in the Australian context. *Front. Psychol.* 10.3389/fpsyg.2020.594837.

Wall, L. D., (2020). Assisting firms during a crisis: Benefits and costs. *Federal Reserve Bank of Atlanta's Policy Hub*, 10, 1–18. https://doi.org/10.29338/ph2020-10.

Wang, S. S., Goh, J. R., Sornette, D., Wang, H. & Yang, E. Y. (2020). Government support for SMEs in response to COVID-19: Theoretical model using Wang transform. *Swiss Finance Institute Research Paper*. https://ssrn.com/abstract=3608646.

Webb, A., McQuaid, R. & Rand, S. (2020). Employment in the informal economy: implications of the COVID-19 pandemic. *International Journal of Sociology and Social Policy*, 40(9–10), 1005–1019.

Wei, S. C., Hsu, W. T., Chiu, C. H., Chang, F. Y., Lo, H. R., Liao C. Y., Yang, H. I., Chou, Y. C., Tsai, C. H. & Chao, Y. C. (2021). An integrated platform for serological detection and vaccination of COVID-19. *Frontiers in Immunology*. 10.3389/fimmu.2021.771011.

CHAPTER 5

The Impact of Government Support on the Employment of Small- and Medium-Sized Enterprises (SMEs) During the COVID-19 Pandemic: A Case of Tunisian Companies

AFEF KHALIL[1], MOHAMMED EL-AMINE ABDELLI[2], NAIMA BENTOUIR[3], and IMEN BACCOUCHE[4]

[1]*University of Manouba-ISCAE, Manouba, Tunisia*

[2]*Laboratory of LEGO, University of Brest-UBO, Brest, France*

[3]*LMELSPM Laboratory, Economics Department, Ain Temouchent University, Ain Temouchent, Algeria*

[4]*University of Manouba-ESC, Manouba, Tunisia*

*Corresponding author

ABSTRACT

The study empirically investigated the impact of government support on the employment of small- and medium-sized enterprises (SMEs) during the Coronavirus disease 2019 (COVID-19) crisis. A questionnaire survey was conducted based on 95 Tunisian SMEs used in this study. Use STATA to analyze the results. The main results show that during the COVID-19 pandemic, government support measures have had a positive impact on employment. This means that companies with higher employment rates need more financial relief and sell them through credit. Besides SMEs' policies, the survey results show that technological innovations improve

Corporate Governance, Digitalization, and Energy Transition: Imen Baccouche and Afef Khalil. (Eds.)

DOI: 10.1201/9781779643407-6

employment in SMEs. This research provides useful and practical enlightenment for scientists, investors, managers, and regulators. It has made a significant contribution to the literature discussing the policies used and their impact on employment in the COVID-19 pandemic. So far, as far as we know, there are no academic papers studying the impact of government support measures on employment during the COVID-19 pandemic. Therefore, this study fills a key research gap in the literature. The chapter can also serve as an initial basis for providing empirical evidence of the influence of government measures on employment during the recent crisis.

5.1 INTRODUCTION

The recent Coronavirus disease 2019 (COVID-19) pandemic is not the first time a coronavirus disease has reached epidemic levels, as seen with severe acute respiratory syndrome and Middle East respiratory syndrome, for example. However, this is the first time a pandemic has had a global impact (Brem et al., 2021). Brem et al. (2021) point out that the current global epidemic of COVID-19 is a catastrophe in several ways. It has impacted not only many people's personal lives but also whole economies, markets, and nations around the world. Deutschmann et al. (2020) claim that the economic impacts of the COVID-19 pandemic may be as significant as its health impacts. The current crisis is worse than the 2008–2009 financial crisis and is equivalent to the great depression in the United States from 1929 to 1933, and the wartime devastation of Europe from 1939 to 1945. Not surprisingly, many politicians have drawn comparisons between battling disease and waging war (Beglaryan and Shakhmuradyan, 2020). Sumner et al. (2020) note that unprecedentedly the COVID-19 pandemic resulted in a rise in poverty rates. Beglaryan and Shakhmuradyan (2020) argue that the coronavirus outbreak triggered a global crisis involving supply and demand shocks. Nicola et al. (2020) add that the lockdowns have disrupted economic growth, unlike any other past demand or supply crisis. Current containment policies could decrease global gross domestic product (GDP) by 2% per month, or 24% annually (According to the Organization for Economic Cooperation and Development (OECD), 2021).

According to Ferrando and Ganoulis (2020), small- and medium-sized enterprises (SMEs) are substantially more vulnerable to pandemic risks than large companies and become financially fragile over the recent pandemic. Moreover, many SMEs were forced to close their doors temporarily or definitively due to the pandemic. Many of these incidents were caused by containment measures, which required nonessential companies to shut their doors during lockdowns (OECD, 2021). Bartik et al. (2020) believe that declining customer demand and staff health problems were the main factors behind the temporary closure. Besides Gourinchas et al. (2020) estimate that COVID-19 would result in an approximately 9 percentage point rise in the failure rate of SMEs. OECD (2021) argues that the COVID-19 crisis has often impacted SMEs rather than large companies. Additionally, Beglaryan and Shakhmuradyan (2020) demonstrate that workers in SMEs have been the hardest hit by the crisis, many of them having been made redundant or having seen their working hours and wages cut. According to experts, working with a small business doubles the chances of being laid off or having your salary reduced. According to the International Labour Organization (2020), around 300 million full-time workers have lost their jobs or have had their working hours and wages reduced because of the lockdown.

To alleviate the employment effects of the COVID-19 pandemic, many SMEs resorted to financial mechanisms such as direct investment, credit sales, tax incentives, credit acquisition, and tax delays (Levashenko and Koval, 2020). Moreover, governments worldwide have introduced temporary support measures to help companies maintain productive relationships with their customers and staff, to cushion the impact of the economic crisis (Bartik et al., 2020; Deutschmann et al., 2020). In 51 nations, the government has implemented over 1300 stimulus measures totaling about $11 trillion, according to Albaz et al. (2020). In Tunisia, SMEs face a lack of financial support. To address this issue, Oxfam in Tunisia works with the organization impact partner that has helped a women's group of pottery producers with technical and financial assistance (Dridi, 2020). The economy in Tunisia is characterized by SMEs, with over 99% of all businesses belonging to the private sector. Tunisian SMEs are confined to low-technology and low-productivity activities, resulting in poor value-added and weak ties with world markets. Tunisian SMEs are also noted for their low upward mobility and low job creation potential, as they lack the financial, human, and technological means to innovate (Bellakhal and Mouelhi, 2020).

The objective of this chapter is to examine the impact of government support on the employment of SMEs during the COVID-19 pandemic. As far as we know, during the COVID-19 pandemic, there are very few empirical studies on government support and its impact on the employment of SMEs. Therefore, current research papers fill the gaps in this literature by studying the impact of government support on the employment of SMEs. To this end, our chapter provides prospective researchers, analysts, and investors with a comprehensive view of the possible impact of government support on the employment of SMEs.

The remainder of this chapter is organized as described below. Section 5.2 deals with the literature review. Section 5.3 describes the sample and variables used. Section 5.4 presents the empirical results and Section 5.5 summarizes.

5.2 LITERATURE REVIEW AND HYPOTHESES

SMEs are often defined in the scientific literature as entrepreneurial structures with less than 250 workers. They are currently the backbone of every economy in the world (Razumovskaia et al., 2020). Over 95% of all firms in the globe are SMEs, which account for around half of employment in the private sector and 40%–60% of the country's total value added (Beglaryan and Shakhmuradyan, 2020). Thus, the destabilization of these business entities' development will have a serious impact on country's macroeconomic and social indicators (Razumovskaia et al., 2020). Albaz et al. (2020) show that the COVID-19 crisis has a dramatic impact on the SMEs. Indeed, the current crisis has left SMEs in a vulnerable situation, and many are at risk of closing down. Albaz et al. (2020) add that since the outbreak of the epidemic, demand has dropped substantially. This is because of the drastic transformation of consumer behaviors due to the implemented measures of social isolation, fear of being infected with the virus, and diminished purchasing capacity. (Razumovskaia et al., 2020). Besides, supply chains have been disrupted by the epidemic, with many SMEs left with no resources to continue operating.

Furthermore, steps aimed at slowing the spread of the disease have affected the production processes of SMEs (Albaz et al., 2020). According to the OECD's monitoring of more than 180 SMEs in 32 countries since February 2020, 70%–80% of SMEs have experienced a significant decline in revenues since the start of the pandemic (OECD, 2021). Pedauga et al. (2021) add that SMEs' reduced income has resulted in serious financial difficulties and solvency issues. Otherwise, SME employees have been severely affected by the crisis, many of them having been made redundant or seen their working hours and wages cut (Beglaryan and Shakhmuradyan, 2020).

Albaz et al. (2020) argue that the ability of SMEs to operate is significantly affected by the dramatic and sudden loss of demand and that the ensuing closure is a source of unemployment. Around 300 million full-time employees have lost their employment or had their working hours and salaries slashed, according to the International Labour Organization (2020). According to some experts, SME employees have been harder hit by the crisis due to a shortage of financial savings and asset guarantees (Reeves and Rothwell, 2020). Palomino et al. (2020) indicate that employees of SMEs with average to advanced professional qualifications were less impacted by the crisis. Saltiel (2020) adds that the pandemic's impact on employment was greatest in areas that rely on proximity, such as transport, trade, and entertainment. Employees who work in services that may be delivered remotely, such as education, information and communications, and banking, were less impacted.

To mitigate the negative effects of the COVID-19 pandemic on employment, SMEs employed digital technologies to retain and resist their employees. In this context, Lukonga (2020) states that digital innovations can increase the productivity and growth of small and medium businesses. Akpan et al. (2020) reveal that technological innovation stimulates demand and creates value. Bartik et al. (2020) and Deutschmann et al. (2020) add that governments all over the world have put in place temporary support measures to assist companies in maintaining positive relationships between their customers and workers and surviving. Furthermore, some SMEs used financial instruments such as direct investment, purchases on credit, tax stimulus, acquisitions on credit, and tax delays (Levashenko and Koval, 2020).

5.2.1 GOVERNMENT SUPPORT AND EMPLOYMENT OF SMES

According to Albaz et al. (2020), governments have established a large number of programs geared at addressing the requirements of SMEs since the outbreak of the recent crisis. Robinson and Kengatharan (2020) argue that the government must assist SMEs that are at risk. Furthermore, the government should enhance its rules to protect both SMEs and employees. According to Razumovskaia et al. (2020), support measures must be systematic, based on precise economic policy objectives, and contain long-term growth priorities for companies. The main objective of government assistance should be to preserve the continuity of the company to rescue as many jobs as feasible while also providing the groundwork for a smoother and speedier recovery by avoiding permanent closures (Razumovskaia et al., 2020). According to a McKinsey study of several small business surveys in the United States, 1.4–2.1 million small businesses (25%–36%) could close down definitively due to the effects of the COVID-19 crisis in just the first four months (Dua et al., 2020). Robinson and Kengatharan (2020) show that government support should be rapid to avoid job losses. According to Carranza et al. (2020), government aid is proposed to help companies maintain their staff, provide insurance to those who lose their jobs, and provide alternative employment and employability support for those who are jobless.

H1. Government support impacts positively SMEs' employment during the COVID-19 crisis.

5.2.2 SMES' POLICIES AND EMPLOYMENT OF SMES

Bartik et al. (2020) claim that during a recession, economic effects are not evenly dispersed throughout productive sectors or enterprises, SMEs are more affected than large enterprises, and industries like tourism, transportation, and construction are more vulnerable to social distance or confinement. Most academics believe that SMEs' greatest vulnerability during a pandemic is caused by the inability to capitalize on external financial resources (Razumovskaia et al., 2020). The COVID-19 crisis appears to be a new form and standard of challenge for SMEs. Businesses use policies that can be categorized as part of different initiatives to respond to the crisis and emerge better in the long term (Kraus et al., 2020). Levashenko and Koval (2020) indicate that many SMEs used financial instruments (e.g., credit purchases) to offset the negative impact of the COVID-19 crisis on employment. Similarly, Ferrando and Ganoulis (2020) show that SMEs may have intended to use trade credit as a substitute for other forms of financing during periods of crisis. Moreover, businesses must sell on credit to keep their employees and customers and, as a result, escape the detrimental effects of the COVID-19 crisis on jobs (Levashenko and Koval, 2020). Apart from credit sales, Fitriasari (2020) focuses on SMEs using and implementing other financial steps, such as late tax payments, to reduce the possibility of default and retain their employees.

H2. SMEs' policies impact positively employment during the COVID-19 pandemic.

5.2.3 DIGITAL TECHNOLOGIES AND EMPLOYMENT OF SMES

The COVID-19 crisis would have a severe effect on our industries and culture. It is important to manage risk and volatility during a pandemic. Risk can be forecasted and quantified using probability techniques (Adžić and Al-Mansour, 2021). According to the OECD (2021), the current crisis has reinforced the use of digital technologies by SMEs. The Internet and web technologies have made a wide range of technological communication solutions available to meet the needs of the recently emerging remote worker (Larson et al., 2020). Kraus et al. (2020) claim that companies use regular mailings, phone calls, WhatsApp messages, messaging, an intelligence blog or podcast, or a service hotline to communicate with their employees. Bacq et al. (2020) add that thanks to digital technologies, SMEs now have innovative and cheaper ways to sell their products and support their brands. Similarly, Akpan et al. (2020) show that technology innovation boosts demand efficiency and adds value. Furthermore, Adžić and Al-Mansour (2021) state that during the COVID-19 crisis, most businesses have implemented work-from-home programs and provided assistance to employees, involving the purchase of additional smartphones, iPads, and computer monitors. Hite and McDonald (2020) argue that employee productivity is improved by digital technologies. Therefore, SMEs who successfully implemented multiple digital technologies were able to maintain their employees and build resilience during the COVID-19 crisis (Razumovskaia et al., 2020). However, Beglaryan and Shakhmuradyan (2020) claim that SME processes are gradually being digitalized to respond to changing circumstances, but temporary employment losses have occurred.

H3. SMEs' digital technologies impact positively employment during the COVID-19 pandemic.

5.3 METHODOLOGY

5.3.1 SAMPLE

To verify our research hypothesis, a quantitative analysis was carried out on a questionnaire from a sample of 95 Tunisian SMEs. This instrument serves as the survey's content support for data collection. It was created to measure the effect of government support on SME employment during the COVID-19 pandemic using a set of variables.

5.3.2 QUESTIONNAIRE DEVELOPMENT

We distributed our survey electronically through an online questionnaire. Since the late 1990s, the use of electronic surveys has increased significantly (Ilieva et al., 2002). Our data were obtained in the first half of January 2021.

We received a total of 139 responses. Participation in the survey is optional, due to the confidentiality of individual details and other ethics set out in the survey guidelines.

Before collecting the data, the survey rules were explained to the participants. They were instructed to respond to as many questions as they can. However, if you were unsure of the answer, you could leave it blank.

5.3.3 DATA PROCESSING AND ANALYSIS

Enter data into Excel for data logging, and use STATA for data analysis. A total of 44 respondents were excluded from this research because they correctly replied to less than 80% of the questions and missed some key information (Table 5.1).

5.3.4 VARIABLES MEASUREMENT

5.3.4.1 DEPENDENT VARIABLE

According to the studies of Phélinas (2014), Beglaryan and Shakhmuradyan (2020), and Cohen (2020), the unemployment variable is measured by one indicator, as shown below:

Y = A binary variable that is equal to 1 if SME workers quit the company and/or have been laid off due to the COVID-19 outbreak and 0 otherwise.

TABLE 5.1 Respondents' Details

Respondents' Details	Frequency (%)
Gender distribution	
Male	82.5
Female	17.5
Age distribution	
<35 years	19.8
Bet 35 and 45 years	43.8
>45 years	36.5
Status of respondents	
General Director	16.5
Financial Director	11.3
Technical Director	9.3
Manager	22.7
Human Resources	14.4
Others	25.8

5.3.4.2 INDEPENDENT VARIABLES

A review of several research studies allowed us to extract three features to analyze the empirical impact of government support measures on unemployment during the COVID-19 pandemic. We found in particular: Government support (GVTSUP) is a binary variable that is equal to 1 if the SMEs obtained government support and 0 otherwise; SMEs' policies (SMEP) is a binary variable that is equal to 1 if the SMEs have used one of these policies: loans from commercial banks, loans from nonbanking financial institutions microfinance institutions, credit cooperatives, credit unions, or finance companies, sales on credit, purchases on credit, government grants, and 0 otherwise; and digital technologies (DIG) is a binary variable that is equal to 1 if the SMEs employ digital technologies and 0 otherwise.

We add five control variables to enhance our empirical results: ACTIV is a binary variable that is equal to 1 if the SMEs' activity decreases and 0 otherwise, SIZE is the SMEs' size, COVID is the mortality rate for COVID-19, GDP is the GDP economic growth rate, and TXF is the inflation rate.[1] Table 5.2 describes the used variables.

1. The World Bank (1), Trading Economies (2), and the World Health Organization (3) websites are often used to obtain the rate of economic growth, the rate of inflation, the number of COVID-19 incidents, and the number of COVID-19 deaths.

TABLE 5.2 Description of Variables Used

Variable	Definition	Measure
Y	Employment	A binary variable that is equal to 1 if SME workers quit the company and/or have been laid off due to the COVID-19 outbreak and 0 otherwise
GVTSUP	Government support	A binary variable that is equal to 1 if the SMEs obtained government support and 0 otherwise
SMEP	SME's policies	A binary variable that is equal to 1 if the SMEs have used one of these policies Loans from commercial banks, Loans from nonbanking financial institutions microfinance institutions, credit cooperatives, credit unions, or finance companies, Delaying payments to suppliers or workers, Sales on credit, Purchases on credit, Government grants), and 0 otherwise
DigTech	Digital technologies	A binary variable that is equal to 1 if the SMEs employ digital technologies and 0 otherwise
ACTIV	SME's activity	A binary variable that is equal to 1 if the SME activity decreases and 0 otherwise
SIZE	The SMEs' size	An ordinal variable measured on four-point scale (1 = 100 and above, 4 = 9 and below)
COVID	Mortality rate for COVID-19	(Deaths' number due to disease/Confirmed cases' number) × 100
GDP	Gross domestic product	The GDP economic growth rate
INF	Inflation	The inflation rate

5.3.5 MODEL SPECIFICATION

We utilize ordinary least squares to evaluate the influence of government support on SMEs' employment during the COVID-19 pandemic, according to Kalezic (2012), Chi et al. (2015), and Rashid et al. (2020). The following model is suggested as follows.

Dichotomous models allow more precise and reliable interpretations compared to descriptive analysis, by highlighting the weight of each characteristic in the realization of the observed event (having left the company) compared to a reference modality (keeping his job). In our work, we regress, using a Probit estimate, the probability of leaving the company on a set of individual characteristics.

$$Pr(Y_i = 1) = C + \beta_1 GVTSUP_i + \beta_2 SMEP_i + \beta_3 DIG_i + \beta_4 ACTIV_i + \beta_5 SIZE_i + \beta_6 COVID_i + \beta_7 GDP_i + \beta_8 TXF_i + \varepsilon_{it}$$

Hence, *C* is the constant. The coefficients of the interest variables range from 1 to 3, whereas the coefficients of control variables range from 4 to 9. In addition, "I" stands for the number of SMEs, which varies from 1 to 95, and ε_{it} designates the error term.

5.4 RESULTS AND DISCUSSION

5.4.1 DESCRIPTIVE STATISTICS

According to Table 5.3, the average of the (SIZE) variable is 1.404, which varies from 0 to 2. The mean of size (SIZE) is 1.404. (COVID) has a range of 1.699 to 5.922 and an average of 2.928. The variable (GDP) has a mean of 105.044.

TABLE 5.3 Descriptive Statistics

	Mean	Std. dev.	Min	Max
SIZE	1.404	0.851	0	2
COVID	2.928	0.903	1.699	5.922
GDP	105.044	145.334	37.87	793
INF	5.048	2.031	-1.86	9.05

Table 5.4 shows that 57.58% of workers quit the company and/or have been laid off due to COVID-19. Government support is provided to 35.35% of SMEs, and 56.57% of businesses have implemented strategies. Furthermore, digital technologies are used by 69.79% of SMEs. Table 5.4 indicates that 46.46% of SMEs activity decreases.

TABLE 5.4 Binary Variable Frequency

Variables	Y		GOVSUPP		DIG		SMEP		Activ	
	0	1	0	1	0	1	0	1	0	1
Frequency %	42.42	57.58	64.65	35.35	30.21	69.79	43.43	56.57	53.54	46.46

5.4.2 CROSS-CORRELATION MATRIX

According to Table 5.5, there is no high correlation between the independent variables, and they are below the limit (0.7) (Kennedy, 2008).

TABLE 5.5 Cross-Correlation Matrix

	GVTSUPP	Gender	SIZE	ACTIV	SMEP	DigTech	COVID
GVTSUPP	1.0000						
Gender	−0.0693	1.0000					
SIZE	0.1077	−0.0121	1.0000				
ACTIV	0.4580	0.1662	0.0020	1.0000			
SMEP	−0.2476	0.0402	−0.0504	−0.0295	1.0000		
DigTech	0.4044	0.1405	−0.0602	0.4241	−0.2035	1.0000	
COVID	0.0894	−0.1471	−0.0073	−0.0126	−0.0960	0.0241	1.0000

5.4.3 DISCUSSION AND POLICY IMPLICATIONS

Table 5.6 summarizes our results on the relationship between firms' policies and government support measures and their effect on employment during the COVID-19 crisis. Government support (GVTSUPP) has a positive impact on the SMEs' employment during the COVID-19 crisis. This positive relationship confirms our hypothesis *H1* and previous research findings (Albaz et al., 2020; Carranza et al., 2020; Dua et al., 2020; Razumovskaia et al., 2020). This result implies that government assistance aids SMEs in reducing the harmful impacts of the COVID-19 epidemic. According to Khalil et al. (2022a, b), government support is essential for companies with limited cash flow to sustain during a crisis. Robinson and Kengatharan (2020) add that to avoid layoffs, the government should take quick action. Therefore, national governments should be instrumental in creating the right measures to enhance the business environment during the current pandemic and keep employees. The coefficient associated with the (SMEP) variable does not significantly impact employment. *H2*, therefore, is not supported. This finding implies that the SMEs' policies do not influence employment during the COVID-19 pandemic. This result contradicts the suggestions of previous research (Bartik et al., 2020; Ferrando and Ganoulis, 2020; Fitriasari, 2020; Levashenko and Koval,

2020). The (DigTech) variable reveals a positive impact on the SMEs' employment. *H3* is, therefore, accepted. Digital technologies improve the SMEs' employment during the COVID-19 crisis, which confirms previous research findings (Adžić and Al-Mansour, 2021; Akpan et al., 2020; Bacq et al., 2020; Hite and McDonald, 2020; Kraus et al., 2020; Larson et al., 2020). Furthermore, the finding is in line with Razumovskaia et al. (2020) predicting that the SMEs who integrated numerous digital technologies successfully were able to keep their staff and develop resilience over the recent crisis. Thus, SMEs should promote the adoption of digital technology. Eventually, concerning the control variables, the (PIB) variable reveals a positive impact on the SMEs' employment. Table 5.6 also shows that other control variables (Size, COVID, INF) do not significantly affect the SMEs' employment.

TABLE 5.6 Panel Regression Results

Y	Coefficient	Z	P >|z|
Govsupp	0.667	2.12	0.034**
SMEP	0.097	0.33	0.743
Dig	0.745	2.23	0.026**
Size	0.197	1.46	0.146
COVID	0.381	1.40	0.160
PIB	0.003	1.89	0.059*
INF	0.033	0.41	0.682
Cons	−2.679	2.72	0.007
R^2	16.53%		
N	95		

5.5 CONCLUSION

The economic response of governments to the COVID-19 pandemic has included a variety of measures to assist companies in keeping their employees during the crisis. SMEs are in a particularly difficult situation. They have had to lay off staff due to falling demand, and many of them do not have the financial means to live in this environment (Albaz et al., 2020). Failure to protect them could threaten the global economy. Thus, the government's policies and recommendations to help SMEs maintain their employees are essential and should be articulated explicitly (Robinson and

Kengatharan, 2020). OECD (2021) states that governments all over the world have reacted quickly and firmly to the unprecedented difficulties that SMEs are facing as a result of the COVID-19 epidemic by enacting a variety of stimulus and support measures. Our purpose is to study the impact of government support on the employment of SMEs during the COVID-19 pandemic. To solve this problem, we used quantitative methodology. Conduct a questionnaire survey to collect data.

According to the results, government support has a positive impact on SMEs' employment. Furthermore, the results show that digital technologies positively impact SMEs' unemployment over the COVID-19 pandemic. This implies that digital technologies assist SMEs but do not ensure their survival. Other independent variables (Size, INF, COVID, SMEP) do not have a significant impact on unemployment during the COVID-19 crisis. As a result, national governments are being called to examine their policies and develop innovative ideas to reduce unemployment and mitigate the damaging effects of the COVID-19 situation on SMEs. Companies must reevaluate their tactics and use new ways. Furthermore, SMEs must employ digital technology to retain employees and survive the current epidemic.

5.5.1 THEORETICAL IMPLICATIONS

This chapter conducts an in-depth study of the current literature from all aspects. First, this research provides a new perspective on how government support affects the employment of SMEs during the COVID-19 pandemic. Previous publications have examined the influence of the recent epidemic, but only a few have addressed relevant government interventions and their impact on SME employment. Second, as far as we know, our research is the first to investigate the impact of government support on the employment of SMEs during the COVID-19 pandemic. Third, this research attempts to fill the gaps in the literature by providing new empirical evidence.

5.5.2 PRACTICAL IMPLICATIONS

For various practitioners, this research chapter provides valuable practical evidence (investors, academics, regulators, etc.). During the COVID-19 pandemic, this chapter provides useful information on how government support affects the employment of SMEs. To update the rules, company officials should consider the results of the research and implement new methods to maintain the effectiveness of government legislation.

5.5.3 STUDY LIMITATIONS AND FUTURE RESEARCH

This chapter discusses the impact of government support on the employment of SMEs during the COVID-19 pandemic. After greater efforts, there are still many ways to be found in future research. First, this research is limited to 2021. The number of researchers in the future should be increased for a few more years because we have taken a step forward, and the impact of government support on the employment of SMEs has become more and more obvious. Second, more empirical analysis of government support and the employment of SMEs is needed. Similarly, during the COVID-19 crisis, future research should pay more attention to the impact of emerging technologies on jobs. Third, more research is needed to address policy questions about how the epidemic affects banks. COVID-19 also faces major obstacles in corporate social responsibility activities. The following problems can be solved by more research.

NOTES

1. www.worldbank.org
2. www.tradingeconomics.com
3. www.who.int

KEYWORDS

- **COVID-19**
- **employment**
- **government support**
- **small- and medium-sized enterprises**

REFERENCES

Adžić, S. & Al-Mansour, J. (2021). Business analysis in the times of COVID-19: Empirical testing of the contemporary academic findings. *Management Science Letters*, 11, 1–10.

Akpan, I. J., Udoh, E. A. P. & Adebisi, B. (2020). Small business awareness and adoption of state-of-the-art technologies in emerging and developing markets, and lessons from the COVID-19 pandemic. *Journal of Small Business and Entrepreneurship*. https://doi.org/10.1080/08276331.2020.1820185.

Albaz, A. Mansour, T., Rida, T. & Schubert, J. (2020). Setting up small and medium-sized enterprises for restart and recovery, McKinsey and Company. https://www.mckinsey.com/industries/public-and-social-sector/our-insights/setting-up-small-and-medium-size-enterprises-for-restart-and-recovery.

Bacq, S., Geoghegan, W., Josefy, M., Stevenson, R. & Williams, T. A. (2020). The COVID-19 virtual idea blitz: Marshaling social entrepreneurship to rapidly respond to urgent grand challenges. *Business Horizons*, 63(6), 705–723.

Bartik, A. W. Bertrand, M., Cullen, Z., Glaeser, E. L., Luca, M. & Stanton, C. (2020). The impact of COVID-19 on small business outcomes and expectations. Working Paper, 20(102), 1–43.

Beglaryan, M. & Shakhmuradyan, G. (2020). The impact of COVID-19 on small and medium-sized enterprises in Armenia: Evidence from a labor force survey. *Small Business International Review*, 4(2), 1–11.

Bellakhal, R. & Mouelhi, R. B. A. (2020). Digitalization and firms performance: Evidence from Tunisian SMEs. Working Paper, 36, EMNES.

Brem, A., Viardot, E. & Nylund, P. A. (2021). Implications of the coronavirus (COVID-19) outbreak for innovation: Which technologies will improve our lives?. *Technological Forecasting and Social Change*, 163, 1–7.

Carranza, E., Farole, T., Gentilini, U., Morgandi, M., Packard, T., Santos, I. & Weber, M. (2020). Managing the employment impacts of the COVID-19 crisis: Policy options for relief and restructuring jobs. Working Paper, 49, 1–33.

Chi, W., Huang, H. & Xie, H. (2015). A quantile regression analysis on corporate governance and the cost of bank loans: A research note. *Review of Accounting and Finance*, 14 (1), 2–19.

Cohen, G. D. (2020). Measuring employment during COVID-19: Challenges and opportunities. *Business Economics*, 55, 229–239.

Dridi, M. (2020). Alternative Business models for start-ups and SMEs in Tunisia with high potential to create jobs for youth and women. Oxfam GB for Oxfam International under ISBN 978-1-78748-582-2. https://doi.org/10.21201/2020.5822.

Dua, A., Ellingrud, K., Mahajan, D. & Silberg, J. (2020). Which small businesses are most vulnerable to COVID-19. McKinsey & Company. https://www.mckinsey.com/featured-insights/americas/which-small-businesses-are-most-vulnerable-to-covid-19-and-when.

Ferrando, A. & Ganoulis, L. (2020). Firms' expectations on access to finance at the early stages of the Covid-19 pandemic. Working Paper Series—The European Central Bank, 2446, 1–46.

Fitriasari, F. (2020). How do small and medium enterprise (SME) survive the COVID-19 outbreak?. *Journal of Economic Innovation*, 5(2), 53–62.

Gourinchas, P. O., Ozcan, S. K., Penciakova, V. & Sander, N. (2020). COVID-19 and SME Failures. IMF Working Paper, 20(207), 1–55.

Hite, L. M. & McDonald, K. S. (2020). Careers after COVID-19: Challenges and changes. *Human Resource Development International*, 23(4), 427–437.

Ilieva, J., Baron, S. & Healey, N. M. (2002). Online surveys in marketing research: Pros and cons. *International Journal of Market Research*, 44(3), 361–382.

International Labour Organization (2020). ILO monitor: COVID-19 and the world of work, 5th edition. http://www.ilo.org/global/topics/coronavirus/impacts-and-responses/WCMS_749399/lang–en/index.htm.

Kalezic, Z. (2012). Corporate governance and firm performance with special reference to the banking system: Empirical evidence from Montenegro. *Journal of Central Banking Theory and Practice*, 2, 19–54.

Kennedy, P. (2008). A Guide to Econometrics, 6th Edition, Wiley.

Khalil, A., Abdelli, M. E. A. & Mogaji, E. (2022a). Do digital technologies influence the relationship between the COVID-19 crisis and SMEs' resilience in developing countries?. *Journal of Open Innovation: Technology, Market, and Complexity*, 8(2), 1–14.

Khalil, A., Bousselmi, H. W., Abdelli, M. E. A., Baccouche, I., Del Río, L. C. Y. L. & Nasr, H. E. (2022b). The impact of digital technologies on SMEs' resilience during the COVID-19 pandemic. Book chapter in Advanced Series in Management, Emreald bookstores.

Kraus, S., Clauss, T., Breier, M., Gast, J., Zardini, A. & Tiberius, V. (2020). The economics of COVID-19: Initial empirical evidence on how family firms in five European countries cope with the corona crisis. *International Journal of Entrepreneurial Behavior & Research*. https://doi.org/10.1108/IJEBR-04-2020-0214.

Larson, B. Z., Vroman, S. R. & Makarius, E. E. (2020). A guide to managing your (newly) remote workers. In Coronavirus and Business: The Insights You Need from Harvard Business Review. *Harvard Business Review*. https://hbr.org/2020/03/a-guide-to-managing-your-newly-remote-workers.

Levashenko, A. & Koval, A. (2020). Measures of financial and non-financial support to small and medium-sized enterprises (SMEs) in the wake of COVID-19 (May 17, 2020). Monitoring of Russia's economic outlook—Trends and challenges of socio-economic development—Moscow. IEP, 9, 7–10.

Lukonga, I. (2020). Harnessing Digital Technologies to Promote SMEs and Inclusive Growth in the Middle East, North Africa, Afghanistan and Pakistan (MENAP) Region. IMF Working Paper, 20(135), 1–46.

Nicola, M., Alsafi, Z., Sohrabi, C., Kerwan, A., Al-Jabir, A., Iosifidis, C., Agha, M. & Agha, R. (2020). The socioeconomic implications of the coronavirus pandemic (COVID-19): A review. *International Journal of Surgery*, 78(185), 1–20.

OECD (2021). One year of SME and entrepreneurship policy responses to COVID-19: Lessons learned to build back better. Tackling coronavirus (COVID-19) Getting it right and emerging stronger-Organization for Economic Co-operation and Development. https://www.oecd.org/coronavirus/en/.

Palomino, J. C., Rodriguez, J. G. & Sebastian, R. (2020). Wage inequality and poverty effects of lockdown and social distancing in Europe. *SSRN Electronic Journal*. https://doi.org/10.2139/ssrn.3615615.

Pedauga, L., Sáez, F. & Márquez, B. L. D (2021). Macroeconomic lockdown and SMEs: the impact of the COVID-19 pandemic in Spain. *Small Business Economics*. https://doi.org/10.1007/s11187-021-00476-7.

Phélinas, P. (2014). Comment mesurer l'emploi dans les pays en développement?. *Third World Review*, 2(218), 15–33.

Rashid, M. H. U., Zobair, S. A. M., Chowdhury, M. A. I. & Islam, A. (2020). Corporate governance and banks' productivity: Evidence from the banking industry in Bangladesh. *Business Research*, 13, 615–637.

Razumovskaia, E., Yuzvovich, L., Kniazeva, E., Klimenko, M. & Shelyakin, V. (2020). The effectiveness of Russian government policy to support SMEs in the COVID-19 pandemic. *Journal of Open Innovation: Technology, Market, and Complexity*, 6(160), 1–20.

Reeves, R. & Rothwell, J. (2020). Class and COVID: How the less affluent face double risks. Brookings Institution. https://www.brookings.edu/blog/up-front/2020/03/27/class-and-covid-how-the-lessaffluent-face-double-risks/.

Robinson, J. & Kengatharan, N. (2020). Exploring the effect of Covid-19 on small and medium enterprises: Early evidence from Sri Lanka. *Journal of Applied Economics and Business Research*, 10(2), 115–125.

Saltiel, F. (2020). Who can work from home in developing countries?. In C. Wyplosz (Ed.), Covid Economics: Vetted and Real-time Papers, CEPR Press, Vol. 6, pp. 104–118. https://cepr.org/content/covideconomics.

Sumner, A., Hoy, C. & Juarez, E. O. (2020). Estimates of the impact of COVID-19 on global poverty. WIDER Working Paper, 2020/43, 1–14.

CHAPTER 6

Paving the Way for Future Responsible Consumers: Educating Children on Healthy Consumption in the Digital Energy Era

SALMA MAHOUACHI[1] and IMED ZAIEM[2]

[1] *ENVIE Laboratory, South Mediterranean University, Mediterranean School of Business, Tunis, Tunisia*

[2] *Faculty of Economics and Management Sciences, Nabeul, Tunisia*

*Corresponding author

ABSTRACT

Consuming properly is a difficult skill that evolves. Children are exposed to a variety of food and beverage options, and they must learn to make good choices to meet their nutritional needs. The environment in which youngsters learn to consume, on the other hand, might be hard. Food marketing is widespread, and harmful meals are frequently less expensive and more convenient than healthy foods. Furthermore, children may lack access to appropriate dietary options or lack the knowledge or skills to make healthy choices. This chapter examines the difficulties that children experience when learning to eat healthily. It also covers the roles of parents, schools, and policymakers in promoting healthy eating among children. The chapter finishes by saying that teaching children to consume healthily is a key skill and that it is critical to create an environment that encourages healthy eating habits.

Corporate Governance, Digitalization, and Energy Transition: Imen Baccouche and Afef Khalil, (Eds.)

DOI: 10.1201/9781779643407-7

6.1 INTRODUCTION

In 2022,[1] the United Nations General Assembly adopted the sustainable development goals, which highlighted tackling overweight and obesity as one of the health challenges for the 2030 agenda for sustainable development. The Global Plan of Action to combat noncommunicable diseases for the period 2013–2020 aims to halt the rise in childhood obesity and sets a target to reduce the percentage of overweight children by 2025. Obesity represents a convergence of health and economic issues. It reflects the food industry's prioritization of profit over consumer health. Disregarding public health and environmental concerns, the products of the agri-food industry exemplify the current trend of prioritizing increased production and reduced costs, even at the expense of quality and the health of certain populations (Brusset, 2018). Obesity and overweight now rank fifth in terms of mortality risk and are recognized as major challenges of the 21st century, obesity extends beyond being a simple public health problem; it intersects with health, economic, and moral issues.[2] It is also an integral part of the challenges faced by thermo-industrial companies' growth models (Tchékémian, 2021).

Many alarming predictions were made years ago, Kelly et al. (2008) predicted that by 2030, approximately 60% of the world's adult population would be overweight or obese. Consequently, obesity-related expenditures, which are already substantial, are expected to double by 2025 (Aitken et al., 2009). This finding is more concerning when we consider that younger generations are gaining weight at a faster pace than their parents (Hebden et al., 2012). World organizations such as the WHO and Food and Agriculture Organization of the United Nations, mainly denounce the aggressive marketing strategies employed by the agri-food industry. Young children are extremely receptive to marketing, which is a probable cause of the increasing rates of overweight and obesity among children. Simply being exposed to an unhealthy food environment twice a day can lead them to develop cravings for unhealthier snacks (Smets and Vandevijvere, 2022).

The reality is that children are exposed to unhealthy eating choices and may lack knowledge and access to nutritious foods. This chapter examines the controversy surrounding commercial practices geared toward children

1. https://www.unep.org/annualreport/2022/
2. WHO (2020). UNICEF/WHO/The World Bank Group Joint Child Malnutrition Estimates: Levels and Trends in Child Malnutrition: Key Findings of the 2020 Edition.

and identifies the challenges they face in learning to consume healthily. Finally, a set of recommendations is put forth to reinforce the role of parents, schools, and policymakers in promoting healthy eating among children.

6.2 MARKETING, CHILDREN, AND OBESITY: THE DEBATE

The significance of targeting children as a primary market for the food industry is undeniable. It represents a rapidly growing and attractive market segment (Grad, 2015). From the initial phase of feeding an infant, where breast milk plays a key role, the industry is already offering alternatives. The global expansion of the baby food industry and its supply chains is accompanied by an increasing intensification and sophistication of its marketing practices. Unfortunately, the policy and regulatory frameworks put in place to protect, promote, and support breastfeeding are generally flawed in most countries, creating an enabling environment for the infant nutrition industry to flourish (Baker et al., 2021). This interest shown by the food industry aligns with the evolving role of children in the market and observable changes in their diets (Benton, 2004; Tarabashkina et al., 2016). There has been a shift toward more energy-dense, sugary, and calorie-rich foods, accompanied by reduced consumption of "healthy foods" such as fruits and vegetables, contrary to current nutritional recommendations (Ustjanauskas et al., 2014).

The debate surrounding marketing strategies targeting children revolves around several key points, as highlighted by Martin and Landon (2006). These include children's rights, the industry's right to promote its products, the regulation of advertising in children's lives, and the actual impact on consumption behavior and children's health. Calvert (2008) emphasizes that promotional activities permeate children's daily lives, exposing them to many unhealthy diets that contribute to obesity. It is important to understand how extensively the food industry shapes what is considered "acceptable to eat," thereby shedding light on the impact of food marketing on children's food-related behaviors and obesity (Cairns et al., 2013; Castronuovo et al., 2021). Children are valuable to food companies because they influence adults' purchasing decisions, spend money themselves, and develop brand loyalty from an early age. Furthermore, children are extensively exposed to food marketing from a young age, which influences their desire to purchase the promoted products, often detrimental to their health (Harris et al., 2009).

The official WHO report acknowledges that many researchers are investigating the link between advertising and obesity. It should be noted that, in addition to the potential impact of advertising, the time spent in front of the television promotes snacking and a sedentary lifestyle, which are major contributors to the obesity epidemic. The most frequently advertised and promoted food products targeted at children are cereals, sweets, soft drinks, salty snacks, and fast food, often presented with colorful packaging and child-oriented imagery (Cook, 2009; Mau et al., 2014; Driessen et al., 2022). This advertising contradicts the recommendations of public health organizations, and the lack of advertising supporting healthy eating practices is also evident (Hasting et al., 2003; Grad, 2015; Nestle, 2022). Children's rights to health and food are compromised by food marketing messages that exploit their cognitive and developmental immaturity, leaving them vulnerable and defenseless against harmful advertising influences (Boyland, 2023). Therefore, regulating the market and marketing techniques, especially television advertising, is necessary to protect young audiences. Children are vulnerable to marketing strategies, and industries approach them without fear or inhibition (Opree et al., 2013; Grad, 2015; Kline, 2022). To counter these trends, several organizations have assumed the responsibility of regulating the media (FCC,[3] FTC,[4] CARU,[5] COPPA[6]). Numerous measures are required, such as ensuring clear transitions between advertisements and program content, prohibiting main characters of TV shows from promoting products during the program or adjacent commercial time slots and avoiding product placements within program content.

Approaching the subject from another perspective, Livingstone and Helsper (2004) argue that while the negative effects of food promotion are an important research concern, public concerns predominantly revolve around children's nutrition and health rather than advertising itself. By

3. FCC: The Federal Communications Commission (FCC) ensures fair communication services and enforces regulations to safeguard consumers' interests.
4. FTC: The Federal Trade Commission (FTC) actively works toward preventing deceptive and unfair business practices, prioritizing consumer protection.
5. CARU: The Children's Advertising Review Unit (CARU) focuses on safeguarding children's rights by promoting ethical standards and monitoring advertising practices targeting young audiences.
6. COPPA: The Children's Online Privacy Protection Act (COPPA) enforces regulations to protect children's online privacy and restricts the collection of personal information from children under the age of 13.

shifting the research question from "Does food advertising influence children's food choices?" to "What factors influence children's food choices?," a broader exploration of the various factors impacting children's diets and health becomes possible. Indeed, children are affected by advertising and are actively participating in family food purchasing decisions (Dikcius et al., 2020). However, it has been established that food preferences are shaped at an early age before children fully comprehend advertising and various factors influence eating habits (Young, 2003). This is supported by Calvert (2008) who highlights the sophisticated environment in which children live and grow, shaping their preferences, choices, and behaviors.

The debate surrounding childhood obesity has generated numerous suggestions for identifying its causes and implementing appropriate solutions. Metcalfe et al. (2018) emphasize the importance of understanding the mechanisms associated with food consumption in children to gain insights into the causes and correlations of unhealthy eating practices in young children. Exploring food preferences early in life can provide valuable information on promoting the consumption of healthier foods and developing sustainable development policies, especially in the context of nutritional education programs (Benton, 2004; Taylor et al., 2005; Anzman et al., 2018) strengthen the role of parents, schools, and policymakers in promoting healthy eating among children.

6.3 CHILDREN'S FOOD PREFERENCES

It is widely acknowledged that children's food preferences strongly influence their eating behavior (Drewnowski, 1997; Birch, 1999; Perez-Rodrigo et al., 2003; Van Der Velde et al., 2019). These preferences are closely linked to decision-making traits and attitudes related to eating habits (Skinner et al., 2002; Livingstone and Helsper, 2004). For children, food preferences mark the initial step in a complex learning process that shapes their food identity throughout adulthood and guides their product choices. These preferences hold significant importance as they determine the healthiness or unhealthiness of children's food consumption. Understanding the mechanisms behind food preference development is crucial for social marketing and sustainable development strategies aimed at promoting healthy eating, by comprehending the reasons behind food choices, health promoters can influence eating habits in line with recommendations (Monterrosa et al.,

2020). Moreover, a better understanding of children's food preferences can inform the design of strategies to reduce obesity and improve nutrition (Laureati et al., 2015), as preferences, particularly in children, play a central role in predicting food choices. Humans, being omnivores, possess a natural inclination to consume a wide variety of foods. Children rapidly learn the context and combinations of feeding through a combination of innate preferences and the ability to acquire new preferences (Wardle and Cooke, 2008). Taste and preferences are often used interchangeably, but taste refers specifically to sensory attributes, while preferences encompass taste for specific foods and preferences between different foods (Birch, 1999; Hastings et al., 2003). The basic tastes of sweet, salty, sour, and bitter are part of the taste system.

Food preferences are shaped by a combination of genetic and environmental factors, underscoring the need for a better understanding to develop effective dietary interventions. Preferences can arise due to exposure, evaluative conditioning, and social influence. Exposure to foods increases liking, but familiarity alone does not explain the underlying mechanism of preference change. Evaluative conditioning occurs when tastes and appearances match, resulting in significant biological responses that can manifest as acquired tastes. Social influence, such as approval from admired individuals, can also impact preferences. Social facilitation, observed in children who are more willing to try new things after seeing someone else use them, is another important phenomenon in food preferences (Wardle and Cooke, 2008).

Genetic predispositions also play a role in children's food preferences (Costa and Oliveira, 2023). Newborns exhibit facial expressions indicating an innate preference for sweet and salty flavors and an aversion to bitter and sour tastes, which reflects evolutionary contexts where sweetness suggests a source of energy and bitterness signifies potential toxicity (Benton, 2004; Wardle and Cooke, 2008; Daniels, 2019). However, it is crucial to move beyond the debate of genetics versus environment and instead explore how genes are expressed in different environmental contexts to produce specific phenotypes (Birch, 1999). Food preferences are phenotypic behaviors resulting from the interaction between genetic predispositions and environmental factors. Three genetic predispositions can limit food preferences: a preference for sweet and salty foods, a rejection of sour and bitter foods, and a neophobic tendency to reject new foods and develop preferences only for the most familiar ones. Food preference development begins early in life, influenced by both genetic and innate predispositions. However, it is a dynamic process that continues to evolve with age through various mechanisms such as exposure, social influence, conditioning, and experience. The interplay between these mechanisms and explanatory factors shapes children's food preferences in a complex manner (Chiva, 1995, 2001; Wardle et al., 2001; Wardle and Cooke, 2008).

Identifying the factors that affect the development of food preferences is challenging. Several variables have been proposed, including food familiarity, age, parental and peer influences, teachers, sensory attributes (flavor, texture, appearance), psychological differences (e.g., personality), psychological effects (e.g., mood, drowsiness), beliefs and attitudes, marketing and economic variables, social, cultural, religious, and demographic factors (Alles-White and Welch, 1985; Cowart and Beauchamp, 1986; Shepherd and Farieigh, 1986; Rogers et al., 1994; Shepherd and Sparks, 1994; Birch, 1999; Rozin, 2006; Letona et al., 2014; Smith et al., 2019; Hirani and Hussain, 2020).

Addressing obesity requires holistic actions and the integration of various social spheres influencing children's food preferences. An encompassing examination of these factors provides valuable guidance for social marketing to plan prevention strategies using integrative models at multiple levels (Norton et al., 2000; Gregson et al., 2001; Laureati et al., 2015; Tarabashkina et al., 2016).

6.4 NUTRITIONAL EDUCATION FOR CHILDREN: A POTENTIAL SOLUTION TO OBESITY

According to authors Brée (1993) and Hill et al. (1998), the establishment of new habits ex nihilo is deemed more feasible compared to the alteration of deeply ingrained unhealthy habits that persist into adulthood and exhibit resistance to modification during later stages of life. One approach to equipping consumers with the skills for making healthy food choices is to enhance their nutritional knowledge (Crites and Aikman, 2005). Shayer (2003) emphasizes the importance of promoting the learning of new nutritional concepts in children's development. Several studies have shown a positive association between nutritional knowledge and the likelihood of consuming healthy foods, indicating that it plays a crucial role in making healthier food choices (Worsley, 2002; Thakur and Mathur, 2021).

The association between nutritional knowledge and overweight/obesity was investigated in Chinese children, revealing a positive correlation. Additionally, higher parental dietary knowledge may play a role in promoting healthier eating behaviors among their children. This study contributes to understanding the importance of parental influence on children's dietary habits and weight status. In Tyrol, Western Austria, Egg et al. (2020) study investigates the relationship between nutrition awareness, education, and eating behaviors among adolescents. Higher nutrition knowledge is connected with attending a rural school, having no migration background, having good physical activity behavior, and being a nontrained instructor, according to the data. Furthermore, additional nutrition education hours are associated with higher consumption of dark bread, lower consumption of meat, and lower use of sweetened energy drinks. These findings emphasize the relevance of nutrition education in encouraging health-conscious food habits among teenagers of all socioeconomic backgrounds.

Nutritional knowledge encompasses various aspects, including perceptions of "good" and "bad" foods, understanding what constitutes a balanced diet, awareness of the nutritional value of different foods, and the ability to comprehend processed foods and nutritional concepts (Hastings et al., 2003). The concept of nutritional knowledge emerged from the interest in modifying unhealthy diets (Stafleu et al., 1996; McDonnell et al., 1998) and reflects a rational engagement of consumers with food (Tarabashkina et al., 2016). Lack of nutritional knowledge is among the factors that can negatively influence eating behaviors, but it is also one of the easiest to address and improve through nutrition education programs, which are common components of obesity interventions (Campbell and Hesketh, 2007). Governments in many countries have taken specific actions to educate young people about healthy lifestyles, with nutrition playing a key role (Hayes et al., 2018).

Childhood eating habits can linger throughout adulthood, highlighting the necessity of early intervention programs such as school-based nutrition instruction. While these programs can help people learn more about nutrition, their impact on real fruit and vegetable consumption may be limited due to the influence of the home environment. Verdonschot et al. (2021) study examined data from a Dutch nutrition education evaluation and discovered that caregivers' health promotion practices influenced children's healthy eating habits favorably. Surprisingly, the program was most beneficial for children who received less encouragement to eat healthily at home, emphasizing the importance of the home environment in fostering healthy eating habits in children.

Nutrition education is defined as "a set of learning experiences designed to facilitate the voluntary adoption of diet and other nutrition-related behaviors that promote health and well-being" (Contento et al., 2002). This definition suggests that behavior change is the appropriate measure to assess the effectiveness of nutrition education. Especially for young consumers, nutrition education should combat the desire for autonomy over food and encourage a preference for healthy diets over unhealthy ones. It empowers young consumers to understand the importance of a balanced diet within their family, school, and social environments. Children should be aware that there are no inherently "good" or "bad" foods but rather a tendency toward balanced food choices (Alcock, 1995). Intervention programs employing nutrition education, as demonstrated by O'Dea (2003) and Gellar et al. (2007), have shown that children can acquire specific knowledge of the health benefits associated with consuming certain foods, such as fruits and vegetables (Lautenschlager and Smith, 2007).

Epstein and Squires (1998) propose that interventions of this nature should modify eating behaviors, allowing healthier behaviors to replace unhealthy ones. Gracey et al. (1996) further emphasize that enhancing young people's self-efficacy in controlling their diet, along with nutrition education, is a critical factor in improving eating behaviors. Additionally, involving parents and schools in providing healthy food is crucial for establishing healthy eating habits early in life.

Schools are a promising setting for interventions targeting obesity prevention. The systematic review of Medeiros et al. (2022) assessed the impact of school-based food and nutrition education programs on the food consumption of adolescents. The findings indicate a significant positive effect of these interventions on fruit and vegetable consumption, with increased servings per day and frequency per week. However, no significant overall effect was observed for fruit and vegetable consumption combined. In conclusion, school-based food and nutrition education interventions show promise in improving the dietary habits of adolescents.

Although nutritional knowledge alone does not guarantee consistent action, it is important for consumers to be aware of their choices and have the freedom to act. Educating children about healthy eating fosters their independence and nurtures their interest in nutrition. It empowers young individuals to become agents of change within their families and schools, potentially leading to a shift in social norms favoring healthy eating (Tallarini et al., 2013). Hayes et al. (2018) highlight that simply knowing what to eat is insufficient to drive behavior change. Effective nutrition education should include elements such as targeting specific behaviors, strengthening children's interests and motivations, employing behavior change strategies and techniques, incorporating practical experiences related to food growth and preparation, providing consistent and focused programs, utilizing active methods including innovative technology tools, allocating sufficient time and intensity for behavior change, and offering appropriate training and support to teachers.

6.5 RECOMMENDATIONS

Several recommendations can be made to address commercial practices targeting unhealthy food preferences and choices in children and to increase the involvement of parents, schools, and political decision-makers in promoting healthy diets among children.

First and foremost, stricter regulations on food advertising to minors should be considered. Policymakers should establish stringent restrictions on advertising low-nutritious foods, while actively supporting the promotion of healthful and nutritious foods. Simultaneously, it is crucial to integrate nutrition education initiatives into school curricula. Schools play a vital role in providing information and developing skills related to food choices. These nutrition education programs would help children gain a comprehensive understanding of the principles of a well-balanced diet, improve their decision-making abilities regarding food, and encourage the adoption of healthy eating habits.

In terms of access to nutritious foods, schools and communities should actively promote the availability of fruits, vegetables, whole grains, and other healthy food options. School food programs need to be assessed to ensure that children have access to healthy and balanced meal choices.

Furthermore, it is essential to enhance parents' understanding of the importance of healthy food for their children. Awareness campaigns and targeted educational tools can assist parents in making informed decisions regarding their family's food choices. Adults, including parents and teachers, should consume a healthy diet and serve as role models to demonstrate the value of eating a balanced diet. Adult eating habits greatly influence children's dietary choices, so setting a good example from an early age is crucial. Collaboration with food stakeholders is another key aspect. Policymakers, health professionals, and the food industry should work together to promote responsible business practices and the development of food products specifically tailored for children, with a focus on nutritional content. Finally, by implementing these recommendations, it is possible to create an environment that promotes healthy eating habits in children. This will enable them to make more informed choices and develop eating habits that promote their long-term health.

6.6 CONCLUSION

The recommendations aimed at increasing the involvement of parents, schools, and governments in promoting healthy diets for children are crucial in addressing the issues related to commercial practices and limited access to nutritious food. However, it is important to note that these recommendations serve as a starting point, and further research is needed to enhance the effectiveness of these interventions and their impact on children's health.

Future research should focus on examining the effectiveness of regulations on food advertising targeting children, as well as their influence on children's food choices and long-term health outcomes. Longitudinal studies could be conducted to track the development of eating behaviors in children who have been exposed to school nutrition education programs. It would also be interesting to investigate the most effective educational practices for imparting nutrition information and encouraging healthy food choices among young individuals. This could involve comparative studies on different teaching models, interactive and participatory techniques, and targeted interventions involving parents to help them adopt healthy eating habits for their children. Regarding access to nutritious foods, future studies could concentrate on identifying the specific challenges faced by disadvantaged groups and exploring potential strategies to improve their access to healthy meals. Intervention studies could be implemented to assess efforts aimed at enhancing access to nutritious foods in schools and communities. Additionally, further investigation into collaboration with the food industry is warranted, focusing on understanding the incentives and mechanisms that drive companies to develop and market healthy food products for children. Additional research could explore incentive techniques, public–private collaborations, and policy incentives to promote ethical business practices within the food industry. By pursuing these research avenues, we can continue to develop evidence-based interventions and policies that support healthy diets in children, contributing to the promotion of a healthier and environmentally conscious future generation. The importance of healthy eating cannot be overstated.

KEYWORDS

- **child consumer**
- **childhood obesity**
- **food industries**
- **food preferences**
- **nutritional education**
- **nutritional knowledge**

REFERENCES

Aitken, R. J., Allman-Farinelli, M. A., King, L. A. & Bauman, A. E. (2009). Current and future costs of cancer, heart disease and stroke attributable to obesity in Australia: A comparison of two birth cohorts. *Asia Pacific Journal of Clinical Nutrition*, 18(1), 63–70.

Alcock, J. P. (1995). The health of the nation campaign: Practical plan or farcical information. *Nutrition & Food Science*, 3, 11–15.

Alles-White, M. L. & Welch, P. (1985). Factors affecting the formation of food preferences in preschool children. *Early Child Development and Care*, 21(4), 265–276.

Anzman-Frasca, S., Ventura, A. K., Ehrenberg, S. & Myers, K. P. (2018). Promoting healthy food preferences from the start: A narrative review of food preference learning from the prenatal period through early childhood. *Obesity Reviews*, 19(4), 576–604.

Baker, P., Santos, T., Neves, P. A., Machado, P., Smith, J., Piwoz, E. & McCoy, D. (2021). First-food systems transformations and the ultra-processing of infant and young child diets: The determinants, dynamics and consequences of the global rise in commercial milk formula consumption. *Maternal & Child Nutrition*, 17(2), 10–19.

Benton, D. (2004). Role of parents in the determination of the food preferences of children and the development of obesity. *International Journal of Obesity*, 28(7), 8–18.

Birch, L. L. (1999). Development of food preferences. *Annual Review of Nutrition*, 19(1), 41–62.

Boyland, E. (2023). Is it ethical to advertise unhealthy foods to children? *Proceedings of the Nutrition Society*, 1–15.

Brée, J. (1993). Les enfants, la consommation et le marketing. Presses Universitaires de France.

Brusset, C. (2018). Et maintenant on mange quoi? Edition Flammarion, France.

Cairns, G., Angus, K., Hastings, G. & Caraher, M. (2013). Systematic reviews of the evidence on the nature, extent and effects of food marketing to children. A retrospective summary. *Appetite*, 62, 209–215.

Calvert, S. L. (2008). Children as consumers: Advertising and marketing. *The Future of Children*, 18(1), 205–234.

Campbell, K. J. & Hesketh, K. D. (2007). Strategies that aim to positively impact weight, physical activity, diet and sedentary behaviors in children from zero to five years. A systematic review of the literature. *Obesity Reviews*, 8, 327–338.

Castronuovo, L., Guarnieri, L., Tiscornia, V. & Allemandi, L. (2021). Food marketing, eating behaviors and gender among children and adolescents: A scoping review. *Nutrition Journal*, 20, 52.

Chiva, M. (1995). L'enfant et la nutrition. Comment apprend-on à manger? *Dietary Information*, 2, 27–31.

Chiva, M. (2001). Emotion et pratiques alimentaires, approches neurophysiologiques. www.lemangeur-ocha.com.

Contento, I. R., Randell, J. S. & Basch, C. E. (2002). Review and analysis of evaluation measures used in nutrition education intervention research. *Journal of Nutrition Education and Behavior*, 34(1), 2–25.

Cook, D. T. (2009). Knowing the child consumer: Historical and conceptual insights on qualitative children's consumer research. *Young Consumers*, 10(4), 269–282.

Costa, A. & Oliveira, A. (2023). Parental feeding practices and children's eating behaviours: An overview of their complex relationship. *Healthcare*, 11(3), 400–410.

Cowart, B. L. & Beauchamp, G. K. (1986). Factors affecting acceptance of salt by human infants and children. In: Kare, M.R. & Brand, I.G. (Eds.), Interaction of the Chemical Senses with Nutrition. Academic Press, Orlando.

Crites Jr, S. L. & Aikman, S. N. (2005). Impact of nutrition knowledge on food evaluations. *European Journal of Clinical Nutrition*, 59(10), 11–19.

Daniels, L. A. (2019). Feeding practices and parenting: A pathway to child health and family happiness. *Annals of Nutrition and Metabolism*, 74(2), 29–42.

Dikcius, V., Urbonavicius, S., Pakalniskiene, V. & Pikturniene, I. (2020). Children's influence on parental purchase decisions: Scale development and validation. *International Journal of Market Research*, 62(4), 449–467.

Drewnowski, A. (1997). Taste preferences and food intake. *Annual Review of Nutrition*, 17(1), 237–253.

Driessen, C., Kelly, B., Sing, F. & Backholer, K. (2022). Parents' perceptions of children's exposure to unhealthy food marketing: A narrative review of the literature. *Current Nutrition Reports*, 11(1), 9–18.

Egg, S., Wakolbinger, M., Reisser, A., Schätzer, M., Wild, B. & Rust, P. (2020). Relationship between nutrition knowledge, education and other determinants of food intake and lifestyle habits among adolescents from urban and rural secondary schools in Tyrol, Western Austria. *Public Health Nutrition*, 23(17), 3136–3147.

Epstein, L. & Squires, S. (1988). The stop-light diet for children: An eight-week program for parents and children. Little Brown, Boston, MA.

Gellar, L. A., Schrader, K. & Nansel, T. R. (2007). Healthy eating practices. *The Diabetes Educator*, 33(4), 671–679.
Grad, I. (2015). Ethical considerations on advertising to children. *Postmodern Openings*, 6(2). 43–57.
Gregson, J., Foerster, S. B., Orr, R., Jones, L., Benedict, J., Clarke, B. & Zotz, K. (2001). System, environmental, and policy changes: Using the social-ecological model as a framework for evaluating nutrition education and social marketing programs with low-income audiences. *Journal of Nutrition Education*, 33, 4–15.
Harris, J. L., Brownell, K. D. & Bargh, J. A. (2009). The food marketing defense model: Integrating psychological research to protect youth and inform public policy. *Social Issues and Policy Review*, 3(1), 211–271.
Harris, J. L., Pomeranz, J. L., Lobstein, T. & Brownell, K. D. (2009). A crisis in the marketplace: How food marketing contributes to childhood obesity and what can be done. *Annual Review of Public Health*, 30, 211–225.
Hastings, G., Stead, M., McDermott, L., Forsyth, A., MacKintosh, A. M., Rayner, M. & Angus, K. (2003). Review of Research on the Effects of Food Promotion on Children. Food Standards Agency, London.
Hayes, D., Contento, I. R. & Weekly, C. (2018). Position of the academy of nutrition and dietetics, Society for Nutrition Education and Behavior, and School Nutrition Association: Comprehensive nutrition programs and services in schools. *Journal of the Academy of Nutrition and Dietetics*, 118(5), 913–919.
Hebden, L., Chey, T. & Allman-Farinelli, M. (2012). Lifestyle intervention for preventing weight gain in young adults: A systematic review and meta-analysis of RCTs. *Obesity Reviews*, 13(8), 692–710.
Hill, L., Casswell, S., Maskill, C., Jones, S. & Wyllie, A. (1998). Fruit and vegetables as adolescent food choices in New Zealand. *Health Promotion International*, 13(1), 55–65.
Hirani, N. S. & Gujarati, M. H. (2020). The effect of product packaging and use of brand mascots in promoting unhealthy food: Product preferences of children and buyer's behavior. *I-Manager's Journal on Management*, 14(3), 47–56.
Kelly, T., Yang, W., Chen, C. S., Reynolds, K. & He, J. (2008). Global burden of obesity in 2005 and projections to 2030. *International Journal of Obesity*, 32(9), 14–22.
Kline, S. (2022). Limits to the Imagination: Marketing and Children's Culture. Cultural Politics in Contemporary America, Routledge.
Laureati, M., Pagliarini, E., Toschi, T. G. & Monteleone, E. (2015). Research challenges and methods to study food preferences in school-aged children: A review of the last 15 years. *Food Quality and Preference*, 46, 92–102.
Lautenschlager, L. & Smith, C. (2007). Beliefs, knowledge, and values held by inner-city youth about gardening, nutrition, and cooking. *Agriculture and Human Values*, 24(2), 24–35.
Letona, P., Chacon, V., Roberto, C. & Barnoya, J. (2014). A qualitative study of children's snack food packaging perceptions and preferences. *BMC Public Health*, 14(1), 12–34.
Livingstone, S. & Helsper, E. (2004). Advertising foods to children: Understanding promotion in the context of children's daily lives. A review of the literature prepared for the Research Department of the Office of Communications (OFCOM).
Martin, C. & Jane, L. (2006). The impact of advertising on food choice: The social context of advertising. In: Shepherd, R., & Raats, M. (Eds.), *The Psychology of Food Choice*, Vol. 10, pp. 227–245.

Mau, G., Schramm-Klein, H. & Reisch, L. (2014). Consumer socialization, buying decisions, and consumer behavior in children: Introduction to the special issue. *Journal of Consumer Policy*, 37(2), 155–160.

McDonnell, G. E., Roberts, D. C. K. & Lee, C. (1998). Stages of change and reduction of dietary fat: Effect of knowledge and attitudes in an Australian university population. *Journal of Nutrition Education*, 30, 37–44.

Medeiros, G. C. B. S. D., Azevedo, K. P. M. D., Garcia, D., Oliveira Segundo, V. H., Mata, Á. N. D. S., Fernandes, A. K. P. & Piuvezam, G. (2022). Effect of school-based food and nutrition education interventions on the food consumption of adolescents: A systematic review and meta-analysis. *International Journal of Environmental Research and Public Health*, 19(17), 10–15.

Metcalfe, J. J. & Fiese, B. H. (2018). Family food involvement is related to healthier dietary intake in preschool-aged children. *Appetite*, 126, 195–200.

Monterrosa, E. C., Frongillo, E. A., Drewnowski, A., De Pee, S. & Vandevijvere, S. (2020). Sociocultural influences on food choices and implications for sustainable healthy diets. *Food and Nutrition Bulletin*, 41(1), 59–73.

Nestle, M. (2022). Regulating the food industry: An aspirational agenda. *American Journal of Public Health*, 112(6), 853–858.

Norton, P. A., Falciglia, G. A. & Ricketts, C. (2000). Motivational determinants of food preferences in adolescents and pre-adolescents. *Ecology of Food and Nutrition*, 39(3), 169–182.

O'Dea, J. A. (2003). Why do kids eat healthful food? Perceived benefits of and barriers to healthful eating and physical activity among children and adolescents. *Journal of the American Dietetic Association*, 103(4), 497–501.

Opree, S. J., Buijzen, M., Van Reijmersdal, E. A. & Valkenburg, P. M. (2014). Children's advertising exposure, advertised product desire, and materialism: A longitudinal study. *Communication Research*, 41(5), 717–735.

Perez-Rodrigo, C., Ribas, L., Serra-Majem, L. L. & Aranceta, J. (2003). Food preferences of Spanish children and young people: The end study. *European Journal of Clinical Nutrition*, 57(1), 45–60.

Rogers, P.J., Green, M. & Edwards, S. (1994). Nutritional influences on mood and cognitive performance: Their measurement and relevance to food. In Thomson, D. M., & MacFie, H. J. H. (Eds.). Measurement of Food Preferences. Blackie Academic.

Rozin, P. (2006). The integration of biological, social, cultural and psychological influences on food choice. *Frontiers in Nutritional Science*, 3, 19–25.

Shayer, M. (2003). Not just Piaget; not just Vygotsky, and certainly not Vygotsky as an alternative to Piaget. *Learning and Instruction*, 13(1), 465–485.

Shepherd, R. & Farleigh, C. A. (1986). Attitudes and personality related to salt intake. *Appetite*, 7, 343–354.

Shepherd, R. & Sparks, P. (1994). Modelling Food Choice. Measurement of Food Preferences. Springer, Boston, MA, USA.

Skinner, J. D., Carruth, B. R., Bounds, W. & Ziegler, P. J. (2002). Children's food preferences: A longitudinal analysis. *Journal of the American Dietetic Association*, 102(11), 1638–1647.

Smets, V. & Vandevijvere, S. (2022). Changes in retail food environments around schools over 12 years and associations with overweight and obesity among children and adolescents in Flanders, Belgium. *BMC Public Health*, 22(1), 15–25.

Smith, R., Kelly, B., Yeatman, H. & Boyland, E. (2019). Food marketing influences children's attitudes, preferences and consumption: A systematic critical review. *Nutrients*, 11(4), 87–92.

Stafleu, A., Van Staveren, W. A., De Graaf, C. & Burema, J. (1996). Nutrition knowledge and attitudes towards high-fat foods and low-fat alternatives in three generations of women. *European Journal of Clinical Nutrition*, 50, 33–41.

Tallarini, A., Zabeo, A. & Ferraretto, A. (2013). Nutritional knowledge in an Italian population of children, pre-adolescents and adolescents. *Public Health Nutrition*, 17(3), 708–714.

Tarabashkina, L., Quester, P. & Crouch, R. (2016). Exploring the moderating effect of children's nutritional knowledge on the relationship between product evaluations and food choice. *Social Science & Medicine*, 149, 145–152.

Taylor, J. P., Evers, S. & McKenna, M. (2005). Les déterminants de la saine alimentation chez les enfants et les jeunes. *Canadian Journal of Public Health*, 12, 22–29.

Tchékémian, A. (2021). La pandémie d'obésité: Signe d'un effondrement civilisationnel? In Session RT38-RT29: Environmental Knowledge, Techniques and Materials in Question. https://shs.hal.science/halshs-03433875.

Thakur, S. & Mathur, P. (2021). Nutrition knowledge and its relation with dietary behavior in children and adolescents: A systematic review. *International Journal of Adolescent Medicine and Health*, 34(6), 381–392.

Ustjanauskas, A. E., Harris, J. L. & Schwartz, M. B. (2014). Food and beverage advertising on children's websites. *Pediatric Obesity*, 9(5), 362–372.

Van Der Velde, L. A., Schuilenburg, L. A., Thrivikraman, J. K., Numans, M. E. & Kiefte-de Jong, J. C. (2019). Needs and perceptions regarding healthy eating among people at risk of food insecurity: A qualitative analysis. *International Journal for Equity in Health*, 18, 1–12.

Verdonschot, A., de Vet, E., Van Seeters, N., Warmer, J., Collins, C. E., Bucher, T. & Haveman-Nies, A. (2021). Caregivers' role in the effectiveness of two Dutch school-based nutrition education programs for children aged 7–12 years old. *Nutrients*, 13(1), 14–26.

Wardle, J. & Cooke, L. (2008). Genetic and environmental determinants of children's food preferences. *British Journal of Nutrition*, 99(1), 15–21.

Wardle, J., Sanderson, S., Gibson, E. L. & Rapoport, L. (2001). Factor-analytic structure of food preferences in four-year-old children in the UK. *Appetite*, 37(3), 217–223.

Worsley, A. (2002). Nutrition knowledge and food consumption: Can nutrition knowledge change food behavior? *Asia Pacific Journal of Clinical Nutrition*, 11(3), 579–585.

Young, B. (2003). Does food advertising influence children's food choices? A critical review of some of the recent literature. *International Journal of Advertising*, 22(4), 441–459.

PART II
Digitalization

DOI: 10.1201/9781779643407-8

CHAPTER 7

Effects of ChatGPT Adoption on Behavioral Intention in the Field of Scientific Research: The Moderating Role of Familiarity

HABIBA BEN AMEUR and KAOUTHER SAIED BEN RACHED

Faculty of Economics and Management of Tunis, University of Tunis El Manar, Business and Research in Marketing (ERMA), Tunis, Tunisia

*Corresponding author

ABSTRACT

Artificial intelligence is being increasingly used in scientific research to help researchers acquire new knowledge, analyze data, and optimize experiments. The interest of this research is to treat the impact of the attitude toward the use of Chat Generative Pretrained Transformer (GPT) on behavioral intention while highlighting the role of familiarity. An empirical investigation using 221 ChatGPT users shows that there is a significant relationship between a person's attitude toward using technology and their intended behavior. Moreover, familiarity positively moderates the relationship between these two variables. These results are discussed in detail, and managerial implications and future avenues of research are presented.

7.1 INTRODUCTION

Artificial intelligence (AI) has gained considerable importance in the world from a practical and scientific approach. Its development is a priority

Corporate Governance, Digitalization, and Energy Transition: Imen Baccouche and Afef Khalil. (Eds.)

DOI: 10.1201/9781779643407-9

for many countries around the world and many companies are devoting significant resources to the study and development of AI. The automated processing of information has made it more efficient, useful, and ubiquitous in several areas (Benabdeouahed and Elkhatibi, 2022). According to Cheng (2023), AI has become a transformative technology in science with the potential to accelerate and improve research in various fields. Chat Generative Pretrained Transformer (GPT) is a popular language model and is one such system that is increasingly being discussed and adapted for scientific research (Cheng, 2023). According to Bala et al. (2017), a chatbot is a computer program that uses AI techniques like natural language processing (NLP) to simulate human conversations in their natural format, whether they are spoken or written. Thus, these conversational agents are used in various domains and contexts (marketing, education, culture, entertainment, and health) (Adamopoulou and Moussiades, 2020). On the other hand, the utilization and acceptance of chatbots remain rarely discussed, especially in the field of scientific research (Benabdeouahed and Elkhatibi, 2022).

The study of the adoption of Chatbot has also affected other areas of research such as the field of business performance (Zouhri, 2019). However, the intention to use and the adoption of Chatbots remains little discussed, especially in the field of scientific research (Benabdeouahed and Elkhatibi, 2022). From this research work, we try to go beyond these fields to deal with a popular field which is that of scientific research. This chapter highlights the important role of AI and more particularly, of the ChatGPT in supporting researchers in their scientific research. The main contribution of this research is to treat the relationship between the attitude toward the use of ChatGPT and the behavioral intention of users in the field of scientific research. In addition, it is a question of highlighting the moderating effect of familiarity on the relationship between attitude and intention to adopt ChatGPT. In this context, we study the attitude of researchers toward the use of ChatGPT and its impact on behavioral intention, highlighting the role of familiarity. The problem of our research is as follows: What is the impact of the adoption of ChatGPT in scientific research on behavioral intention?

To carry out this research chapter, we conducted an empirical study of 221 ChatGPT users. First, we will introduce the conceptual framework of our research by identifying the concept of AI, ChatGPT, the attitude toward the adoption of ChatGPT, and behavioral intention. Next, we will specify the relationships that exist between these different variables. Finally, we will present the research methodology and we will discuss the results.

7.2 LITERATURE REVIEW AND HYPOTHESES

7.2.1 ARTIFICIAL INTELLIGENCE

7.2.1.1 ORIGIN AND DEFINITION OF AI

AI was born in 1956 by Mc Carthy (Zouhri, 2019). It finds its origins in the research of Turing who works on the possibilities of attributing consciousness to machines and proposes an experiment known as the "Turing test" (Véry and Cailluet, 2019). Then, it developed with the progress of knowledge in the fields of neural networks of mathematical logic and computer science (Véry and Cailluet, 2019). Several researchers are interested in defining AI. According to Minsky (1976), this concept is defined as the development of computer programs that perform tasks that are currently performed more satisfactorily by humans due to the high-level mental processes required. For his part, Shapiro (1992) considers AI as the field of science and engineering that deals with understanding with the help of the computer, intelligent behavior, and the creation of artificial systems that reproduce this behavior.

In the future, AI's goal is the mechanization of human intelligence (Nilsson, 2005). Véry and Cailluet (2019) say that the concept of AI refers to machines and/or algorithms that learn from their own experience and can perform tasks performed by humans by simulating human cognitive techniques. It covers an extensive variety of strategies and methods that enable machines to perform tasks that typically require human intelligence such as problem-solving, learning, language perception, and understanding (Russell, 2010). According to Soudoplatoff (2018), there are three main approaches to AI, namely the human approach, which is founded on imitation of human reasoning in the context of discussion with an expert and translation into a language understandable by the machine. The approach is based on the factorial analysis of data, which uses statistical tools and the modeling of the human brain through algorithms, making it possible to propose solutions to sophisticated problems.

7.2.1.2 AI IN SCIENTIFIC RESEARCH

AI become an interesting tool in scientific research. It helps researchers to quickly obtain information and access databases to accomplish their research projects. According to Mijwi (2023), several AI techniques can be used in scientific production, namely:

- Text generation: AI models can be trained on a large amount of data scientific research papers and then used to generate new research papers on a given topic.
- Text summarization: AI models can be used to summarize scientific research articles, making it easier for researchers to quickly understand the main findings of an article.
- Grammar and language checking: AI models can be used to check grammar and language errors in research papers, making it easier for researchers to produce error-free papers.
- Literature review: AI models can be used to help researchers identify relevant articles to assist them in carrying out their research projects.

7.2.2 THE CHATBOT: AN AI CHATBOT

7.2.2.1 DEFINITION OF CHATBOT

Eliza is the first Chatbo created by Joseph Weizenbaum in 1966 (Gümüş and Çark, 2023). The term "Chatbot" is derived from the words "Chat" and "Robot," which mimics human conversation and allows humans to respond as an intelligent entity through text or voice (Bansal et al., 2018). Colic et al. (2022) claim that a Chatbot or conversational agent is a computer program that uses technologies based on automated algorithms, such as AI, machine learning, and NLP to imitate interactions and conversations with humans. According to Gümüş and Çark (2023), Chatbots are also known as Chatterbots, conversational robots, or artificial conversational entities, which are software designed to simulate an intelligent dialogue using voice commands and text chats with one or more users. There are many applications for chatbots. They can give consumers' comprehensive details regarding products and services, manage their schedules, and help them save time and money (Ambawat and Wadera, 2019).

Chatbots are classified according to their type of existence—virtual or physical, embodied or disembodied), the type of communication (textual or vocal), and their abilities (mechanical Chatbots for routine tasks and thinking

Chatbots for idiosyncratic tasks) (Araujo, 2018; Huang and Rust, 2021). According to Gümüş and Çark (2023), there are several types of Chatbots:

- Flow-based Chatbots use developer-defined conversational flows. They are designated "Rule-Based Chatbots" because they are made for multiple tasks based on rules established by their developers.
- AI chatbots enable natural language communication and unrestricted user interaction. A sentence entered by the user can be analyzed by the bot with several parameters to understand it. In this research, we are interested in dealing with the AI Chatbot which is the ChatGPT.

7.2.2.2 ChatGPT AND ITS IMPORTANCE IN SCIENTIFIC RESEARCH

The most promising feature of ChatGPT is its capacity to use deep learning techniques to provide responses to text input that are human-like at a level far beyond any other AI model (Wen and Wang, 2023). This Chatbot works through programmed algorithms to understand natural language and give suitable answers, either freshly created or prewritten by AI (Silva et al., 2023). ChatGPT is constantly being enhanced using machine learning, reinforcement learning, and NLP to increase its capacity to comprehensively understand and respond to user needs (Silva et al., 2023). Chatbots apply to scientific research as well. Indeed, ChatGPT can become a powerful and encouraging instrument for jobs such as automatic draft generation, article summarization, and language translation. These can be beneficial in academic activities work faster and easier to write. On the other hand, this tool's use in scientific writing raises ethical concerns and should thus be regulated.

7.2.3 ATTITUDES TOWARD ADOPTION OF CHATBOT

7.2.3.1 ATTITUDE TOWARD THE USE OF ChatGPT

According to Fishbein and Ajzen (1975), the attitude contains the feelings (positive and negative) about the behavior they intend to adopt and this is particularly important because these beliefs and evaluations determine the voluntary behavior (Ajzen, 2012). Attitude is an essential prerequisite factor for the intention to develop a particular skill (Ajzen and Fishbein, 1980;

Pee et al., 2008). Fishbein and Ajzen (1975) argue that attitude is a multidimensional construct, composed of a cognitive, emotional, and conative or behavioral component. The cognitive component refers to an individual's knowledge of a product or service (experience, beliefs, and opinions). The emotional component refers to the set of feelings, emotions, and evaluations. Finally, the intention is referred to by the conative component. Several theories and models have used attitude, including reasoned action To explain behavioral intention, use theory and the technology acceptance model. On the whole, the attitude toward the employment of a certain technology should determine the intention to use it (Davis et al., 1989). Additionally, other researchers find that attitude toward using Chatbots significantly influences intent to use, and unsatisfactory interactions with Chatbots reduce intent to apply them (Kasilingam, 2021; Kwangsawad and Jattamart, 2022).

7.2.3.2 FACTORS INFLUENCING ChatGPT ADOPTION ATTITUDE

7.2.3.2.1 Perceived Ease

The degree to which a consumer finds it easy to use a computer system is defined as perceived ease of use (Venkatesh and Davis, 2000). It is distinguished by the robot's convenience and ease of operation (Zhong et al., 2021). Perceived usability refers to a person's belief that using a system will be simple (Venkatesh and Davis, 2000). The more easy to use a system is, the better it can enhance efficiency at work (Gumus and Çark, 2023). Referring to the literature, Kasilingam (2021) clarified that there is a significant positive relationship between ease of use of Chatbot and attitude. Similarly, Murtarelli et al. (2022) notes that perceived usability is an important determinant of attitude toward Chatbot adoption. Therefore, our hypothesis is as follows:

H1. Perceived ease of use positively influences the attitude of adopting a ChatGPT.

7.2.3.2.2 Perceived Usefulness

According to Davis et al. (1989), perceived utility is the extent to which a consumer thinks that believing in the system's implementation would enhance their ability to carry out a specific task or perform a given task. Rogers (1998) indicates that perceived utility is considered the extent to which an invention is thought to be superior to the previous one. It is also defined as the ability of a robot to implement the expected services (Zhong et al., 2021). Perceived usefulness is an antecedent of the attitude to adopt a Chatbot (Silva et al., 2023). Indeed, several researchers show that utility is an important factor in the adoption of a technology (Elmorshidy et al., 2015; Selamat et al., 2021). According to empirical studies, perceived usefulness has a significant impact on people's attitudes toward Chatbot use (Gümü and Çark, 2021; Murtarelli et al., 2022). According to Rose et al. (2012), when users perceive a Chatbot to be effective (well designed, informative, and convenient to use), they will consequently have a more positive feeling about its adoption. As a result, we hypothesize:

H2. Perceived usefulness acts positively on the attitude of adopting a ChatGPT.

7.2.3.2.3 Perceived Intelligence

The term perceived intelligence was created by AI (Ho and Mac Dorman, 2010), including the skill, transmission of knowledge, responsiveness, intelligence, and reasonable response of the Chatbot (McGinn et al., 2019). According to Rajaobelina et al. (2021), perceived intelligence is an experiment in which participants interpret robot's characteristics of speech, voice, and appearance are used to assess intelligence. Zhang et al. (2022) show that bots that provide personalized information are more likely to be adopted if they interact with their users. According to Tussyadiah and Park (2018), perceived intelligence is one of the key determinants of robot adoption. Furthermore, cognitive and reasoning ability in data processing become an essential component of many AI algorithms (Hossain et al., 2020). Rafiq et al. (2012) say that there is a significant and positive relationship between perceived intelligence and the willingness to adopt a ChatGPT. Our hypothesis is then stated as follows:

H3. Perceived intelligence acts positively on the attitude of adopting a ChatGPT.

7.2.4 BEHAVIORAL INTENT AND FAMILIARITY WITH THE ADOPTION OF ChatGPT

7.2.4.1 INTENTION TO ADOPT ChatGPT

Intention to adopt Chatbots refers to the likelihood of using this technology (Gümüş and Çark, 2023). The study of users' behavioral intentions aims to illuminate and forecast the way through which they will collaborate with emerging technologies (Chatterjee et al., 2021). Behavioral intention is a powerful predictor of actual usage behavior (Cosmo et al., 2021). According to Chhikara et al. (2022), usage intention is the user's disposition to use a technology. Previous studies claim that the intention to use can be a determinant of the actual application of a new technology (Yi-Cheng et al., 2007; Zhang et al., 2008). Theory of Planned Behavior from the Theory of Reasoned Actions states that the behavior of an individual is influenced by his intention, which is influenced in turn by attitudes. According to this theory, the behavioral intentions of users toward Chatbots are preceded by their attitudes toward this technology. Similarly, Cabanillas et al. (2014) and Belanche et al. (2019) show that there is a significant and positive relationship between the attitude of users and their behavioral intention toward Chatbot. We propose the following hypothesis:

H4. The attitude of adopting a ChatGPT acts positively on behavioral intention.

7.2.4.2 FAMILIARITY WITH ChatGPT

According to Blanche et al. (2019), familiarity with robotic systems plays an important role in the adoption of robotic advisers. Thus, customers may differ in their level of familiarity with these innovations (Davis et al., 1989). Familiarity is a concept intimately linked to past interactions and experiences (Gefen, 2000; Komiak and Benbast, 2006). It assesses the degree of understanding of experience (Gefen, 2000). It is assimilated to specific knowledge that develops from an activity and is based on learning to use a particular interface (Gefen, 2000). The feeling of intimacy leads the individual to feel protected against any risk that can affect their privacy (Komiak and Benbasat, 2006). Familiarity with AI and robots acts as a moderating variable between attitude and behavioral intention to adopt Chatbots (Blanche et al., 2019). Indeed, users with a higher level of familiarity will have positive attitudes toward the use of Chatbots and a strong personal predisposition to their behavior (Castañeda et al., 2007) because they have more vague and indirect knowledge about robo-advisors (Venkatesh and Davis, 2000). Thus, we suggest the following hypothesis:

H5. Familiarity moderates the relationship between the attitude of using a ChatGPT and behavioral intention.

7.3 METHODOLOGY

The objective of this empirical part is to treat the impact of the attitude of the users toward the ChatGPT on behavioral intention. To validate the theoretical model of this academic work, we conducted an online survey with a sample of 221 users, including 51.6% women and 48.4% men. This sample is divided into several categories: 18.6% students, 10.9% doctoral students, 21.3% engineers, 28.5% doctors, and 20.8% teacher-researchers. The questionnaire allows us to evaluate the attitude toward the use of ChatGPT by addressing its determinants, which are: perceived intelligence, perceived usability, and ease of use. We use the scale of Ponte et al. (2015), to measure perceived intelligence. The scale of Oh et al. (2013) is applied to measure perceived usefulness and ease of use. To measure the attitude of the users, we employ the scale of Bhattacherjee (2000). For behavioral intention, we refer to the scale of Pillai and Sivathanu (2020). Familiarity is measured using the scale of Blanche et al. (2019). The items relating to these scales are noted on a scale from 1 to 5. In addition, the results are generated by the SPSS 22 (version 22.0, IBM Corp., New York, NY) and AMOS 22 software. We carry out an exploratory analysis and a confirmatory analysis. Finally, the structural analysis makes it possible to validate the adjustment of the structural model as well as its research hypotheses.

7.4 RESULTS AND DISCUSSION

The results of the exploratory and confirmatory analyses are successively exposed before validating the structural model of the research and studying the moderating role of familiarity.

7.4.1 RESULTS OF THE EXPLORATORY ANALYSIS AND VALIDATION OF MEASUREMENT SCALES

The results of the exploratory analysis are presented as follows:

- The perceived ease of use measurement scale shows that there is a meritorious predisposition of the data to be factored. The null hypothesis indicates that there is no significant correlation in the data matrix and is rejected. The perceived ease of use measurement scale has very good internal consistency (α = 0.892). The confirmatory analysis of this scale gives us acceptable fit indices. For absolute indices: goodness of fit index (GFI): 2.740; adjusted goodness-of-fit index (AGFI): 0.942; root mean square residual (RMR): 0.034; and root mean square error of approximation (RMSEA): 0.089. Incremental indices: Tucker–Lewis Index (TLI): 0.980 and Comparative Fit Index (CFI): 0.993 Parsimonious indices: χ^2/dl = 2.740; Bayesian information criterion (BIC): 48.665; Ms: 53.982; Consistent Akaike Information Criterion (CAIC): 56.665; and Ms: 63.982. The convergent validity is good with a value of 0.673 (ρvc > 0.5) and the Rho of Joreskog is 0.891, which shows that this scale has satisfactory reliability.

- The perceived usefulness measurement scale indicates that there is a meritorious predisposition of the data to be factored. Similarly, Bartlett's sphericity test is significant at 5% risk, and therefore the correlation matrix of each variable is different from the identity matrix. The perceived usefulness measurement scale has very good internal consistency (α = 0.873). The fit indices are compatible with the critical acceptance levels (GFI: 2.810; RMR: 0.039; RMSEA: 0.081; TLI: 0.977; CFI: 0.992; χ^2/ dl=2.810; BIC: 48.80; Ms: 53.982; CAIC: 56.805; Ms: 63.982). The Rho of Joreskhog is 0.875, which shows that there is very good internal consistency. The convergent validity is good (ρvc = 0.638).
- For perceived intelligence, the measurement scale indicates a very good internal consistency (α = 0.884). Rho of Joreskhog is about 0.887. Convergent validity is good (ρvc = 0.724). The confirmatory analysis of this scale gives us acceptable fit indices.
- For absolute indices, we note that GFI is 0.992; AGFI is 0.955; RMR is 0.062; and RMSEA is 0.083.
- Incremental indices indicate that TLI is 0.988 and CFI is 0.992. Parsimonious indices show that: χ^2/ dl=2.512; BIC: 29.503; Ms: 32.389; CAIC: 34.503; and Ms: 38.389.
- The attitude measurement scale indicates that the internal consistency is good (α = 0.772), and the Rho of Joreskhog is 0.782. The convergent validity is good because (ρvc > 0.5). The adjustment

indices are satisfactory (GFI: 0.989; AGFI: 0.934; RMR: 0.074; and RMSEA: 0.111; TLI: 0.959; CFI: 0.986; χ^2/dl=3.700; BIC: 30.691; Ms: 32.389; CAIC: 35.691; and Ms: 38.389).

- For the behavioral intention, there is a meritorious predisposition of the data to be factored. The measurement scale indicates a very good internal consistency (α = 0.825) and the Rho of Joreskhog is 0.835. Convergent validity is good at 0.633. Confirmatory analysis of this scale gives acceptable fit indices (GFI: 0.996; RMR: 0.042; RMSEA: 0.028; TLI: 0.998; CFI: 0.9; χ^2/dl= 1.170; BIC: 28.161; Ms: 32.389; CAIC: 33.161; and Ms: 38.389).
- The familiarity measurement scale shows that the internal consistency is good (α = 0.794), and the Rho of Joreskhog is 0.806. The convergent validity is satisfactory (0.591). Confirmatory analysis of this scale gives acceptable fit indices: (GFI: 0.997; RMR: 0.043; RMSEA: 0.017; TLI: 0.999; CFI: 0.998; χ^2/dl= 1.060; BIC: 28.05; Ms: 32.389; CAIC: 33.051; and Ms: 38.389). Table 7.1 indicates that the global measurement model fit indices are acceptable.

TABLE 7.1 Global Measurement Fit Indices

Absolute Indices				Incremental Indices			Parsimonious Indices		
X²	**GFI**	**AGFI**	**RMR**	**RMSEA**	**TLI**	**CFI**	**X²/DDL**	**BIC**	**CAIC**
353.295	0.912	0.889	0.068	0.088	0.930	0.943	3.183	580.018	622.018
								Ms	Ms
								825.919	978.919

Table 7.2 shows the test of the hypotheses of our model. Results indicate that there is a significant and positive relationship between perceived ease of use and users' attitude toward ChatGPT (c.r = 5.767 >1.96 and P = 0.000). The same goes for the relationship between perceived usefulness and attitude (c.r = 5.738 >1.96 and P = 0.000) and the relationship between perceived intelligence and attitude (c.r = 4.987 >1.96 and P = 0.000). So hypotheses *H1*, *H2*, and *H3* are confirmed. Also, Hypothesis *H4* states that there is a significant and positive relationship between users' attitudes toward ChatGPT and behavioral intention.

TABLE 7.2 Testing the Model Hypotheses

Hypothesis	Links	Standardized Structural Link	CR	P	Significance
H1	Attitude ← Ease of use	0.421	5.767	***	Significant
H2	Attitude ← Usefulness	0.434	5.738	***	Significant
H3	Attitude ← Perceived intelligence	0.472	4.987	***	Significant
H4	Behavioral intention ← Attitude	0.562	6.865	***	Significant

7.4.2 TESTING THE MODERATING EFFECT OF FAMILIARITY BETWEEN ATTITUDE AND BEHAVIORAL INTENTION

7.4.2.1 IDENTIFICATION OF GROUPS BY THE CLASSIFICATION OF DYNAMIC CLUSTERS (K-MEANS)

We have two groups: 51.59% represent the percentage of individuals who are not very familiar with the use of robots and ChatGPT, and 48.41% represent the percentage of people who are very familiar with the use of this technology (Table 7.3).

TABLE 7.3 Number of Observations

Classes	Number	Percentage (%)
1: Low Familiarity	114,000	51.59
2: Strong Familiarity	107,000	48.41
Total	221,000	100

7.4.2.2 CHI-SQUARE DIFFERENCE TEST RESULTS

To test the moderating role of familiarity, we employ multigroup analysis. The calculation of the Chi-square difference test allows the determination of a level of probability that we must compare to the recommended minimum threshold of 5%. Table 7.4 shows that the Chi-square difference test is significant. Thus, the link between attitude toward ChatGPT and behavioral intention is moderated by familiarity.

TABLE 7.4 Results of the Chi-Square Difference Test

Hypothesis	Chi-deux	DDL	Probability Level
Constrained model	22.184	20	0
Free model	32.242	23	0
Difference	10.058	3	0.018

7.4.2.3 SPECIFICITY OF THE MODERATING VARIABLE

Table 7.5 indicates that the evolution of the link between attitude and behavioral intention is associated with an increase in familiarity. We conclude that familiarity positively moderates the relationship between attitude and intention behavior. Results show that perceived usefulness, ease of use, and perceived intelligence act positively on the attitude of using ChatGPT. Research conducted by Gümüs and Çark, (2021), Murtarelli et al. (2022), and Silva et al. (2023) confirm our results and argue that perceived usefulness positively influences users' attitude toward ChatGPT. Indeed, when users perceive that the use of ChatGPT adds value to them, enriches their knowledge, and provides a concise and unambiguous response to their inquiries. This will lead to a positive attitude toward the use of this technology. Also, the perceived ease of use is one of the factors that improve attitude toward using ChatGPT (Kasilingam, 2021; Murtarelli et al., 2022). Indeed, when users perceive that this technology is easy to apply, they become accustomed to exploiting it in their work and research. This fosters a positive attitude toward the technology's adoption. Similarly, Tussyadiah and Park (2018) and Hossain et al. (2020) specify that perceived intelligence positively influences the attitude of using ChatGPT, which confirms our findings. Intelligent robots that provide data processing, good communication, and clear answers give a positive perception among users. According to Cabanillas et al. (2014) and Blanche et al. (2019), there is a favorable correlation between the attitude of using ChatGPT and behavioral intention. Indeed, attitude is considered to be an important determinant of behavioral intention. We argue that the rise in the quantity of users is linked to their perception of this technology. Results allow us to verify the moderating role of familiarity. In other words, the habit of using this kind of technology is an important factor that will strengthen the relationship between attitude and behavioral intention.

TABLE 7.5 Comparison Between Groups

Groups	G1 : Low Familiarity			G2: High Familiarity		
	Estimate	CR	*P*	Estimate	CR	*P*
Attitude → Behavioral Intention	0.409	3.490	0.000	0.721	7.325	0.000

7.5 CONCLUSION

This research looks at the variables that affect the attitudes of students, researchers, and graduates toward the use of ChatGPT. It deals with the impact of the attitude toward this technology on their behavioral intention while highlighting the moderating role of familiarity.

This chapter provides an overview of the current literature in several respects. First, the research paper offers a new perspective on the influence of attitude on behavioral intention toward the use of ChatGPT in the field of scientific research. Second, we address the role of familiarity as a moderating variable. To our knowledge, there are gaps in the literature regarding the study of the link between behavioral intention and attitude. As methodological implications, we use the model of structural equations under AMOS 22. This chapter offers useful information for professionals (academics, retailers, investors). Scientific writing requires specialized knowledge, innovative ideas, or opinions always requiring a human touch that cannot be replaced by AI.

Despite the current gaps in the literature, there are still areas to explore for further studies. First, the framework of our study is limited to studying the use of ChatGPT only in the field of scientific research. It is possible to broaden this field of research to other fields (e.g., e-commerce, e-learning). Second, the number of people interviewed is limited. It would therefore be important to widen the sample. Third, future studies should introduce other moderating or mediating variables that can enrich the conceptual model of our research (e.g. trust, involvement, technology anxiety).

KEYWORDS

- **artificial intelligence**
- **attitude**
- **behavioral intention**
- **ChatGPT**
- **familiarity**
- **scientific research**

REFERENCES

Adamopoulou, E. & Moussiades, L. (2020). Chatbots: History, technology, and applications. *Machine Learning with Applications*, 2(15), 10–16.

Ajzen, I. & Fishbein, M. (1980). Understanding attitudes and predicting social behavior. Organizational Behavior and Human Decision Processes.

Ajzen, I. (2012). The theory of planned behavior. In: Handbook of Theories of Social Psychology, New York, pp. 438–459.

Ambawat, M. & Wadera, D. (2019). A review of chatbot adoption from the consumer's perspectives. *Journal of the Gujarat Research Society*, 21(11), 15–23.

Araujo, T. (2018). Living up to the chatbot hype: the influence of anthropomorphic design cues and communicative agency framing on conversational agent and company perceptions. *Computers in Human Behavior*, 85, 183–189.

Bala, K., Kumar, M., Hulawale, S. & Pandita, S. (2017). Chatbot for college management system using AI. *International Research Journal of Engineering and Technology*, 4(11), 2030–2033.

Bansal, H. & Khan, R. (2018). A review paper on human-computer interaction. *International Journal of Advanced Research in Computer Science and Software Engineering*, 8(53), 53–56.

Belanche, D., Casalo, L. V. & Flavian, C. (2019). Artificial intelligence in FinTech: Understanding robo-advisors adoption among customers. *Industrial Management & Data Systems*, 1–20.

Benabdeouahed, R. & Elkhatibi, Y. (2022). Chatbots: Towards a revolution in customer relations. *Review of Management and Culture*, 7, 611–631.

Bhattacherjee, A. (2000). Acceptance of e-commerce services: The case of courtage électronique, Transactions IEEE sur les systèmes, l'homme et la cybernétique. *Systems and Humans*, 411–420.

Cabanillas, F. L., Fernandez, J. & Leiva, F. M. (2014). The moderating effect of experience in the adoption of mobile payment tools in virtual social networks: The m-Payment acceptance model in virtual social networks (MPAM-VSN). *International Journal of Information Management*, 34, 151–166.

Castañeda, J. A., Muñoz-Leiva, F. & Luque, T. (2007). Web acceptance model (WAM): Moderating effects of user experience. *Information and Management*, 44(4), 384–396.

Cheng, H. W. (2023). Challenges and limitations of ChatGPT and artificial intelligence for scientific research: A perspective from organic materials. *Artificial Intelligence*, 4(2), 401–405.

Chatterjee, S., Rana, N. P., Dwivedi, Y. K. & Baabdullah, A. M. (2021). Understanding AI adoption in manufacturing and production firms using an integrated TAM-TOE model. *Technological Forecasting and Social Change*, 170,12–18.

Chhikara, D., Sharma, R. & Kaushik, K. (2022). Indian E-commerce consumer and their acceptance towards Chatbots. *Academy of Marketing Studies Journal*, 26(1), 1–10.

Colic, C., Hadi, R., Stephen, A. T. & Thomaz, F. (2022). Express: Blame the bot: Anthropomorphism and anger in customer-chatbot interactions. *Journal of Marketing*, 86(4), 132–148.

Cosmo, L. M., Piper, L. & Di Vittorio, A. (2021). The role of attitude toward chatbots and privacy concerning the relationship between attitude toward mobile advertising and behavioral intention to use chatbots. *Italian Journal of Marketing*, 6(2), 83–102.

Davis, F. D., Bagozzi, R. P. & Warshaw, P. R. (1989). User acceptance of computer technology: A comparison of two theoretical models. *Management Science*, 35, 982–1003.

Elmorshidy, A., Mostafa, M. M., El-Moughrabi, I. & Al-Mezen, H. (2015). Factors influencing live customer support chat services: An empirical investigation in Kuwait. *Journal of Theoretical Applied Electronic Commerce Research*, 10, 63–76.

Fishbein, M. & Ajzen, I. (1975). Belief, Attitude, Intention, and Behavior: An Introduction to Theory and Research. Addison-Wesley, Reading, MA, USA.

Gefen, D. (2000). E-Commerce: The rôle of familiarity and trust. *The International Journal of Management Science*, 28(6), 725–737.

Gümüş, N. & Çark, Ö. (2021). The effect of customers' attitudes towards chatbots on their experience and behavioural intention in Turkey. *Interdisciplinary Description of Complex System,* 19(3), 420–436.

Ho, C. C. & Mac Dorman, K. F. (2010). Revisiting the uncanny valley theory: Developing and validating an alternative to the Godspeed indices. *Computer in Human Behavior,* 26(6), 1508–1518.

Hossain, M. A., Akter, S. & Yanamandram, V. (2020). Revisiting customer analytics capability for data-driven retailing. *Journal of Retail. Consumer Service*, 56, 10–21.

Huang, M. H. & Rust, R. T. (2021). A strategic framework for artificial intelligence in marketing. *Journal of the Academy of Marketing Science*, 49(1), 30–50.

Kasilingam, D. L. (2021). Understanding the attitude and intention to use smartphone chatbots for shopping. *Technology in Society*, 62, 10–18.

Komiak, S. Y. X. & Benbasat, I. (2006). The effects of personalization and familiarity on trust and adoption of recommendation agents. *MIS Quarterly*, 30(4), 941–960.

Kwangsawad, A. & Jattamart, A. (2022). Overcoming customer innovation resistance to the sustainable adoption of chatbot services: A community-enterprise perspective in Thailand. *Journal of Innovation and Knowledge*, 7, 10–22.

McGinn, C., Cullinan, M. F., Otubela, M. & Kelly, K. (2019). Design of a terrain adaptive wheeled robot for human-orientated environments. *Autonomous Robots*, 43, 63–78.

Mijwil, M. (2023). ChatGPT: The Future of Artificial Intelligence in the Scientific. https://www.researchgate.net/publication/368788743_ChatGPT.

Minsky, H. P. (1976). John Maynard Keynes. Macmillan, London.

Murtarelli, G., Collina, C. & Romenti, S. (2022). Hi! How can I help you today?: Investigating the quality of chatbots–millennials relationship within the fashion industry. *The TQM Journal,* 35(3), 719–733.

Nilsson, N. J. (2005). Human-level artificial intelligence? Be serious. *AI Magazine Magazine*, 26(4), 68–75.

Oh, O., Agrawal, M. & Rao, H. R. (2013). Community intelligence and social media services: A rumor theoreticanalysis of tweets during social crises. *MIS Quarterly,* 37, 407–442.

Pee, L. G., Woon, I. M. Y. & Kankanhalli, A. (2008). Explaining non-work related computing in the workplace: A comparison of alternative models. *Information and Management*, 45, 120–130.

Pillai, R. & Sivathanu, B. (2020). Adoption of AI-based chatbots for hospitality and tourism. *International Journal of Contemporary Hospitality Management*, 32, 3199–3226.

Rafiq, F., Dogra, N., Adil, M. & Wu, J. Z. (2012). Examining consumer's intention to adopt AI-chatbots in tourism using partial least squares structural equation modeling method. *Mathematics*, 10, 21–39.

Rajaobelina, L., Prom Tep, S., Arcand, M. & Ricard, L. (2021). Creepiness: Its antecedents and impact on loyalty when interacting with a chatbot. *Psychology and Marketing*, 38, 2339–2356.

Rogers, E. M. (1998). Diffusion of Innovations (3rd Edition), The Free Press, New York.

Rose, S., Clark, M., Samuel, P. & Hair, N. (2012). Online customer experience in retailing: An empirical model of antecedents and outcomes. *Journal of Retailing*, 88(2), 308–322.

Russell, S. J. (2010). Artificial Intelligence is a Modern Approach. Pearson Education.

Selamat, M. A. & Windasari, N. A. (2021). Chatbot for SMEs: Integrating customer and business owner perspectives. *Technology in Society*, 66, 10–16.

Shapiro, S. (1992). Encyclopedia of Artificial Intelligence (2nd Edition), Wiley, New York.

Silva, F. A., Shojaei, A. S. & Barbosa, B. (2023). Chatbot-based services: A study on customers' reuse intention. *Journal of Theoretical and Applied Electronic Commerce Research*, 18, 457–474.

Soudoplatoff, S. (2018). Report. The Foundation for Political Innovation.

Tussyadiah, I. P. & Park, S. (2018). Consumer evaluation of hotel service robots. Information and Communication Technologies in Tourism, Springer, Cham, Switzerland, 308–320.

Venkatesh, V. & Davis, F. (2000). A theoretical extension of the technology acceptance model: Four longitudinal field studies. *Management Science*, 46, 186–204.

Véry, P. & Cailluet, L. (2019). Artificial intelligence and research in management. *French Management Review*, 285, 121–134.

Wen, J. & Wang, W. (2023). The future of ChatGPT in academic research and publishing: A commentary for clinical and translational medicine. *Clinical and Translational Medicine, 22,* 1–3.

Yi-Cheng, C., Chun-Yu, C., Yi-Chen, L. & Ron-Chen, Y. (2007). Predicting college students of e-learning systems: An attempt to extend technology acceptance model. PACIS Proceedings, 12–31.

Zhang, B., Zhu, Y., Deng, J., Zheng, W., Liu, Y., Wang, C. & Zeng, R. (2022). I am here to assist your tourism: Predicting continuance intention to use AI-based chatbots for tourism. DoesGenderReallyMatter? *International Journal of Human-Computer Interaction*, 39, 1–17.

Zhang, L. J., Gu, Y. P. & Hu, G. (2008). A cognitive perspective on Singaporean bilingual children's use of reading strategies in learning to read in English. *British Journal of Educational Psychology*, 78, 245–271.

Zhong B., Huang Y. & Liu, Q. (2021). Mental health toll from the coronavirus: Social media usage reveals Wuhan residents' depression and secondary trauma in the COVID-19 outbreak. *Computers in human behavior*, 114, 10–25.

Zouhri, A. (2019). Big data, artificial intelligence, and the performance of companies. *Review of Control, Accounting and Audit*, 4(3), 916–931.

CHAPTER 8

The Artificial Intelligence (AI) Application for an Automated Education System

ALESSIO FACCIA[1], MANJEET RIDON,[2] and
LUIGI PIO LEONARDO CAVALIERE[3]

[1]*School of Business, University of Birmingham Dubai, Dubai, United Arab Emirates*

[2]*De Montfort University, Leicester, United Kingdom*

[3]*Università di Foggia, Foggia, Italy*

*Corresponding author

ABSTRACT

This chapter explores the application of artificial intelligence (AI) in automating various aspects of the education system, including assignments, teaching, learning, support, and marking. The chapter discusses the benefits and challenges of using AI in education and explores its potential to enhance student engagement, academic performance, and institutional efficiency. The analysis focuses on the benefits and limitations of using AI in education, including its potential to personalize learning and provide timely feedback to students, as well as concerns around data privacy, bias, and the potential for AI to replace human instructors. The chapter also discusses the role of educators and other stakeholders in the effective use of AI in education. The study highlights the importance of collaboration between educators, intelligent tutoring professionals, and other stakeholders in designing, developing, and implementing AI-powered education systems. It concludes by discussing the potential for AI to transform the

Corporate Governance, Digitalization, and Energy Transition: Imen Baccouche and Afef Khalil. (Eds.)

DOI: 10.1201/9781779643407-10

education system and the implications of its use for teaching and learning. The findings of this study demonstrate the potential of AI to enhance various aspects of the education system and provide guidance to educators and policymakers seeking to implement AI-powered education systems.

8.1 INTRODUCTION

In our constantly transforming world, combining technology with multiple domains revolutionizes our operations. Education is one sector profoundly impacted by this wave of change. There is an escalating interest in leveraging artificial intelligence (AI) to automate various facets of the educational landscape, igniting intriguing conversations. This chapter takes you on an exploratory journey into AI-enriched educational architectures, shedding light on their benefits, challenges, and potential to reshape how we dispense and assimilate knowledge (Cox, 2021). AI's vast expanse within education enables the automation of assignments and pedagogical procedures, providing personalized assistance and smoothing the cumbersome assessment process. As we set sail on this transformative voyage, it is imperative to understand the multifaceted dynamics that AI introduces into the education sphere. This chapter invites you on an exciting expedition of AI's diverse applications in education. We will unpack the potential of intelligent tutoring (IT) systems, automated writing evaluation tools, and adaptive learning platforms, highlighting their attributes, functions, and impact on instructional and learning outcomes.

Deeper exploration reveals that AI possesses the potential to revamp education by boosting learner engagement, lifting academic performance, and enhancing institutional efficiency. By customizing learning experiences and offering prompt feedback, AI can morph conventional education paradigms into responsive, adaptable processes that serve individual needs and learning styles. Nonetheless, like all technological progressions, infusing AI into education brings challenges and considerations. Concerns around data privacy, biases, and the possibility of AI usurping human educators must be critically inspected (Da'u and Salim, 2020). This chapter tackles these issues, analyzing AI's educational constraints and prospects. Understanding that the triumphant integration of AI in education requires a coalition of multiple stakeholders is critical. Educators, IT experts, policymakers, and others must collaborate to architect, create, and deploy AI-empowered educational frameworks that resonate with our educational institution's mission and values. By cultivating a culture of innovation and collaboration, we can fully leverage AI to enrich teaching and learning experiences (Hussin et al., 2019). With AI's steady advancement, the potential to revolutionize education grows more evident. Personalized learning is one field where AI has exhibited remarkable potential. Traditional education methods often follow a uniform model, ignoring students' strengths, weaknesses, and learning styles.

AI-driven adaptive learning platforms have the potential to counter this issue (Pantelimon et al., 2021). By analyzing extensive data on student performance, preferences, and progress, these platforms can customize learning resources and activities to cater to each student's unique needs. This personalized approach enhances student engagement and understanding, as they can learn independently, focusing on areas requiring additional assistance (Wang et al., 2023). Intelligent Tutoring Systems (ITS) represent another thrilling AI application in education (Steenbergen-Hu and Cooper, 2014). These systems use natural language processing (NLP) and machine learning algorithms to engage with students, reminiscent of one-on-one tutoring, providing personalized feedback and guidance (Baker et al., 2006). Moreover, AI can automate and streamline administrative tasks within the education system (Votto et al., 2021). AI-infused tools can automate the grading of multiple-choice exams, enabling teachers to concentrate on more enriching activities such as providing feedback and engaging in student discussions (Kommey et al., 2022). However, while the merits of AI in education are abundant, addressing its implementation challenges and considerations is crucial. Privacy concerns (Prinsloo et al., 2022) arise as AI systems gather and analyze important student data, necessitating robust data protection measures. Equally vital is addressing potential bias in AI algorithms and ensuring AI systems supplement, not substitute, human educators. As educators navigate the AI-powered education environment, their roles become even more pivotal, employing AI tools to augment teaching practices and nurture critical skills such as critical thinking, problem-solving, and social-emotional learning.

8.1.1 UNLEASHING THE POTENTIAL: AI-DRIVEN LEARNING ENVIRONMENT

In the rapidly evolving landscape of education, integrating AI can potentially transform learning environments into dynamic and immersive spaces

(Smuts et al., 2019). AI-driven learning environments harness the power of technology to create personalized and engaging educational experiences for learners. By leveraging AI algorithms, virtual reality simulations, and NLP, these environments offer innovative pathways for acquiring knowledge and developing skills. One of the most remarkable aspects of AI-driven learning environments is their ability to adapt to individual learners' needs and preferences. Traditional classrooms often follow a one-size-fits-all approach, where instruction is delivered in a standardized manner. However, AI-powered systems can analyze vast data, including learners' performance, learning styles, and preferences, to provide tailored content and experiences. This level of personalization enhances learner engagement and motivation, ensuring that the educational material aligns with their unique interests and abilities.

Moreover, AI-driven learning environments have the potential to foster critical thinking and problem-solving skills. Through interactive simulations and virtual scenarios, learners can engage in authentic, real-world situations (Koivisto et al., 2017) that require them to apply their knowledge and make decisions. AI algorithms can analyze learners' actions, provide immediate feedback, and offer guidance to help them refine their problem-solving approaches. This iterative learning and improvement process creates a rich and immersive educational experience that mirrors the complexities of the real world. Collaboration is another key component of AI-driven learning environments (Jones, 2010). By incorporating AI technologies, learners can engage in collaborative projects and connect with peers from diverse backgrounds and locations. Virtual platforms facilitate seamless communication and enable learners to collaborate on tasks, share ideas, and learn from each other's perspectives (Wong et al., 2016). These collaborative experiences foster essential skills such as teamwork, communication, and cultural awareness, which are increasingly valuable in our interconnected global society.

While AI-driven learning environments offer exciting possibilities, it is essential to address the challenges that arise. Data privacy and security concerns must be carefully considered, as these systems gather and analyze sensitive learner data (Xue et al., 2014). Striking a balance between data collection for personalization purposes and ensuring the protection of individuals' privacy is of utmost importance. Additionally, there may be concerns about the reliability and accuracy of AI algorithms (Shin, 2022). Transparent evaluation and continuous monitoring are necessary to ensure that the AI systems function effectively and provide reliable educational experiences. AI-driven learning environments hold immense potential to revolutionist the educational landscape. By leveraging AI algorithms, virtual reality simulations, and NLP, these environments can provide personalized, engaging, and adaptive educational experiences (Kamruzzaman, 2023). Learners benefit from tailored content, immersive simulations, and collaborative opportunities that enhance their engagement, critical thinking, and problem-solving skills. However, careful consideration must be given to data privacy and security, as well as the reliability and accuracy of AI algorithms. Through thoughtful implementation and ongoing evaluation, AI-driven learning environments can shape the future of education, empowering learners and educators alike (Table 8.1).

TABLE 8.1 Summary

	Benefits of AI-Driven Learning Environments	**Challenges of AI-Driven Learning Environments**
Personalization	Allows individualized instruction based on learners' performance, learning styles, and preferences, enhancing engagement and motivation.	Striking a balance between data collection for personalization and protecting individuals' privacy.
Critical Thinking and Problem-Solving Skills	Fosters these skills through interactive simulations and virtual scenarios that require applying knowledge and decision-making. Provides immediate feedback to refine problem-solving approaches.	There may be concerns about the reliability and accuracy of AI algorithms in providing meaningful scenarios and accurate feedback.
Collaboration	Facilitates collaboration and communication between learners from diverse backgrounds and locations, enhancing teamwork, communication, and cultural awareness skills.	Not explicitly mentioned, but could include issues of the digital divide and ensuring equitable access to technology.
Data Privacy and Security	Not explicitly mentioned as a benefit.	Raises concerns as AI systems gather and analyze sensitive learner data. Requires careful consideration and management.
Reliability and Accuracy of AI Algorithms	Not explicitly mentioned as a benefit.	There may be concerns about the reliability and accuracy of AI algorithms. Transparent evaluation and continuous monitoring are necessary.

8.1.2 FROM ASSISTIVE TO AUGMENTATIVE: REDEFINING THE ROLE OF EDUCATORS

In the realm of AI-powered education, the role of educators is undergoing a significant transformation. Rather than solely being information providers, educators become facilitators, mentors, and orchestrators of learning experiences (Laurillard et al., 2009). AI technologies offer unprecedented opportunities to assist and augment educators in their instructional practices, ultimately enhancing the quality and effectiveness of education (Hernandez-de-Menendez et al., 2020). One of the key aspects of AI's impact on educators is its ability to provide personalized support and guidance to individual learners (Alam, 2021). Through AI-powered adaptive learning systems, educators can gain insights into students' learning styles, preferences, and areas of strength or challenge. By leveraging this information, educators can tailor their instructional approaches, adapt content delivery, and provide targeted interventions to meet the specific needs of each learner. Furthermore, AI technologies can automate routine administrative tasks, allowing educators to focus more on instructional design and individualized instruction (Alam and Mohanty, 2023). Grading and assessment processes can be streamlined with the help of automated evaluation tools, freeing up valuable time for educators to engage in more meaningful interactions with their students. This shift in focus from administrative burdens to instructional excellence enables educators to provide the necessary support and guidance to foster students' intellectual growth and development.

In addition to assisting educators, AI technologies augment their instructional practices by offering valuable insights and resources (Dwivedi et al., 2021). AI-powered analytics can provide educators with real-time data on students' progress, highlighting areas where additional support may be needed or identifying patterns that can inform instructional decisions. This data-driven approach empowers educators to make evidence-based interventions, allowing them to address learning gaps promptly and effectively. Moreover, AI can facilitate the creation of personalized learning pathways and adaptive curricula (Xie et al., 2019). By analyzing vast amounts of data on learner performance, AI algorithms can generate tailored learning plans that cater to each student's individual needs and pace of learning. This personalized approach maximizes the potential for academic growth and nurtures students' motivation and engagement, as they feel a sense of ownership and relevance in their learning journey. However, as we embrace the augmentation provided by

AI, it is crucial to maintain a human-centered approach to education (Bacciu et al., 2021). While AI can offer valuable insights and automate certain tasks, the role of human educators remains irreplaceable. The human touch is essential in fostering meaningful connections, empathetic understanding, and social-emotional development in learners. Educators bring their expertise, intuition, and passion for creating nurturing and inclusive learning environments beyond what AI can offer alone (Ainscow and Sandill, 2010). Integrating AI in education redefines the role of educators from being solely instructors to facilitators, mentors, and designers of personalized learning experiences (Guilherme, 2019). AI technologies assist educators by providing personalized support, automating administrative tasks, and offering valuable insights. Additionally, AI augments educators' instructional practices by enabling data-driven decision-making, facilitating personalized learning pathways, and promoting student engagement. As we harness the power of AI, it is essential to strike a balance between technological advancements and the invaluable human qualities that educators bring to the table, ultimately creating a harmonious synergy that empowers learners and enhances the educational experience (Goulart et al., 2022).

As we stride confidently into the dynamic world of AI-integrated education, we find ourselves standing at the precipice of a new era of learning. Environments sculpted with the chisel of AI showcase the marvels of technology, offering personalized, immersive educational experiences that carry the promise of revolutionizing the way we learn. By leveraging the power of AI algorithms, NLP, and the spellbinding allure of virtual reality simulations, we see the birth of novel methods for knowledge acquisition and skill development. Arguably, the most compelling facet of these AI-driven learning environments is their innate ability to adapt and mold themselves to cater to learners' needs and preferences. A paradigm shift from the traditional "one-size-fits-all" approach of classical classrooms (Haniya, 2023), these environments harness the immense processing power of AI to analyze enormous volumes of data about learners, from their academic performance and learning styles to their preferences and inclinations. The resultant content and experiences are finely tuned to enhance learner engagement and motivation, offering personalization that ensures alignment between the educational material and each student's unique interests and abilities (Kamruzzaman, 2023). Beyond mere personalization, AI-driven learning environments harbor the potential to cultivate critical thinking and problem-solving skills among learners. Through engaging interactive simulations and immersive virtual scenarios, learners are placed within authentic, real-world situations that mandate the application of their acquired knowledge and decision-making skills (Calandra et al., 2022). AI algorithms dissect learners' actions (Ochoa et al., 2022), providing immediate feedback and offering guidance to refine their problem-solving approaches. The resulting iterative process of learning and self-improvement constructs a rich educational experience that faithfully mirrors the complexities and challenges of the real world.

Collaboration is another cornerstone of AI-driven learning environments. These environments employ AI technologies to facilitate cooperative projects (Yang, 2022) and foster connections among peers from diverse backgrounds and locations. Virtual platforms act as a conduit for seamless communication, empowering learners to work together on tasks, exchange ideas, and glean insights from each other's perspectives (Guache et al., 2023). Such collaborative experiences engender crucial skills, including teamwork, communication, and cultural awareness, which hold immense value in our increasingly interconnected global society (Markauskaite et al., 2022). While the promise of AI-driven learning environments is captivating, we must address this nascent revolution's formidable challenges. Primary among these concerns are issues related to data privacy and security. AI systems gather and analyze sensitive learner data, raising questions about the adequacy of data protection measures (Meszaros, 2022). A delicate balance must be struck between the collection of data for personalization and the paramount necessity of preserving individual privacy. As mentioned before, the potential concerns regarding the reliability and accuracy of AI algorithms cannot be overlooked. The systems must be transparent in their operation, and continuous monitoring is crucial to ensure that the AI functions effectively and delivers reliable, beneficial educational experiences (Mhlanga, 2023). It includes periodically reviewing the systems to rectify inherent or emergent biases and ensuring fairness and equity in educational opportunities. AI-driven learning environments, therefore, embody an exciting paradox of immense potential coupled with significant challenges (Khogali and Mekid, 2023). By leveraging AI algorithms, virtual reality simulations, and NLP, these environments can offer tailored, engaging, and adaptive educational experiences. They open doors to personalized content, immerse learners in compelling simulations, and provide platforms for collaborative efforts that nurture critical thinking, problem-solving skills, and the spirit of teamwork. However, these environments also demand meticulous attention to data privacy and security and the reliability and accuracy of the AI algorithms driving them. Through thoughtful implementation, ongoing evaluation, and proactive addressing of potential issues, AI-driven learning environments can shape the future of education (Schiff et al., 2021). They stand as a testament to the prowess of AI in empowering learners and educators alike, redefining the contours of knowledge acquisition and skill development, and, ultimately, driving us toward a more enlightened world.

While opening doors to unprecedented opportunities for personalized and immersive learning, AI-powered education also calls for a deeper understanding of its underlying technologies (Dai and Ke, 2022). This knowledge empowers stakeholders to make informed decisions, design effective strategies, and ensure that AI is a robust and reliable tool for enhancing educational experiences. Furthermore, ethical considerations must always be at the forefront of AI discussions in education. As we forge a future where AI plays an increasingly significant role, we must also ensure that principles of fairness, equity, transparency, and privacy are firmly embedded within the fabric of our AI-powered educational systems. In an era where data is an invaluable asset, maintaining the privacy and security of learner data must be a non-negotiable priority. Ultimately, the integration of AI into education must be seen not as a replacement for human teachers but rather as a powerful tool that complements and enhances the skills of educators. AI has the potential to relieve educators of administrative burdens, freeing up time for more practical pedagogical activities. Teachers can then focus on fostering creativity, critical thinking, emotional intelligence, and other skills that are challenging to automate but vital for the holistic development of learners. The true power of AI in education lies in its ability to democratize learning. With AI, quality education can be accessible to all, regardless of geographical location, economic status, or learning abilities. With AI at its helm, the future of education promises to be one where every learner is empowered, every teacher is equipped, and every barrier to quality education is surmountable.

As we continue our journey into the landscape of AI-driven education, we must keep these considerations in mind. By balancing the promise of AI with the responsibilities that come with it, we can ensure that AI serves to enhance and enrich our educational experiences rather than overshadow them. Therefore, AI's influence on education presents an exciting opportunity and considerable responsibility. It necessitates a delicate balancing act that acknowledges and harnesses the potential of AI and recognizes and addresses the challenges that come along. By doing so, we will not only shape the educational landscape of the future but also ensure that it upholds our values and serves the needs of all learners (Table 8.2).

TABLE 8.2 Summary

Topic	Benefits of AI in Education	Challenges and Considerations in AI-Driven Education
Role of Educators	The transformation from information providers to facilitators, mentors, and orchestrators of learning experiences. AI assists educators by providing personalized support, automating administrative tasks, and offering valuable insights.	Preserving the human touch in education is crucial. The human element is vital in fostering meaningful connections, empathetic understanding, and social-emotional development in learners.
Personalization	AI allows for creating personalized learning pathways and adaptive curricula tailored to each student's individual needs and pace of learning.	Data privacy and security concerns as AI systems gather and analyze sensitive learner data. A balance between data collection for personalization and privacy preservation is essential.
Critical Thinking and Problem-Solving Skills	AI helps cultivate these skills among learners through engaging interactive simulations and immersive virtual scenarios.	Concerns regarding the reliability and accuracy of AI algorithms in providing meaningful scenarios and accurate feedback.
Collaboration	AI facilitates cooperative projects and fosters connections among peers from diverse backgrounds and locations.	Not explicitly mentioned, but could include issues of the digital divide and ensuring equitable access to technology.
Data Privacy and Security	Not explicitly mentioned as a benefit.	AI systems gather and analyze sensitive learner data, raising questions about the adequacy of data protection measures.
Reliability and Accuracy of AI Algorithms	Not explicitly mentioned as a benefit.	Concerns about the reliability and accuracy of AI algorithms. The systems must be transparent in their operation, and continuous monitoring is necessary.
Ethical Considerations	Not explicitly mentioned as a benefit.	Principles of fairness, equity, transparency, and privacy must be firmly embedded within AI-powered educational systems.
Democratization of Education	AI has the potential to make quality education accessible to all, regardless of geographical location, economic status, or learning abilities.	Not explicitly mentioned, but it could include the risk of increased digital divide if not properly managed.

8.2 PROBLEM STATEMENT

In education, integrating AI brings forth a range of opportunities and challenges. This chapter explores the challenges of incorporating AI into the automated education system. As educators and policymakers embrace AI technologies to enhance teaching and learning experiences, it is important to understand and address the potential drawbacks and concerns that arise. This problem statement examines the limitations, ethical considerations, and potential risks of AI implementation while emphasizing the need for a balanced approach that values the human element in education. By critically analyzing these challenges and providing insights into effective strategies and solutions, this chapter aims to guide educators and policymakers in harnessing the transformative potential of AI while navigating the complexities in the realm of education. Integrating AI into the education system presents numerous opportunities for enhancing teaching and learning experiences. However, this chapter explores the challenges and potential drawbacks of incorporating AI into the automated education system. As educators and policymakers embrace AI technologies to revolutionize education, it is essential to understand and address the limitations, ethical considerations, and potential risks that may arise. One of the key challenges is data privacy and security. AI-powered systems gather and analyze sensitive learner data to personalize learning experiences. However, this raises concerns about the adequacy of data protection measures. Striking a balance between collecting data for personalization and ensuring the privacy and security of individuals' information is critical to building trust in AI-powered education.

Moreover, the reliability and accuracy of AI algorithms need careful attention. AI systems heavily rely on data analysis and machine learning to provide personalized feedback and content. Ensuring that these algorithms function effectively and deliver reliable educational experiences is paramount. Transparent evaluation and continuous monitoring are necessary to identify and rectify any inherent or emergent biases in AI systems. Another important consideration is the potential for AI to replace human educators. While AI can offer valuable insights and automate certain tasks, it is crucial to maintain a human-centered approach to education. The role of human educators remains irreplaceable in fostering meaningful connections, empathetic understanding, and social-emotional development in learners. Educators bring expertise, intuition, and passion to create nurturing and inclusive learning environments beyond what AI can offer alone. Additionally, ethical considerations must be at the forefront of AI discussions in education. As AI plays an increasingly significant role in the education system, fairness, equity, transparency, and privacy principles must be firmly embedded in AI-powered educational systems. Ensuring AI systems do not perpetuate biases and provide equitable opportunities for all learners is vital. Furthermore, the potential risk of a digital divide must be addressed. While AI has the potential to democratize education and make it accessible to all, it could exacerbate existing inequalities if not properly managed. Ensuring equitable access to AI-powered education technologies is crucial in bridging the digital divide.

A balanced approach is necessary to harness AI's transformative potential in education. AI can assist educators by providing personalized support, automating administrative tasks, and offering valuable insights. It can foster critical thinking, problem-solving skills, and collaborative learning experiences. However, educators must retain their roles as facilitators, mentors, and designers of personalized learning journeys. Integrating AI into education requires careful planning, ongoing evaluation, and proactive addressing of potential challenges. Data privacy and security emerge as critical concerns when implementing AI-powered education systems. As these systems collect and analyze vast amounts of learner data, there is a heightened risk of unauthorized access and data breaches. Protecting students' privacy and ensuring the secure handling of their sensitive information become paramount. Robust data protection measures must be implemented to safeguard against potential vulnerabilities and uphold the trust of students, parents, and educational institutions. Ensuring the reliability and accuracy of AI algorithms is of utmost importance. AI-driven personalized learning experiences heavily rely on data analysis to make informed decisions. However, if the algorithms are flawed or biased, they may lead to incorrect assessments and inappropriate content recommendations. Transparent evaluation and continuous monitoring are vital to identify and address any biases and inaccuracies, ensuring that AI systems deliver meaningful and reliable educational outcomes.

A significant concern relates to the potential for AI to replace human educators. While AI can provide valuable support and automate certain tasks, it should not be perceived as a substitute for human interaction and personalized guidance. Educators play a crucial role in fostering creativity, critical thinking, emotional intelligence, and other essential skills that are challenging to automate but vital for learners' holistic development. Emphasizing the human element in education is essential to maintain a well-rounded and empathetic learning environment. Ethical considerations also come to the forefront when implementing AI-powered education systems. Fairness, equity, transparency, and privacy must be deeply embedded in the design and deployment of AI technologies. AI algorithms must be designed to minimize biases and ensure that all learners have equal access to educational opportunities. Policymakers and educators must work collaboratively to create ethical guidelines and standards for the responsible use of AI in education. Additionally, the potential risk of exacerbating the digital divide must be addressed. While AI has the potential to democratize education and level the playing field for learners worldwide, it could inadvertently widen disparities in access to technology. Ensuring equitable access to AI-powered educational tools and resources is crucial to bridging the digital divide and promoting inclusive education for all learners. Balancing AI's promise with its complexities requires a thoughtful and strategic approach. Educators and policymakers must collaborate to design effective strategies for integrating AI into the education system. It is crucial to strike a harmonious balance between leveraging AI technologies to enhance learning experiences and preserving human educators' unique qualities and expertise.

8.3 UNDERSTANDING THE AI TECHNOLOGIES IN EDUCATION

8.3.1 MACHINE LEARNING AND PREDICTIVE ANALYTICS

AI in education signifies a paradigm shift in teaching and learning (Rodney, 2020). A major driving force behind AI is the concept of neural networks (NNs) and deep learning (Perrotta and Selwyn, 2020). These powerful tools enable AI applications to deliver personalized, dynamic, and engaging learning experiences. To understand the role of these technologies in education, we must first comprehend the basics. NNs are AI systems modeled after the human brain, consisting of interconnected layers of nodes, or "neurons," that process information (Katal and Singh, 2022). These layers constitute an input layer, one or more hidden layers, and an output layer. Each node processes the input it receives and passes on the result, simulating the process of human brain cells transmitting signals. Deep learning, a subset of machine learning, involves using NNs with multiple hidden layers. These layers enable the system to learn from data inputs and adjust its internal parameters to make accurate predictions or decisions.

The "depth" in deep learning denotes these multiple layers, and it is this depth that facilitates more complex, nuanced learning and prediction capabilities. In the context of education, these technologies present immense possibilities. Personalized learning is one of the most compelling applications of NNs and deep learning in education (Wu et al., 2020). These technologies can analyze vast data on student performance and learning styles. By processing this data, AI systems can adapt teaching materials and instructional strategies to cater to the unique needs of each learner, thereby enhancing the efficacy of teaching and learning. AI can identify patterns in a student's learning behavior, detect areas of weakness or strength, and then modify the content delivery accordingly. It could mean presenting concepts in different formats, adjusting the difficulty level of questions, or suggesting additional resources for further learning. The system evolves and learns over time, continually refining its strategies to ensure optimal learner engagement and understanding. Another significant application is ITS (Taub et al., 2021). These systems, driven by NNs and deep learning, can provide one-on-one tutoring to students, adapting to their learning pace and offering instant feedback. These systems can detect when a student struggles with a concept and provide additional explanations or examples, just as a human tutor would. Furthermore, these technologies can facilitate the automated evaluation of assignments and exams, relieving teachers of time-consuming grading tasks (Alam, 2022). Deep learning algorithms can even evaluate more complex responses, like essays, by analyzing structure, grammar, and relevance to the topic (Salloum et al., 2020). It provides students with instant feedback, helping them to improve faster. However, while NNs and deep learning can revolutionize education, it is essential to consider potential challenges. Understanding how these systems arrive at a decision—also known as "explainability"—can be complex due to the multiple layers of computation (Ali et al., 2023). Ensuring transparency and fairness in their operations is critical. Furthermore, educators must be mindful not to let technology replace the vital human element in education. While AI can adapt to individual learning styles and offer personalized feedback, it cannot replicate the social interactions and emotional support that teachers provide. Balancing the use of AI with the invaluable human touch will be vital to successfully integrate these technologies into education.

8.3.2 NNS AND DEEP LEARNING

NNs and Deep Learning represent two of the most fascinating and significant advancements in AI. Through these technologies, machines can learn, adapt, and even make decisions in a manner previously thought to be the exclusive domain of the human brain. NNs draw inspiration from the human brain (Brabazon and O'Neill, 2006). They constitute an interconnected web of artificial neurons or nodes modeled after biological neurons. Each node in this network processes the information it receives, and if the information is significant, the node passes it on to other nodes. This interconnected web creates a system capable of learning and adapting, much like our brains. Each neuron in a neural network takes several inputs, applies a function to them, and then passes the output to the next layer. These functions are typically nonlinear, allowing the network to learn complex patterns. Importantly, each input has an associated weight, which adjusts as the model learns. The weight indicates the importance of that particular input in the calculation performed by the neuron.

Conversely, deep learning is a subset of machine learning that uses NNs with three or more layers. These deep neural networks enable the model to learn and represent the world through a hierarchy of concepts, each defined through its relation to simpler ones. By assembling these simple concepts, a deep neural network can comprehend intricate structures flexibly and efficiently. One of the most striking examples of deep learning applications is image recognition. Convolutional neural networks, a class of deep learning models (Jogin et al., 2018), have significantly improved image recognition. They can identify faces, diagnose diseases from medical images, and even generate startlingly real images. In addition to image recognition, deep learning has revolutionized NLP. Recurrent neural networks (Sherstinsky, 2020) and more recent models like Transformers have been used to develop language translation tools, sentiment analysis models, and even AI language models capable of generating human-like text. As we delve deeper into the potential of deep learning, one emerging area of interest is generative adversarial networks (GANs) (Pan et al., 2019). GANs pit two NNs against each other, with one trying to generate real data (the generator) and the other (the discriminator) trying to distinguish the generated data from the real thing. This dynamic creates a feedback loop that allows both networks to improve over time, resulting in a powerful model that can generate highly realistic outputs. However, while the implications of NNs and deep learning are profound, they are not without challenges (Kumar and Manash, 2019). One key issue is interpretability, often called the "black box" problem. Deep learning models, due to their complexity, often lack transparency, making it hard to understand why they have made a certain decision. Another challenge is the requirement for large amounts of data. Deep learning models typically need vast quantities of data to learn effectively. This requirement can present practical difficulties and ethical concerns, particularly around data privacy.

8.3.3 ROBOTIC PROCESS AUTOMATION (RPA)

AI is transforming the landscape of education, and one of the standout technologies contributing to this change is RPA (Lasso-Rodríguez and Gil-Herrera, 2019). RPA, at its core, involves automating repetitive tasks through software robots or "bots." These bots are programmed to follow rule-based procedures, performing tasks much quicker and more accurately than humans, freeing up time for more complex, creative tasks. RPA is unique in its ability to interact with computer systems at the user interface (UI) level, just like a human user. It follows preset rules and can handle structured data to perform repetitive tasks. RPA differs from traditional automation because it can adapt to different situations and handle exceptions, allowing for a higher degree of automation without requiring significant changes to existing systems (Syed et al., 2020). RPA has enormous potential in education to streamline operations and enhance efficiency. Many administrative tasks in educational institutions are repetitive and time-consuming. Automating these tasks through RPA can save time and resources, allowing staff to focus on more strategic activities, such as improving the quality of education. For instance, one of the most labor-intensive tasks in any educational institution is the admissions process (Ahmad et al., 2022). With hundreds, if not thousands, of applications to review, each consisting of multiple documents and data points, the process is highly time-consuming. With RPA, data extraction from application forms can be automated, ensuring quicker turnaround times and removing the possibility of human error.

Another example is the grading process. Teachers spend significant amounts of time grading student work. RPA, in conjunction with AI technologies like machine learning and NLP, can be used to automate certain aspects of this process. It saves teachers' time and provides students with quick and consistent feedback (Darvishi et al., 2022). Furthermore, RPA can also streamline routine communications (Turcu and Turcu, 2020). Many educational institutions send out regular notifications to students and parents about class schedules, assignments, grades, and more. Automating these communications with RPA can ensure timely and error-free notifications. RPA can also play a role in data management and reporting. Educational institutions often must generate regular reports on student performance, attendance, and curriculum effectiveness (Issac et al., 2018). Automating this process ensures that the reports are generated quickly and accurately, allowing institutions to analyze these reports more frequently and make data-driven decisions. However, while the potential of RPA is immense, it does not come without challenges. Implementation can be costly and requires careful planning to ensure compatibility with existing systems. Furthermore, there are concerns about job displacement as tasks become automated, necessitating a careful approach to balance efficiency gains with workforce implications (Bursley, 2021). Moreover, as with any technology handling sensitive data, security and privacy issues must be considered. The bots used in RPA must adhere to strict data privacy rules to protect the sensitive information of students and staff.

8.4 THE ARCHITECTURE OF AI-DRIVEN AUTOMATED EDUCATION SYSTEM

8.4.1 DATA INFRASTRUCTURE AND MANAGEMENT

At the heart of any AI-driven system, including an automated education system, lies a robust data infrastructure and efficient data management practices. As the saying goes, "data is the new oil," and this could not be truer for AI technologies. The architecture of an AI-driven automated education system starts with establishing a well-structured data infrastructure (Cao, 2022). This infrastructure is the backbone that enables data collection, storage, and processing. It encompasses databases, data warehouses, cloud storage systems, and data processing tools. A well-designed data infrastructure supports the efficient management and utilization of data, ensuring it can be easily accessed and used for AI applications. When building the data infrastructure for an AI-driven education system, the first consideration is the type and volume of data that will be handled. Education systems generate diverse data, including student demographics, academic performance data, administrative data, and more. The data infrastructure must handle this variety and volume of data. The infrastructure must also be scalable (Buitrago et al., 2020). As the education system evolves and grows, the data infrastructure should be able to scale accordingly to accommodate more data and more complex data processing tasks. It is where cloud-based infrastructure becomes valuable, as it allows for easy scaling and access to advanced data processing tools.

Data management is another critical component of an AI-driven automated education system (Ciolacu et al., 2017). Effective data management involves governance, quality control, and security. These elements ensure data is accurate, reliable, and secure, making it a solid foundation for AI applications. Data governance involves defining who within an organization has authority and control over data assets and how those data assets may be used. It includes creating rules and policies for data management and usage. Good data governance ensures that data is used and managed ethically and that data-related practices align with organizational objectives and regulations. Data quality control is about ensuring the accuracy and consistency of data. Data quality is paramount in AI because AI models' performance heavily depends on the data quality they are trained on. Techniques such as data cleaning, data validation, and data integration are used to improve data quality.

Lastly, data security is vital in protecting sensitive information (Puthal et al., 2021). It includes student personal data, academic records, and staff information in an educational context. Effective data security practices, including encryption, access control, and regular security audits, help prevent unauthorized access and data breaches. Implementing effective data infrastructure and management is no small task. It requires significant planning, investment, and ongoing maintenance. However, the effort is worth it. With robust data infrastructure and management, an AI-driven automated education system can deliver personalized learning experiences, efficient administrative processes, and valuable insights that improve education outcomes.

8.4.2 AI ALGORITHMS AND MODEL TRAINING

AI is reshaping the education sector, and a critical part of this transformation is the use of AI algorithms and the training of AI models. In an AI-driven automated education system, the "intelligence" results from these algorithms trained on data to make decisions, offer predictions, and perform tasks. AI algorithms can range from relatively simple decision trees to complex deep learning models, depending on the specific application within the education system. These algorithms are mathematical formulas or statistical processes used to find patterns in data. They are the core of any AI system and directly influence its ability to perform tasks and make decisions. In the context of an AI-driven automated education system, AI algorithms play various roles. For instance, machine learning algorithms can personalize learning by adapting content to individual student's needs based on their learning styles and progress. They can also assist in administrative tasks, such as scheduling and grading, and provide predictive analytics for student performance and attrition rates.

Once the appropriate algorithms have been selected, training the AI models is the next step. Model training involves feeding the algorithm with data and allowing it to adjust its parameters to predict better or classify the output. This process involves splitting the available data into training and validation sets. The algorithm learns from the training data and then fine-tunes its parameters based on the validation data to avoid overfitting (where the model learns too well and performs poorly on unseen data) (Lucchese et al., 2016). Model training might involve feeding the algorithm data about students' past performance, engagement levels, learning preferences, and other relevant factors in an educational setting. The model then learns from this data to predict future performance or recommend personalized learning resources.

It is worth noting that the training process often requires significant computational resources, especially for complex models like deep neural networks. Cloud computing platforms and specialized hardware like Graphics Processing Units are commonly used. Furthermore, the choice of training data is crucial. The data needs to be representative of the problem at hand. The resulting AI model will also be biased if the training data is biased. For instance, if an AI model designed to predict student success is only trained on data from a specific demographic, its predictions for other demographics might not be accurate. Model training is iterative. After the initial training, the model's performance needs to be evaluated, and if necessary, the model needs to be retrained or fine-tuned. The evaluation process often involves using a separate test data set to check the model's performance on unseen data. The training and implementation of AI models also involve ethical considerations. Data privacy is paramount, particularly when dealing with sensitive student data. Appropriate measures should be taken to anonymize data and protect student identities.

8.4.3 SYSTEM INTEGRATION AND TESTING

Implementing an AI-driven automated education system is not just about the data infrastructure or AI algorithms. System integration and testing are equally important parts of this process (Savadjiev et al., 2019). These process stages ensure that the AI system functions well within the existing education infrastructure and performs as expected. System integration is the process of combining the different components of the AI system and ensuring they function together seamlessly. In an AI-driven automated education system, this involves integrating the AI algorithms and models with the existing educational software and databases. This integration must be executed so that the AI system can interact with the existing components efficiently and effectively. The integration process often involves Application Programming Interfaces (APIs) that allow different software components to communicate with each other (Perrotta et al., 2021). For example, an AI algorithm designed to personalize learning content may need to interact with a Learning Management System (LMS) to access course content and student performance data. A well-designed API can facilitate this interaction. The next step is system testing once the AI system has been integrated into the broader education system. Testing is crucial to ensure the system functions as expected and to identify and address any issues or bugs.

Testing an AI system is somewhat different from testing traditional software. Because AI systems learn and adapt over time, their behavior can be less predictable, and the output for a given input might change as the system learns. As such, testing an AI system often involves checking if the system is working correctly and evaluating the quality of its predictions or decisions. In an educational context, testing an AI system might involve verifying that it can correctly access and process data from the LMS, make accurate predictions about student performance, and that its recommendations for personalized learning are appropriate and effective. Importantly, testing should not be a one-time activity. Given the dynamic nature of AI systems, regular testing and monitoring are necessary to ensure that the system continues to perform well as it interacts with new data and as the educational environment evolves. Beyond functional testing, it is also crucial to test the system from a user perspective. It means evaluating the system's usability and effectiveness in achieving its educational objectives. User testing can provide valuable feedback and help identify areas for improvement. Lastly, integrating an AI system into education is not just a technical challenge. It also involves considering how the system will affect the users educators and students. Data privacy, fairness, and transparency must be addressed to ensure that the AI system is ethical and beneficial.

8.4.4 UI AND EXPERIENCE DESIGN

Implementing an AI-driven automated education system is incomplete without a robust UI and a thoughtfully designed user experience (UX) (Grigera et al., 2023). After all, it is through this interface that students, educators, and administrators will interact with the AI system. A well-designed interface and UX can make the difference between a system that frustrates users and enhances the educational process.

The UI is the point of human–computer interaction and communication in a device. In an AI-driven automated education system, this could be a web portal, a mobile app, or a voice-based interface. The interface's design directly affects the user's perception of and ability to use the system effectively. Designing the UI for an AI-driven system presents unique challenges and opportunities. Unlike traditional software, AI systems often can learn and adapt to individual users. The interface may need to change and evolve based on the user's interactions and preferences. This adaptability can provide a more personalized and engaging UX, but it also requires careful design to ensure that changes in the interface do not confuse or frustrate users. The UX goes beyond the UI (Rajeshkumar et al., 2013). It encompasses all aspects of the user's interaction with the system, including how easy it is to use, how it makes the user feel, and how well it meets their needs and expectations. In an AI-driven automated education system, the UX design should focus on enhancing the learning process, supporting educators, and streamlining administrative tasks. For students, a well-designed UX could mean a system that adapts to their learning style, provides personalized feedback, and helps them stay engaged and motivated. For educators, it could mean a system that reduces administrative workload, offers insights into student performance, and supports differentiated instruction. For administrators, it could mean a system that automates routine tasks, provides data-driven insights, and helps improve the efficiency and effectiveness of the educational institution. A key aspect of UX design is user testing (Kuniavsky, 2010). It involves testing the system with actual users to get feedback and identify areas for improvement. In the context of an AI-driven automated education system, user testing could involve students, teachers, and administrators using the system and providing feedback on its usability, usefulness, and overall experience.

Another important consideration in UX design for AI systems is transparency and control. Users should clearly understand what the AI system is doing, why it is doing it, and how it is making its decisions. They should also have some level of control over the system's actions. For example, if the system is making recommendations for personalized learning, students and teachers should understand the basis for these recommendations and have the ability to override them if necessary.

8.5 ETHICAL CONSIDERATIONS IN AI-POWERED EDUCATION

8.5.1 DATA PRIVACY AND SECURITY

As we embrace the transformative power of AI in education, it is equally important to address the ethical considerations that come with it. Among these, data privacy and security emerge as paramount concerns. Given the sensitive nature of information in an educational setting, these issues cannot be overlooked. AI-driven automated education systems rely heavily on data. From personal details of students to their learning patterns and academic performance, an array of information is used to personalize learning experiences, predict performance, and manage administrative tasks. This heavy reliance on data raises critical questions about how this information is collected, used, and protected. Data privacy revolves around the right to control personal information (Nair and Tyagi, 2021). In an AI-driven education system, this means ensuring that students, parents, and educators are fully aware of the data being collected and its use. Transparency is a key principle here. Users should be provided with clear, understandable information about the system's data practices and be able to opt in or out of data collection and use.

Another key aspect of data privacy is the concept of data minimization (Antignac et al., 2017). This principle suggests that only the data necessary to achieve a specific purpose should be collected and used. Applying this principle in an AI-driven education system could mean, for instance, only collecting student performance data relevant to personalizing a learning experience and avoiding unnecessary personal information. Data security, on the other hand, is about protecting data from unauthorized access and breaches. As AI-driven education systems store and process vast amounts of sensitive data, they can become cyberattack targets. It makes robust security measures indispensable. Effective data security involves a range of practices, such as encryption, access control, and regular security audits. Encryption involves transforming data into a format that can only be read with a decryption key, providing a robust defense against unauthorized access. Access control means ensuring that only authorized individuals can access certain data, and regular security audits involve systematically checking the system's security measures and addressing any vulnerabilities. Furthermore, any data breaches should be promptly addressed, with affected parties notified as data protection regulations require. In addition, organizations should have contingency plans to respond to and recover from security incidents.

Balancing the benefits of AI with these ethical considerations is a challenge. Striking the right balance requires ongoing dialogue among educators, administrators, technologists, and policymakers. Legal frameworks, such as the European Union's General Data Protection Regulation, can provide useful guidelines, but given the rapid pace of AI technology, ongoing vigilance and proactive ethical considerations are necessary.

8.5.2 AI BIAS AND FAIRNESS

Implementing AI in education is a powerful tool that can revolutionize learning but also brings forth important ethical considerations. Among these, the issues of AI bias and fairness are particularly significant. AI bias refers to the tendencies of AI systems to make unjust, prejudiced, or inequitable decisions. It typically happens when the data used to train the AI system reflects societal or historical biases or when the AI algorithms unintentionally favor certain groups over others. In AI-powered education, bias can manifest in numerous ways, including skewed performance predictions, unfair personalization of learning content, or discriminatory administrative decisions.

One common form of bias is selection bias, which can occur if the data used to train the AI system does not represent all student groups.

For instance, if an AI model intended to predict student success is trained predominantly on data from urban students, its predictions may be less accurate for rural students (Simpson, 2006). Another form of bias is confirmation bias, which happens when an AI system reinforces existing prejudices. For example, if an AI tutoring system consistently recommends advanced math topics to boys more than to girls based on partial historical data, it could perpetuate gender stereotypes.

Addressing AI bias requires a combination of technical and nontechnical strategies (Glauner et al., 2016). On the technical side, efforts should be made to ensure that the data used to train the AI system is diverse and representative. Techniques like bias detection and mitigation can also be employed during the AI model development process. These techniques aim to identify and reduce bias in the AI model's predictions. On the nontechnical side, involving a diverse group in the AI development process can help bring multiple perspectives and identify potential biases that might not be obvious to a more homogenous group. In addition, transparency about the AI system's decision-making process can help users understand and question its predictions or decisions. Closely related to the issue of bias is fairness. In AI-powered education, fairness can mean that the system provides equitable learning opportunities for all students, regardless of their background or characteristics. It can also mean that the system's predictions or decisions do not unfairly disadvantage any student group.

In AI-powered education, achieving fairness is challenging because fairness can mean different things in different contexts (Hakami et al., 2020). However, some general strategies can help promote fairness. These include involving stakeholders in decision-making about the AI system, regularly reviewing and updating the AI system to address any emerging fairness issues, and prioritizing transparency so that users can understand and challenge the system's decisions.

8.5.3 THE DIGITAL DIVIDE AND ACCESSIBILITY

Incorporating AI in education holds immense promise for enhancing learning experiences and outcomes. However, it also comes with ethical considerations that we must address: the digital divide and accessibility. The "digital divide" refers to the gap between those with ready access to computers and the internet and those without access (Luttrell et al., 2020). In an AI-powered education system, the digital divide can be exacerbated if some students lack the necessary technology or internet connectivity to engage with AI tools fully. For instance, AI-driven personalized learning tools can provide rich, customized educational experiences. Still, these benefits can only be realized if students can access a device and a reliable internet connection. Without these, students can be left behind, widening educational disparities. Addressing the digital divide requires multifaceted solutions involving technological, policy, and community initiatives. Efforts to provide affordable devices and internet access are critical on the technology front. On the policy side, legislation can help ensure equitable access to technology through grants or public Wi-Fi initiatives. Community programs can also help by providing technology resources and training for students and families who lack them. Even when students have access to technology, there is another crucial consideration: accessibility. AI-driven education systems should be designed so that all students, including those with disabilities, can engage with them fully and effectively.

Accessibility in this context goes beyond compliance with regulations such as the Americans with Disabilities Act in the United States or the Web Content Accessibility Guidelines internationally (Bozkurt, 2023). It ensures that all students benefit from the AI-driven education system, regardless of their abilities or disabilities. Designing for accessibility can involve a range of practices. For instance, an AI-driven tutoring system might include text-to-speech functionality to support students with visual impairments or speech-to-text functionality to assist students with hearing impairments. AI systems can also be designed to be compatible with assistive technologies like screen readers. Nevertheless, accessibility is not just about technical features. It is also about designing the UX to be intuitive and inclusive. It might involve user testing with a diverse group of students, including those with disabilities, to ensure the system is easy to use and meets the needs of all learners. Beyond these considerations, ethical AI design in education should also be mindful of students' varying learning needs and preferences. AI systems should strive to offer a customizable UX, accommodating the diverse ways students engage with educational content.

8.6 CONCLUSION

Integrating AI in education is a transformative venture with opportunities and challenges. The benefits of AI-powered education are numerous, from personalized learning experiences to efficient administrative processes and insightful data analytics. However, these benefits come with significant ethical considerations, including data privacy, AI bias, the digital divide, and accessibility. As we strive toward an era of AI-powered education, it becomes crucial to strike a balance between harnessing the potential of AI and addressing these ethical considerations. As discussed earlier, machine learning and predictive analytics provide remarkable tools for understanding and shaping students' learning journeys. They enable adaptive learning paths, informed predictions on student performance, and efficient administrative functions. However, the proper handling and interpretation of data, in adherence to ethical standards, will determine the effectiveness and acceptability of these technologies.

NNs and deep learning, the core of many advanced AI systems, offer unprecedented capabilities for understanding complex patterns in student data and crafting personalized educational experiences. However, the same power that makes these technologies exciting makes them susceptible to bias and fairness concerns. RPA also brings an immense potential for improving efficiency in educational processes, allowing educators to focus more on their core teaching responsibilities. Nevertheless, it, too, like other AI technologies, must be implemented thoughtfully to respect privacy and maintain security. From a system's perspective, we dove into the data infrastructure, AI algorithms, system integration, and UI and experience. Each element forms a crucial part of an AI-driven automated education system. However, as we construct these systems, we must ensure they are designed to be technically robust, ethically sound, accessible, and equitable. Finally, we delved into critical ethical considerations of AI-powered education. Data privacy and security, AI bias and fairness, the digital divide, and accessibility are issues that demand our attention as we design and implement these systems. Addressing these ethical considerations is not just a legal obligation or a nice-to-have feature. It is a critical prerequisite for building trust among students, educators, and parents, which, in turn, is key for successfully adopting AI in education.

A few key conclusions emerge as we reflect on our journey through this chapter. First, AI offers immense potential for enhancing education, but this potential can only be fully realized if we address the ethical considerations it brings. Second, while each AI technology offers unique benefits and challenges, common themes of data privacy, bias, fairness, the digital divide, and accessibility run across them all. Third, the success of AI in education hinges not just on the technologies themselves but on how they are implemented—from the data infrastructure and AI algorithms to the UI, UX, and system integration.

KEYWORDS

- **artificial intelligence**
- **benefits and challenges**
- **education system**
- **personalized learning**

REFERENCES

Ahmad, S. F., Alam, M. M., Rahmat, M. K., Mubarik, M. S. & Hyder, S.I . (2022). Academic and administrative role of artificial intelligence in education. *Sustainability*, 14(3), 11–22.

Ainscow, M. & Sandill, A. (2010). Developing inclusive education systems: The role of organisational cultures and leadership. *International Journal of Inclusive Education*, 14(4), 401–416.

Alam, A. & Mohanty, A. (2023). Foundation for the future of higher education or 'misplaced optimism'? Being human in the age of artificial intelligence. *First International Conference*, ICIICC. Springer International Publishing.

Alam, A. (2021). Should robots replace teachers? Mobilisation of AI and learning analytics in education. *International Conference on Advances in Computing, Communication, and Control (ICAC3)*, IEEE.

Alam, A. (2022). Employing adaptive learning and intelligent tutoring robots for virtual classrooms and smart campuses: Reforming education in the age of artificial intelligence. *Advanced Computing and Intelligent Technologies: Proceedings of ICACIT*. Springer Nature Singapore.

Ali, S., Abuhmed, T., El-Sappagh, S., Muhammad, K., Alonso-Moral, J. M., Confalonieri, R., Guidotti, R., Del Ser, J., Díaz-Rodríguez, N. & Herrera, F. (2023). Explainable artificial intelligence (XAI): What we know and what is left to attain trustworthy artificial intelligence. *Information Fusion*, 2, 10–18.

Antignac, T., Sands, D. & Schneider, G. (2017). Data minimisation: A language-based approach. *ICT Systems Security and Privacy Protection: 32nd IFIP TC 11 International Conference, Proceedings 32*. Springer International Publishing.

Bacciu, D., Akarmazyan, S., Armengaud, E., Bacco, M., Bravos, G. C., Calandra, C., Carlini, E., Carta, A., Cassarà, P., Coppola, M. & Davalas, C. (2021). Teaching-trustworthy autonomous cyber-physical applications through human-centered intelligence. *International Conference on Omni-Layer Intelligent Systems (COINS)*. IEEE.

Baker, R. S. D., Corbett, A. T., Koedinger, K. R., Evenson, S., Roll, I., Wagner, A. Z., Naim, M., Raspat, J., Baker, D. J. & Beck, J. E. (2006). Adapting to when students game an intelligent tutoring system. *8th International Conference, ITS, Proceedings 8*. Springer.

Bozkurt, A. (2023). Generative artificial intelligence (AI) powered conversational educational agents: The inevitable paradigm shift. *Asian Journal of Distance Education*. https://doi.org/10.5281/zenodo.7716416.

Brabazon, A. & O'Neill, M. (2006). Neural network methodologies. *Biologically Inspired Algorithms for Financial Modelling*. https://link.springer.com/book/10.1007/3-540-31307-9.

Buitrago, P. A., Nystrom, N. A., Gupta, R. & Saltz, J. (2020). Delivering scalable deep learning to research with bridges-AI. *6th Latin American Conference*, CARLA. Springer International Publishing.

Bursley, M. (2021). Job impact on automation in accounting: What will happen to job availability?, *Journal for Global Business and Community*, 12(1), 10–10.

Calandra, D., De Lorenzis, F., Cannavò, A. & Lamberti, F. (2022). Immersive virtual reality and passive haptic interfaces to improve procedural learning in a formal training course for first responders. *Virtual Reality*, 6, 1–28.

Cao, L. (2022). A new age of AI: Features and futures. *Intelligent Systems*, 37(1), 25–37.

Ciolacu, M., Svasta, P. M., Berg, W. & Popp, H. (2017). Education 4.0 for tall thin engineers in a data-driven society. *23rd International Symposium for Design and Technology in Electronic Packaging (SIITME)*, IEEE.

Cox, A. M. (2021). Exploring the impact of Artificial Intelligence and robots on higher education through literature-based design fiction. *International Journal of Educational Technology in Higher Education*, 18(1), 3–10.

Da'u, A. & Salim, N. (2020). Recommendation system based on deep learning methods: a systematic review and new directions. *Artificial Intelligence Review*, 53(4), 2709–2748.

Dai, C. P. & Ke, F. (2022). Educational applications of artificial intelligence in simulation-based learning: A systematic mapping review. *Computers and Education: Artificial Intelligence*, 12, 10–27.

Darvishi, A., Khosravi, H., Abdi, S., Sadiq, S. & Gašević, D. (2022). June. Incorporating training, self-monitoring and AI-assistance to improve peer feedback quality. *The Ninth ACM Conference on Learning@ Scale*.

Dwivedi, Y. K., Hughes, L., Ismagilova, E., Aarts, G., Coombs, C., Crick, T., Duan, Y., Dwivedi, R., Edwards, J., Eirug, A. & Galanos, V. (2021). Artificial Intelligence (AI): Multidisciplinary perspectives on emerging challenges, opportunities, and agenda for research, practice and policy. *International Journal of Information Management*, 57, 10–19.

Glauner, P., Meira, J. A., Valtchev, P., State, R. & Bettinger, F. (2016). The challenge of non-technical loss detection using artificial intelligence: A survey. https://arxiv.org/abs/1606.00626.

Goulart, V. G., Liboni, L. B. & Cezarino, L. O. (2022). Balancing skills in the digital transformation era: The future of jobs and the role of higher education. *Industry and Higher Education*, 36(2), 118–127.

Grigera, J., Espada, J. P. & Rossi, G. (2023). AI in User Interface Design and Evaluation. *IT Professional*, 25(2), 20–22.

Guache, M., Manaig, K., Tesoro, J. F., Yazon, A. & Sapin, S. (2023). Beyond words: Uncovering the untold stories of multilingual students' lived experiences in online distance learning. *Journal of Elementary and Secondary School*, 1(1), 2–15.

Guilherme, A. (2019). AI and education: the importance of teacher and student relations. *AI & Society*, 34, 47–54.

Hakami, E. & Davinia, H. L. (2020). How are learning analytics considering the societal values of fairness, accountability, transparency and human well-being?: A literature review. https://ceur-ws.org/Vol-2671/paper12.pdf.

Haniya, S. (2023). Transcending the spatial boundaries in large lecture settings via e-learning: Strategies for a Change. *Society for Information Technology & Teacher Education International Conference*. https://www.learntechlib.org/p/222183/.

Hernandez-de-Menendez, M., Escobar, D. C. & Morales-Menendez, R. (2020). Technologies for the future of learning: state of the art. *International Journal on Interactive Design and Manufacturing*, 14, 683–695.

Hussin, H., Jiea, P. Y., Rosly, R. N. R. & Omar, S. R. (2019). Integrated 21st century science, technology, engineering, mathematics (STEM) intelligent tutoring system. 8th International Conference, ITS. Proceedings 8. Springer Berlin Heidelberg.

Issac, R., Muni, R. & Desai, K. (2018). Delineated analysis of robotic process automation tools. *Second International Conference on Advances in Electronics, Computers and Communications (ICAECC)*, IEEE.

Jogin, M., Madhulika, M. S., Divya, G. D., Meghana, R. K. & Apoorva, S. (2018). Feature extraction using convolution neural networks (CNN) and deep learning. 3rd IEEE *International Conference on Recent Trends in Electronics, Information & Communication Technology (RTEICT)*, IEEE.

Jones, P. (2010). Collaboration at a distance: Using a wiki to create a collaborative learning environment for distance education and on-campus students in a social work course. *Journal of Teaching in Social Work*, 30(2), 225–236.

Kamruzzaman, M. M., Alanazi, S., Alruwaili, M., Alshammari, N., Elaiwat, S., Abu-Zanona, M., Innab, N., Mohammad, E. B. & Ahmed A. B. (2023). AI-and IoT-assisted sustainable education systems during pandemics, such as COVID-19, for smart cities. *Sustainability*, 15(10), 12–33.

Katal, A. & Singh, N. (2022). Artificial neural network: Models, applications, and challenges. *Innovative Trends in Computational Intelligence*, 12, 235–257.

Khogali, H. O. & Mekid, S. (2023). The blended future of automation and AI: Examining some long-term societal and ethical impact features. *Technology in Society*, 73, 10–22.

Koivisto, J. M., Niemi, H., Multisilta, J. & Eriksson, E. (2017). Nursing students' experiential learning processes using an online 3D simulation game. *Education & Information Technologies*, 22, 383–398.

Kommey, B., Keelson, E., Samuel, F., Twum-Asare, S. & Akuffo, K. K. (2022). Automatic Multiple Choice Examination Questions Marking and Grade Generator Software. *The Journal for Technology and Science*, 33(3), 175–189.

Kumar, P. R. & Manash, E. B. K. (2019). Deep learning: A branch of machine learning. *Journal of Physics*, 1228(1), 12–45.

Kuniavsky, M. (2010). Smart things: ubiquitous computing user experience design. https://www.sciencedirect.com/book/9780123748997/smart-things?via=ihub.

Lasso-Rodríguez, G. & Gil-Herrera, R. (2019). Robotic process automation applied to education: A new kind of robot teacher? *12th Annual International Conference of Education, Research and Innovation*, IATED.

Laurillard, D., Oliver, M., Wasson, B. & Hoppe, U. (2009). Implementing technology-enhanced learning. technology-enhanced learning: Principles and Products. https://link.springer.com/book/10.1007/978-1-4020-9827-7.

Lucchese, C., Nardini, F. M., Orlando, S., Perego, R., Silvestri, F. & Trani, S. (2016). Post-learning optimisation of tree ensembles for efficient ranking. *The 39th International ACM SIGIR Conference on Research and Development in Information Retrieval*.

Luttrell, R., Wallace, A., McCollough, C. & Lee, J. (2020). The digital divide: Addressing artificial intelligence in communication education. *Journalism & Mass Communication Educator*, 75(4), 470–482.

Markauskaite, L., Marrone, R., Poquet, O., Knight, S., Martinez-Maldonado, R., Howard, S., Tondeur, J., De Laat, M., Shum, S. B., Gašević, D. & Siemens, G. (2022). Rethinking the entwinement between artificial intelligence and human learning: What capabilities do learners need for a world with AI? *Computers and Education: Artificial Intelligence*, 3, 10–16.

Meszaros, J. (2022). The next challenge for data protection law: AI revolution in automated scientific research. https://papers.ssrn.com/sol3/papers.cfm?abstract_id=4030901.

Mhlanga, D. (2023). Open AI in education, the responsible and ethical use of ChatGPT towards lifelong learning. Education, the responsible and ethical use of ChatGPT towards lifelong learning. https://papers.ssrn.com/sol3/papers.cfm?abstract_id=4354422.

Nair, M. M. & Tyagi, A. K. (2021). Privacy: History, statistics, policy, laws, preservation and threat analysis. *Journal of Information Assurance & Security*, 16(1), 12–14.

Ochoa, X., Lang, C., Siemens, G., Wise, A., Gasevic, D. & Merceron, A. (2022). Multimodal learning analytics-Rationale, process, examples, and direction. The Handbook of Learning Analytics, 54–65.

Pan, Z., Yu, W., Yi, X., Khan, A., Yuan, F. & Zheng, Y. (2019). Recent progress on generative adversarial networks (GANs): A survey. *IEEE Access*, 7, 36322–36333.

Pantelimon, F. V., Bologa, R., Toma, A. & Posedaru, B. S. (2021). The evolution of AI-driven educational systems during the COVID-19 pandemic. *Sustainability*, 13(23), 13–25.

Perrotta, C. & Selwyn, N. (2020). Deep learning goes to school: Toward a relational understanding of AI in education. *Learning, Media and Technology*, 45(3), 251–269.

Perrotta, C., Gulson, K. N., Williamson, B. & Witzenberger, K. (2021). Automation, APIs and the distributed labour of platform pedagogies in Google Classroom. *Critical Studies in Education*, 62(1), 97–113.

Prinsloo, P., Slade, S. & Khalil, M. (2022). The answer is (not only) technological: Considering student data privacy in learning analytics. *British Journal of Educational Technology*, 53(4), 876–893.

Puthal, D., Mishra, A. K. & Sharma, S. (2021). AI-driven security solutions for the internet of everything. *IEEE Consumer Electronics Magazine*, 10(5), 70–71.

Rajeshkumar, S., Omar, R. & Mahmud, M. (2013). Taxonomies of user experience (UX) evaluation methods. *International Conference on Research and Innovation in Information Systems (ICRIIS)*. IEEE.

Rodney, B. D. (2020). Understanding the paradigm shift in education in the twenty-first century: The role of technology and the Internet of Things. *Worldwide Hospitality and Tourism Themes*. https://doi.org/10.1108/WHATT-10-2019-0068.

Salloum, S. A., Khan, R. & Shaalan, K. (2020). A survey of semantic analysis approaches. *International Conference on Artificial Intelligence and Computer Vision (AICV)*. Springer International Publishing.

Savadjiev, P., Chong, J., Dohan, A., Vakalopoulou, M., Reinhold, C., Paragios, N. & Gallix, B. (2019). Demystification of AI-driven medical image interpretation: past, present and future. *European Radiology*, 29, 1616–1624.

Schiff, D., Rakova, B., Ayesh, A., Fanti, A. & Lennon, M. (2021). Explaining the principles to practices gap in AI. *IEEE Technology and Society Magazine*, 40(2), 81–94.

Sherstinsky, A. (2020). Fundamentals of recurrent neural network (RNN) and long short-term memory (LSTM) network. *Physica D: Non-linear Phenomena*, 404, 13–23.

Shin, D. (2022). How do people judge the credibility of algorithmic sources? *AI & Society*, 8, 1–16.

Simpson, O. (2006). Predicting student success in open and distance learning. *The Journal of Open, Distance and e-Learning*, 21(2), 125–138.

Smuts, M., Gardner, M., Callaghan, V. & Gutierrez, A. G. (2019). Towards Dynamically Adaptable Immersive Spaces for Learning. *11th Computer Science and Electronic Engineering (CEEC)*, IEEE.

Steenbergen-Hu, S. & Cooper, H. (2014). A meta-analysis of the effectiveness of intelligent tutoring systems on college students' academic learning. *Journal of Educational Psychology*, 106(2), 331–344.

Syed, R., Suriadi, S., Adams, M., Bandara, W., Leemans, S. J., Ouyang, C., Hofstede, T. A. H., Weerd, I. V. D., Wynn, M. T. & Reijers, H. A. (2020). Robotic process automation: contemporary themes and challenges. *Computers in Industry*, 115, 10–31.

Taub, M., Azevedo, R., Rajendran, R., Cloude, E. B., Biswas, G. & Price, M. J. (2021). How are students' emotions related to the accuracy of cognitive and metacognitive processes during learning with an intelligent tutoring system? *Learning and Instruction*, 72, 10–22.

Turcu, C. & Turcu, C. (2020). On robotic process automation and its integration in higher education. *Conference Proceedings, The Future of Education*.

Votto, A. M., Valecha, R., Najafirad, P. & Rao, H. R. (2021). Artificial intelligence in tactical human resource management: A systematic literature review. *International Journal of Information Management*, 58, 10–24.

Wang, L., Zhao, H., Wang, D., Liu, Z., Alok, R. & Cheng, S. (2017). Integrating cloud computing and internet of things: A future roadmap. *13th International Conference on Natural Computation, Fuzzy Systems and Knowledge Discovery (ICNC-FSKD)*, IEEE.

Wong, L. H., King, R. B., Chai, C. S. & Liu, M. (2016). Seamlessly learning Chinese: Contextual meaning making and vocabulary growth in a seamless Chinese as a second language learning environment. *Instructional Science*, 44, 399–422.

Wu, M., Vo, H. T., Vo, B. T., Vo, B. & Hwang, D. (2020). Review on the application of robotic process automation in blockchain for decentralized autonomous organizations. *4th Advanced Information Management, Communicates, Electronic and Automation Control Conference (IMCEC)*, IEEE.

Xie, H., Chu, H. C., Hwang, G. J. & Wang, C. C. (2019). Trends and development in technology-enhanced adaptive/personalised learning: A systematic review of journal publications from 2007 to 2017. *Computers & Education*, 140, 10–35.

Xue, Y., Hensman, J. & Rasmussen, C. E. (2020). Data-efficient learning of feedback policies from image pixels using deep dynamical models. https://arxiv.org/abs/1510.02173.

Yang, B., Liu, D., He, Q., Zhang, M. & Zhang, Y. (2019). A survey on deep learning-based fine-grained object recognition and attribute detection. *The 27th ACM International Conference on Multimedia.*

Yang, J., Lin, Q., Qi, B., Zhang, L., Lu, T. & Qi, J. (2022). Edge intelligence for 5G-enabled internet of things: A comprehensive survey and future perspectives. *IEEE Internet of Things Journal*, 10(2), 2221–2243.

Yang, S. (2022). Recognizing Textual Entailment with BERT and GPT-2-based Models. https://medium.com/@livajorge7/gpt-3-bert-and-roberta-ai-model-analysis-comparison-7dfab049367d.

CHAPTER 9

Digitalization of Education: Postpandemic Indian Perspective

RITU PAREEK

Birla Institute of Technology, Mesra, Jaipur Campus, India

ABSTRACT

The COVID-19 pandemic has had a significant impact on education systems worldwide, forcing institutions to switch to online and virtual platforms to continue their activities. India, like many other countries, has been forced to move to virtual education. However, this country has a significant digital divide, with limited access to devices and affordability, making the digitization of education difficult. This situation is further exacerbated by disparities in digital literacy, which are significantly lower in rural areas and among disadvantaged populations. In addition, the digital divide between men and women has become a major concern in India. Women face significant barriers to education, and the shift to e-learning has only exacerbated the situation. The use of satellite programs that can be broadcast on community TV sets, as well as the installation of projection screens, are proposed in this chapter for the vocational and academic training of disadvantaged female populations.

9.1 INTRODUCTION

COVID-19, scientifically known as severe acute respiratory syndrome coronavirus 2, emerged as a novel coronavirus in late 2019 in Wuhan

Corporate Governance, Digitalization, and Energy Transition: Imen Baccouche and Afef Khalil. (Eds.)

DOI: 10.1201/9781779643407-11

City, China. It has since caused the global pandemic known as COVID-19. Numerous international organizations (IOs) and policy entrepreneurs promptly recognized the health crisis as a political opening to acquire global credibility and exert influence over public policy agendas (Debre & Dijkstra, 2021). Before the pandemic, the world was already grappling with a learning crisis, characterized by high levels of learning poverty. However, the outbreak of COVID-19 resulted in the temporary closure of schools in over 160 countries, affecting more than 90% of the global student population. Additional localized closures impacted millions of learners worldwide. The World Bank estimates that school closures have affected approximately 1.6 billion children and youth globally. In India, the government implemented a nationwide lockdown, leading to the complete cessation of the learning process as schools and universities were shut down. Concerns have been raised regarding the long-term consequences of widespread school closures, including a potential loss of learning, diminished human capital, and reduced economic opportunities.

Governments across the globe have implemented various measures to mitigate the impact of COVID-19, including the adoption of remote learning approaches to manage the crisis. According to a recent publication by the United Nations Educational, Scientific and Cultural Organization (UNESCO, 2015), global closures of educational institutions have affected more than 60% of the global student population (UNESCO, 2020). Furthermore, numerous other nations have also enforced localized closures, impacting millions more learners (Charissi et al., 2020). The World Bank has been collaborating with numerous countries to provide support to Ministries of Education in offering remote learning opportunities during school closures. The COVID-19 pandemic has brought about an extraordinary situation, one that has not been experienced before. Due to its unprecedented nature, there has been a lack of comprehensive research on the widespread use and effectiveness of online learning platforms during such crises. Hence, the primary focus of this chapter is to delve into how COVID-19 has catalyzed the digital revolution in education. By doing so, the researcher aims to understand the ramifications and consequences of this abrupt shift in the educational paradigm.

One significant implication of this rapid transition to online learning was the apparent need for reliable and accessible technology. Inequities in technology access among students and educators were brought to the forefront. Another crucial aspect to consider is the potential complexity of accessing computers and Wi-Fi in certain regions. Consequently, mobile learning emerges as a significant solution to overcome these technical obstacles (Al-Adwan, 2020). While some students easily adapted to digital learning, others faced challenges due to a lack of devices, internet connectivity, or digital literacy. This stark digital divide exposed the urgency of addressing technological disparities to ensure inclusive and equitable education for all.

The shift to online education also had an impact on teaching methodologies and instructional strategies. In many situations, the pandemic caused a shift in the typical priorities of schools and teachers. They moved away from performance-driven obligations and outcomes-based management, focusing instead on more fundamental concerns like ensuring educational access and delivery, as well as promoting students' well-being (Netolicky, 2020; Lepp et al., 2021). Educators had to rethink their approaches to engage students effectively in a virtual environment. Traditional classroom techniques had to be modified to suit online platforms, emphasizing the importance of interactive and engaging content. This necessitated the exploration and development of new pedagogical tools and practices tailored to the digital realm.

Acknowledging the forthcoming "new normal" that will follow the COVID-19 phase, it is imperative to make adjustments to the educational landscape from the perspective of curriculum studies (Khan et al., 2021). Furthermore, the pandemic accelerated the adoption of artificial intelligence (AI) and machine learning technologies in the educational landscape. Educational institutions began leveraging AI for personalized learning experiences, intelligent tutoring systems, and data analytics to assess student progress and identify areas for improvement. The integration of AI-based learning tools has shown great potential in enhancing the efficiency and effectiveness of education, offering tailored learning experiences to students. Nevertheless, the sudden reliance on online learning also highlighted some challenges. Maintaining student motivation and preventing feelings of isolation proved to be significant obstacles in the virtual environment. Additionally, ensuring the integrity of online assessments and tackling issues related to academic integrity became crucial concerns for educators and institutions. Our chapter aims to:

1. Address several key objectives related to the impact of the COVID-19 pandemic on the education sector in India.

2. Emphasize the diverse challenges and opportunities that have emerged as a result of COVID-19 in the realm of education.
3. Identify and list the trends that have emerged in the education sector post-COVID-19.
4. Propose effective suggestions to ensure the continuity of educational activities during the postpandemic situation.

9.2 LITERATURE REVIEW

According to Sansa (2020), animals serve as the source of COVID-19, and the primary mode of transmission is human-to-human through respiratory droplets expelled during sneezing, coughing, or exhaling. In their article titled "Seven Scenarios," McKibbin and Roshen (2020) examined the global macroeconomic impacts of COVID-19. They emphasized the uncertain nature of the virus's evolution, making it challenging for policymakers to formulate appropriate macroeconomic policies. To understand potential economic outcomes, McKibbin and Roshen (2020) employed a modeling technique and explored seven different scenarios for the future development of the virus. By utilizing a global hybrid dynamic stochastic general equilibrium/computable general equilibrium model, they assessed the effects of these scenarios on macroeconomic outcomes and financial markets. The study revealed that even if the pandemic is contained, it can still have significant short-term impacts on the global economy. These scenarios highlight the potential costs that could be mitigated through increased investment in public health systems across all economies, particularly in less developed regions with high population density and underdeveloped healthcare systems.

Wenham et al. (2020) found a lack of gender analysis conducted by global health institutions or affected governments during the COVID-19 outbreak or in the preparedness phases. The closure of schools in countries like China, Hong Kong, Italy, and South Korea, which were implemented to control virus transmission, may have had a differential impact on women. As women predominantly provide informal care within families, the closure of schools limited their ability to work and restricted their economic opportunities.

9.3 METHODOLOGY

The methodology employed in this study primarily involves a comprehensive review of secondary data sources, such as newspaper articles, magazines, and journals. Additionally, insights were gathered from recently published journals, policy papers, and reports released by national and IOs. It is essential to acknowledge that the conceptual nature of the chapter poses a specific limitation. This limitation arises from the constrained availability of data, considering that the COVID-19 pandemic is an ongoing and evolving event. As a result, the study's findings should be interpreted with caution, considering the dynamic nature of the pandemic and the potential for new information to emerge.

9.4 EDUCATION IN INDIA

The present situation of education in India is a mixed bag. On the one hand, there has been significant progress in terms of access to education. The literacy rate has increased from 52.2% in 1991 to 77.0% in 2011. While the literacy rate for males was 82.14%, it was only 65.46% for females. Moreover, while urban areas boasted a literacy rate of 84.11%, rural areas had a much lower literacy rate of just 68.91%. On the other hand, there are still many challenges that need to be addressed. The quality of education is often poor, and there are significant disparities in access to education between different social groups. Education in India is overseen by both central and state governments and is offered in both public and private sectors. However, despite efforts to enhance educational access, a substantial portion of the inhabitants, especially in countryside areas, remain illiterate. According to the 2011 Census, the literacy rate in India stood at 74.04%, with marked disparities in terms of gender and geography. Hence, the disparity in education based on gender is not solely an outcome of the limited economic benefits associated with women's education; it also serves as an indicator of deep-seated prejudices that dampen the ambitions of women and other marginalized groups (McDougall, 2000).

The COVID-19 pandemic has exacerbated these challenges. The national lockdown that was imposed in March 2020 forced schools and colleges to close their doors. This led to a sudden and massive disruption in education. Millions of students were unable to attend school or college, and many teachers were unable to teach. The government responded to this crisis by launching various initiatives to support digital learning.

These initiatives included the launch of the National Digital Education Mission and the Pradhan Mantri Free Online Course scheme. However, these initiatives have faced several challenges, including the absence of an approach to digital tools and cyberspace connectivity in rural areas.

While the challenges posed by the pandemic are undeniable, it has also created an opportunity to expedite the digital transformation of education in India. In recent years, there has been a notable increase in the number of internet users across the country. However, it is important to acknowledge that the low penetration of internet access has primarily restricted its availability to privileged groups (Illavarasan, 2013). Despite this limitation, the current situation calls for concerted efforts to bridge the digital divide and ensure equitable access to digital education for all segments of society. By leveraging the potential of technology and expanding internet infrastructure, India can seize the opportunity to promote inclusive and accessible digital education, thereby fostering a more equitable and sustainable learning ecosystem. Despite the overall increase in internet usage, a significant portion of the population remains excluded from its benefits due to limited access and infrastructure constraints. The government has announced several initiatives to promote digital learning, including the launch of the National Education Policy (NEP) 2020. The NEP 2020 envisages a "digital-first" approach to education, and it calls for the use of technology to improve the quality and access to education. During times of crisis, numerous educational apps have been introduced as a means of providing education to students (Li & Lalani, 2020). These educational apps serve as valuable tools that facilitate remote learning, offering students access to a wide range of educational resources, interactive activities, and instructional materials. The digitalization of education has the potential to address many of the challenges that India faces in the edification sector. It can help to improve the quality of education by requiring access to high-quality resources and by making it possible for teachers to personalize instruction. It can also help to increase access to education by making it possible for students to learn from anywhere.

However, the process of digitalizing education is not without its challenges. A study conducted among school students in Delhi shed light on some of these obstacles, revealing that the lack of interaction and the presence of distractions in the home environment significantly hindered online learning (Khan et al., 2021). The shift to remote learning has exposed students to a new learning environment where the absence of face-to-face interaction with peers and teachers has had an impact on their engagement and motivation levels. Addressing these challenges requires a multifaceted approach. First, it is crucial to ensure that all students have equal access to digital devices and reliable internet connectivity, regardless of their socioeconomic background. This calls for infrastructure development and investment in remote areas to bridge the digital divide. Second, equipping teachers with the necessary skills and training to effectively integrate technology into their teaching practices is paramount. Professional development programs should focus on enhancing teachers' digital literacy, enabling them to leverage digital tools and platforms to deliver engaging and interactive lessons. Additionally, the digitalization of education necessitates the development of appropriate digital content and resources that align with the curriculum and cater to diverse learning styles. Collaborative efforts between educators, content creators, and policymakers are essential to ensure the availability of high-quality digital learning materials.

Furthermore, ensuring data privacy and cybersecurity measures is crucial to safeguard student information and protect it from potential risks associated with online platforms. Lastly, addressing the sociocultural barriers and mindset challenges related to digital education is vital. Parents, guardians, and community members should be engaged in understanding the benefits of digital education and be provided with support and resources to facilitate their involvement.

By addressing these challenges and implementing comprehensive strategies, India can successfully navigate the path of digitalizing education and enhance the quality and accessibility of education for all its learners. It is a complex process, but with careful planning, collaboration, and continuous evaluation, the digitalization of education holds immense potential to transform the educational landscape in India and empower learners for a brighter future. Despite these challenges, the digitalization of education has the potential to transform the education landscape in India. By addressing these challenges, India can reap the benefits of a more equitable and accessible education system.

9.5 EDUCATION CHALLENGES

In India, achieving education for all is impeded by various hurdles, including limited access to education in rural regions, which is highlighted as one of the most significant challenges. A report from the Ministry of Education indicates that over 70% of India's population resides in rural areas where access to quality education is often restricted due to inadequate infrastructure, including classrooms, teaching resources, and a shortage of skilled teachers.

Additionally, affordability is a major concern, particularly for impoverished families. Even though the government aims to provide free education, various expenses such as books, uniforms, and transportation costs can be prohibitive for many. Over 320 million pupils in India were affected by various measures and the nationwide COVID-19 lockout (Jena, 2020). Gender disparities further exacerbate the problem, as girls face social discrimination and pressure that discourages them from attending school. As per the 2011 Census, the literacy rate for females was only 65.46%, compared to males' literacy rate of 82.14%, emphasizing the gravity of the challenge.

9.5.1 DIGITAL GENDER GAP

The digital gender gap is an important aspect that requires attention in light of the digitalization of education in postpandemic India. This gap refers to the disparities between males and females in terms of access to and usage of digital technologies. The main causes include a lack of technical expertise, customs-related restrictions, inadequate education and skills, a lack of network connectivity (especially common in rural areas with poor broadband access), a lack of financial independence and exposure, underdeveloped infrastructure, and more (Upadhyay, 2021). According to Khokhar (2016), policy changes are necessary to improve digital literacy to close the digital divide. When examining the digital gender gap within the realm of education, several key points should be considered:

- Access to digital infrastructure: Girls in India face limited access to digital infrastructure, including internet connectivity and digital devices. This lack of access can hinder their participation in digital education initiatives and limit their ability to fully benefit from online learning resources.
- Sociocultural barriers: Gender biases, social norms, and cultural expectations can influence girls' access to and usage of digital technologies. Societal perceptions of gender roles may discourage

girls from pursuing digital education, leading to lower enrolment rates and reduced engagement in digital learning activities.

- Digital literacy and skills: There may be disparities in digital literacy and skills between boys and girls. Girls may have less exposure to digital technologies and, therefore, be less confident and proficient in using them. This lack of digital literacy can create barriers to their active participation in digital education programs.
- Safety and security concerns: Girls may face unique safety and security concerns while accessing digital platforms, particularly in online spaces. These concerns can lead to parental restrictions on digital access, further exacerbating the digital gender gap in education.
- Role of stereotypes and bias: Gender stereotypes and biases can influence the types of subjects or fields of study that girls are encouraged to pursue in digital education. Addressing these biases and promoting inclusive digital learning environments can help bridge the gender gap and foster equal opportunities for all.
- Empowerment and leadership: Digital education has the potential to empower girls by providing them with skills, knowledge, and opportunities for leadership. Research should explore the impact of digital education on girls' empowerment, their career aspirations, and their ability to participate in decision-making processes.
- Best practices and interventions: Research should identify and analyze successful interventions and best practices aimed at reducing the digital gender gap in education. This includes initiatives that promote digital literacy, provide mentorship and role models for girls, and create safe and inclusive learning environments.
- Policy recommendations: Based on research findings, policy recommendations should be developed to address the digital gender gap in education. These policies should focus on promoting equal access, providing digital literacy training for girls and women, and creating an enabling environment that encourages girls' active participation in digital education.

By examining the digital gender gap in the digitalization of education in postpandemic India, the chapter is an attempt to shed light on the specific challenges faced by girls and identify strategies and policies to promote gender equality in accessing and benefiting from digital education initiatives. Bridging the digital gender gap is crucial to ensure that girls have equal opportunities to thrive and contribute to a digitally inclusive society.

9.5.2 RURAL AREAS

The COVID-19 pandemic has highlighted the glaring digital divide in India, especially in rural areas and among underprivileged children. Recent data from the National Sample Survey Organization reveals that internet access is available to only 24% of rural households, in stark contrast to the 42% in urban areas. This stark disparity has posed significant challenges for schools in rural regions, particularly in facilitating online education during the pandemic. The lack of reliable internet connectivity and access to digital devices has further widened the educational gap, leaving many rural students unable to fully participate in remote learning initiatives. In a developing country like India with vast socioeconomic disparities, the digital divide has further widened the learning handicap and needs urgent attention from both public and private sector players to minimize the differences in opportunities for online learning (Sharma, 2020). Bridging this digital divide and ensuring equitable access to online education is a pressing need for India to promote inclusive and quality education for all learners, regardless of their geographical location or socioeconomic background.

- Limited internet connectivity: Rural areas in India often face challenges in terms of internet connectivity. Access to high-speed internet remains limited, and connectivity issues can hinder the implementation of digital education initiatives. However, efforts are being made to improve internet infrastructure in rural regions to bridge the digital divide.
- Availability of digital devices: The availability of digital devices such as computers, laptops, and smartphones in rural areas can be limited. Many households may lack the necessary hardware and devices required for online learning. However, initiatives like the government's Digital India campaign aim to increase digital literacy and provide access to affordable devices in rural areas.
- Infrastructure challenges: Rural areas often lack the necessary infrastructure to support digital education. Schools may have limited or no access to computer labs, high-speed internet, and other digital learning resources. Infrastructure development is

crucial to ensure the successful implementation of digital education initiatives in rural schools.

- Teacher training and digital literacy: There may be a need for teacher training programs focused on technological proficiency and the effective use of electronic devices in education in rural areas. Building the capacity of teachers to use digital tools and platforms can enhance the quality of digital education delivery in rural schools.
- Local language content: Many rural areas in India have a significant population that primarily communicates in regional or local languages. To make digital education more accessible and effective, there is a need for localized digital content and resources in regional languages that cater to the specific needs and cultural context of rural students.
- Community engagement and awareness: Engaging the local community is essential for the successful implementation of digital education initiatives in rural areas. Community participation can help create awareness, build support, and address concerns related to digital education. Involving parents, local leaders, and community organizations can contribute to the acceptance and integration of digital learning in rural communities.
- Power supply: A reliable electricity supply is crucial for the effective implementation of digital education in rural areas. Ensuring uninterrupted power availability is a significant challenge in many rural regions. Alternative energy sources and infrastructure development are needed to address this issue.
- Cost considerations: Affordability of digital devices and internet services is a significant concern in rural areas where households may have limited financial resources. Making digital education affordable and accessible for rural students requires considerations of cost-effective solutions and government support in terms of subsidies and schemes.
- Customized learning solutions: Considering the diverse learning needs and challenges in rural areas, there is a need for customized learning solutions that cater to the specific requirements of rural students. Tailoring digital education initiatives to address the unique educational context of rural areas can lead to better learning outcomes.

- The digitalization of education in rural areas is an ongoing process in India. While challenges exist, efforts are being made to address infrastructure limitations, improve connectivity, provide digital devices, and enhance digital literacy in rural communities. The goal is to provide students from rural areas with equivalent opportunities for quality education and the advantages of digital learning.
- Furthermore, many children from economically disadvantaged backgrounds are unable to access digital devices such as smartphones, tablets, or laptops, which hinders their participation in online classes and access to digital study materials. Even if they have access to devices, a reliable internet connection may be lacking, further impeding their ability to engage in remote learning.
- Additionally, the pandemic has exacerbated economic hardships for many families, making it difficult for them to afford digital devices or internet connectivity for their children. Consequently, an educational access gap has widened, disproportionately affecting those from low-income backgrounds. As a result, numerous children in rural areas and from economically disadvantaged backgrounds have faced significant obstacles in accessing education during the pandemic.

To address these challenges, the government and educational institutions need to provide devices and internet connectivity to all students, particularly those from rural areas and economically disadvantaged backgrounds. According to a report by the Telecom Regulatory Authority of India (TRAI, 2019), the Internet has experienced significant growth and penetration in Indian society, particularly after 2017. Despite the overall progress, the limited availability and accessibility of Internet services in rural areas continue to pose challenges, hindering equitable digital inclusion. This would ensure equal access to education for all, bridging the existing gap and promoting inclusive learning opportunities.

9.5.3 SUGGESTIVE MEASURES

Several solutions have been proposed to address the challenges of achieving universal education in India. One significant approach is the improvement of education quality in rural areas through enhanced infrastructure and teacher training programs. Donaghy (2021) noted that achieving greater access to digital resources relies on a variety of elements: the financial means for acquisition, the training and expertise required for utilization, and the infrastructure necessary for maintenance. The government has launched initiatives such as the Sarva Shiksha Abhiyan, which intends to deliver basic education to all citizens. Additionally, the recently launched Samagra Shiksha scheme is a centrally sponsored program focused on improving educational outcomes.

Another solution involves providing financial assistance to economically disadvantaged families, particularly those living below the poverty line, to support education-related expenses. Government schemes like the Mid-Day Meal Scheme play a crucial role in this regard by offering free meals to students in government schools, reducing the financial burden on families, and ensuring better access to education.

Addressing gender disparities in education is also essential. Initiatives such as the Beti Bachao and Beti Padhao (Save the Daughter, Teach the Daughter) campaigns have been launched to promote the education and empowerment of girls. These efforts aim to uplift the status of girls and women through increased access to education, creating a more inclusive and equal educational environment.

However, to effectively address these challenges, it is imperative to leverage digitalization in education. Digital technologies can play a transformative role by expanding access to education, improving educational quality, and bridging geographical and socioeconomic gaps. By embracing digital tools and platforms, students can access learning resources beyond the constraints of traditional classrooms and teachers can enhance their teaching methods and reach a wider audience. Additionally, digitalization enables personalized learning experiences, adaptive assessments, and interactive educational content, promoting student engagement and motivation.

Moreover, digitalization can facilitate the integration of innovative teaching methodologies such as blended learning, flipped classrooms, and online collaborations, fostering critical thinking, problem-solving skills, and creativity among students. It also enables the use of data analytics and educational software to monitor student progress, identify learning gaps, and provide personalized support, ensuring that no child is left behind.

While various solutions have been proposed to address educational challenges in India, the importance of digitalization cannot be overstated.

By harnessing the power of digital technologies, barriers to education can be overcome, quality can be enhanced, and a more inclusive and equitable educational system can be created that empowers all learners, regardless of their background or circumstances.

9.6 IMPACT OF COVID-19 ON EDUCATION IN INDIA: CHALLENGES AND SOLUTIONS FOR DISTANCE LEARNING

The COVID-19 outbreak has had a significant impact on the global education landscape, including in India. With schools closed to prevent the growth of the virus, educational institutions had to swiftly adjust to remote learning. This transition, however, has created numerous challenges for Indian students, teachers, and policymakers. Various approaches can be implemented to conquer the difficulties caused by the consequences of COVID-19 on educational institutions in India:

- A significant hurdle has been the digital divide. Many students in India lack access to computers, tablets, or smartphones, making it difficult for them to engage in online classes or complete digital assignments. This disparity predominantly affects students from low-income families or those residing in rural areas. To address this issue, some states have implemented initiatives to distribute smartphones or tablets to students, while others have leveraged television and radio broadcasts to deliver educational content. It is equally important to improve internet connectivity and infrastructure in rural and underserved areas, provide devices such as tablets or laptops to students who lack access to technology, and collaborate with telecommunications companies to offer affordable internet packages or zero-rated educational content.
- Promoting digital literacy and training: Conduct digital literacy programs for teachers, students, and parents to enhance their proficiency in using digital tools and platforms. The lack of student participation and engagement in online classes, combined with the technological challenges faced by teachers, has resulted in a decline in job satisfaction compared to their previous experience in traditional classroom teaching (Nambiar, 2020). The shift to online teaching has presented various obstacles that have affected both students and teachers, impacting the overall teaching and learning experience. Offer professional development

opportunities for teachers to acquire the necessary skills for effective online instruction. Create online repositories of resources and tutorials for self-paced learning.

- Inadequate infrastructure and resources to support remote learning have also posed challenges. Many schools in India lack reliable internet connectivity, appropriate software, and effective learning management systems (LMS), hindering teachers' ability to deliver engaging and interactive lessons and students' access to educational materials. Moreover, educators have had to quickly adapt to new teaching methods and technologies, leading to a learning curve for many.
- Developing contextualized digital content: Design digital educational content that caters to the diverse linguistic, cultural, and regional needs of students in India. Collaborate with local content creators and educators to ensure the relevance and accuracy of digital resources. Utilize open educational resources and promote content-sharing platforms to enhance resource availability.
- Strengthening teacher–student engagement: Implement interactive and engaging online teaching methodologies such as virtual classrooms, multimedia presentations, and gamified learning experiences. Foster regular communication channels between teachers and students through online platforms and discussion forums. Encourage peer collaboration and group projects through virtual platforms.
- Supportive policies and partnerships: Develop policies that promote digital infrastructure development, including improved internet connectivity and availability of digital devices. Establish partnerships between government bodies, educational institutions, private sector organizations, and civil society to leverage resources and expertise for the effective implementation of digital education initiatives. Allocate adequate funding for digital education initiatives, including investments in infrastructure, teacher training, and content development.
- Monitoring and evaluation: Establish mechanisms for monitoring the effectiveness and impact of digital education initiatives. Regularly assess students' learning outcomes and engagement levels to identify areas for improvement. Students' emotional maturity is critical regarding their modification and reactions

within an internet-based educational setting (Matulessy et al., 2021). Emotional maturity enables students to navigate through the virtual learning space with resilience, handle the demands of remote learning, and effectively engage with online learning materials and activities. By conducting research and studies, the long-term effects of remote learning on educational outcomes and student well-being can be evaluated. The pandemic has also taken a toll on the mental health and well-being of students and teachers. The sudden shift to remote learning has resulted in feelings of isolation and disconnection, as the face-to-face interaction between students and teachers has been significantly reduced. This has had adverse effects on the emotional and mental well-being of many, particularly those who were already vulnerable. A proposition suggests that the government and colleges/institutes should join forces to address this problem by providing students with high-quality, accessible, and crisis-oriented mental health services (Cao et al., 2020). Additionally, the financial instability and uncertainty caused by the pandemic have heightened stress and anxiety levels among students and their families.

In response to these challenges, policymakers, educational institutions, and stakeholders must address the digital divide by ensuring equitable access to technology and internet connectivity. Efforts should be made to enhance digital infrastructure in schools and provide necessary training and support for teachers to effectively navigate remote learning environments. Prioritizing the mental health and well-being of students and educators through counseling services and support systems is essential. By implementing these strategies, the challenges posed by the effects of COVID-19 on education in India can be overcome. This will help ensure that students have equitable access to quality education, even in times of crises, and lay the foundation for a resilient and inclusive education system in the postpandemic era. By acknowledging and proactively addressing these challenges, India can also pave the way for more inclusive and resilient educational systems, even in times of crisis.

9.7 MEASURES TAKEN BY THE INDIAN GOVERNMENT

Numerous additional digital initiatives such as PM eVidya and Swayam Prabha TV, including a channel tailored for individuals with disabilities and the distribution of e-textbooks, have been launched during the COVID era (Kadam, 2021). The Government of India has taken different measures to promote the digitalization of education in the postpandemic era. These measures include:

- Despite the challenges mentioned earlier, numerous solutions and initiatives have emerged to support remote learning in India. One notable effort is the "PM eVIDYA" program launched by the Government of India, which aims to provide digital education to all students across the nation. This initiative involves collaborations with educational technology companies to develop digital content and platforms for students. Furthermore, certain states have introduced innovative solutions such as "smart classrooms" and virtual laboratories, aiming to recreate the traditional classroom experience in a digital format.
- To address the digital divide, private companies and nonprofit organizations have played a crucial role by providing students with essential technology and resources. Many companies have donated laptops, tablets, and internet connectivity to students in need, while nonprofits have initiated crowdfunding campaigns to support digital education initiatives.
- In addition, teachers and schools have shown remarkable adaptability by embracing creative and engaging teaching methods. Educators have turned to social media platforms to interact with their students, creating a virtual classroom environment. They have also developed interactive digital content, including quizzes and games, to enhance student engagement and participation. Some schools have gone as far as organizing "virtual school trips" to provide students with an immersive and adventurous learning experience.

These solutions and initiatives demonstrate the resilience and commitment of various stakeholders in ensuring that remote learning remains effective and accessible despite the challenges posed by the COVID-19 pandemic. By leveraging technology, fostering collaborations, and embracing innovative teaching approaches, India continues to pave the way for a transformed education system that can thrive even in challenging circumstances. The COVID-19 pandemic has brought forth significant challenges for education in India; however, it has also highlighted the resilience and adaptability of the education system. Various solutions and initiatives have been introduced to support remote learning and ensure the continuity of education. These efforts must be sustained and expanded to address underlying inequalities and challenges within the education system, making education equally accessible to all, regardless of their background or circumstances.

The pandemic has prompted a shift in teaching and learning methodologies, replacing traditional classrooms with online classes and e-learning modules. While some students have thrived in the online environment, others have struggled with the lack of personal interaction and support. While the COVID-19 pandemic has presented significant challenges for education in India, it has also opened doors for innovation and adaptation. Education can be made more accessible during these difficult times by prioritizing technological technology and infrastructure, assistance with mental health issues, and stakeholder collaboration. Adopting suitable strategies and campaigns will not only assist in overcoming current challenges but will also result in an even more adaptable and proper education system in the future.

9.7.1 INITIATIVES DURING THE COVID-19

Teachers and students are adjusting to the unique changes brought about by the COVID-19 epidemic, while the government works to become familiar with the advancements in developing a comprehensive virtual learning environment (Abbasi et al., 2020). Amid the COVID-19 pandemic, numerous initiatives were launched in India to bolster remote learning and uphold the continuity of education. These initiatives encompass:

- DIKSHA: Developed by the Ministry of Education, DIKSHA is a national platform offering digital infrastructure and e-learning resources for students and teachers.
- SWAYAM: Established by the Ministry of Education, SWAYAM is a Massive Open Online Course platform that provides online courses from esteemed Indian institutions.
- E-Pathshala: Launched by the Ministry of Education, E-Pathshala provides an approach to e-books, e-journals, and other digital assets for students and teachers.
- Online classes and webinars: Many educational institutions and teachers have taken to conducting online classes and webinars to ensure uninterrupted learning amid school and college closures.

- Collaboration and partnerships: Government bodies, educational institutions, and nonprofit organizations have collaborated to extend support and resources to students and teachers throughout the pandemic.
- Mental health support: Schools and educational institutions have prioritized mental health support and counseling services to aid students and teachers in managing the stress and anxiety induced by the pandemic.

These initiatives have been critical in ensuring the continuation of education in the face of the pandemic's challenges. They have demonstrated the potential for innovation and adaptation within the education system, emphasizing the significance of collaboration and partnerships among stakeholders. These initiatives are still ongoing in India, as the pandemic continues to impact the country. Remote learning has become an essential aspect of the education system, making initiatives like DIKSHA, SWAYAM, and E-Pathshala vital in providing digital infrastructure and e-learning resources to students and teachers. Many educational institutions and teachers persist in conducting online classes and webinars to facilitate uninterrupted learning.

Collaboration and partnerships among stakeholders within the education system continue to be a priority, with organizations joining forces to offer support and resources to students and teachers. Furthermore, schools and educational institutions remain committed to prioritizing mental health support and counseling services. As the pandemic persists in India, these initiatives retain their significance in ensuring that education remains accessible to all students, regardless of the challenges posed by the ongoing crisis. They also underscore the importance of embracing innovation and adaptation within the education system as we navigate the evolving educational landscape in the aftermath of the pandemic.

9.7.2 SCHOOL PREPARATION IN TERMS OF RESOURCES AND INFRASTRUCTURE

To foster a positive learning environment and safeguard the safety and well-being of students, teachers, and staff, schools must be ready in terms of resources and infrastructure. The following are some critical components of preparedness in various areas:

- Indian schools have been proactive in addressing the challenges of remote learning by investing in essential technology and infrastructure. They have made significant efforts to equip students and teachers with devices such as laptops, desktop computers, and tablets, enabling them to engage in online learning effectively. Furthermore, schools have prioritized improving their internet connectivity to ensure reliable and high-speed internet access for seamless online interactions.
- In addition to hardware and internet connectivity, schools have also focused on developing comprehensive digital resources and e-learning materials. This includes the creation of online textbooks, e-books, and other digital learning materials that students can access from their homes. Many schools have embraced LMS and educational software to manage online classes and assignments efficiently.
- As a result of the pandemic, teachers' roles expanded beyond just imparting knowledge to also encompass ensuring the engagement of students in online classes (Burgess et al., 2021). Recognizing the need for teachers to adapt to the new digital environment, schools have invested in training programs and workshops. These initiatives aim to enhance teachers' digital teaching skills and provide them with a comprehensive understanding of the intricacies of remote learning. By empowering teachers with the necessary tools and knowledge, schools have ensured a smooth transition to online instruction.

Overall, schools in India have demonstrated remarkable resilience and adaptability in their efforts to support remote learning during the pandemic. Despite the challenges encountered, they have successfully equipped themselves with the required technology, infrastructure, and resources. This dedication has enabled them to continue delivering quality education to their students amid the adversities posed by the pandemic.

9.7.3 AVAILABILITY AND ACCESSIBILITY OF COMPUTERS, AND INTERNET CONNECTIONS IN SCHOOLS

The availability and accessibility of computers and internet connectivity in schools are pivotal factors that significantly influence modern education.

These resources have become integral tools for both teaching and learning, shaping the way students acquire knowledge and skills in the following ways:

- Access to computers and high-speed internet has become increasingly crucial in the education system of India, especially during the COVID-19 pandemic where remote learning has become the norm. Recognizing this, many schools have made investments in computers, laptops, and tablets for students and teachers to facilitate online learning.
- Furthermore, schools have prioritized improving internet connectivity and upgrading their infrastructure to ensure high-speed internet access for online classes and webinars. In areas with limited connectivity, schools have even established Wi-Fi hotspots to enable students without internet access at home to participate in online classes.
- However, it is important to acknowledge that the digital divide remains a significant challenge, particularly in rural areas. Not all students and teachers have equal access to computers and internet connectivity, creating disparities in accessing online learning resources. To bridge this gap, both government and nongovernment organizations (NGOs) have launched initiatives to provide computers and internet connectivity to underprivileged students and teachers in rural areas.
- Despite these efforts, universal access to computers and high-speed internet across India is still a long-term goal. The National Sample Survey conducted in 2017–2018 revealed that only a fraction of households in India had internet access, particularly in rural areas where access was even more limited. This digital divide has made it exceptionally challenging for students and teachers in rural areas to access online learning resources.
- To address this issue, government initiatives like Digital India aim to provide high-speed internet connectivity to all citizens, with a particular focus on rural areas. Additionally, NGOs such as Pratham and Akshaya Patra have implemented programs to provide computers and internet connectivity to underprivileged students in rural areas. Electronic tools, such as tablets and other devices, have played a crucial role in enabling students to independently complete their tasks in a shorter timeframe compared

to traditional methods (Makosa, 2014). Despite these efforts, many students and teachers in India continue to face obstacles in accessing computers and high-speed internet, particularly in rural areas. Closing the digital divide and ensuring universal access to these resources remains a crucial goal for India's education system.

9.7.4 ADAPTIVE MEASURES BY SCHOOL DURING THE COVID-19

In the absence of devices and internet access, schools in India have had to adapt their teaching methods during the COVID-19 pandemic. Some of the alternative methods employed include:

- Radio and TV broadcasts: The government initiated the Swayam Prabha program, which broadcasts educational content through 32 Direct-to-Home channels. This enables students in remote areas to access educational resources through radio and television.
- Printed study materials: Schools have provided printed study materials, such as worksheets, textbooks, and assignments, to students who lack access to digital devices. This ensures that they have tangible resources to continue their studies.
- WhatsApp groups: Teachers have utilized WhatsApp groups to share study materials, communicate with students, and engage with parents. This platform enables easy dissemination of information and fosters communication.
- Community-based learning: In certain areas, teachers have organized small-group learning sessions in open spaces, adhering to social distancing norms. This approach allows for face-to-face interaction while maintaining safety measures.

However, these alternative methods present their challenges. Printed study materials may not adequately cover complex concepts, and community-based learning might not be feasible in all areas due to infrastructure limitations. Additionally, these methods may struggle to engage students who lack the structure and environment of a regular classroom.

Prominent experts have expressed skepticism on social media regarding the motivations driving certain individuals, organizations, and companies to provide guidance, questioning whether market interests have influenced their actions (Siemens, 2020). Moreover, there is growing apprehension regarding the potential adverse effects of hastily implementing quick technological fixes in education without carefully considering their long-term consequences (Selwyn, 2020; St. Amour, 2020). The swift adoption of learning platforms and online education has also raised concerns surrounding privacy, surveillance, and their impact on students' personal lives and dignity (Harwell, 2020). It is imperative to address these concerns and ensure that any digital solutions implemented in education are ethically sound, prioritize student well-being, and respect individuals' rights to privacy and autonomy. Taking a thoughtful and measured approach to the integration of educational technology will help safeguard students' interests and ensure the long-term effectiveness and sustainability of digital education initiatives. These critical observations remind us of the importance of thoughtfully considering the pedagogical and ethical dimensions when embracing technology in education.

Therefore, the government and educational institutions must persist in their efforts to provide devices and internet connectivity to all students in India. By ensuring access to quality education remotely, even in challenging times like the COVID-19 pandemic, they can mitigate the limitations of alternative teaching methods and promote equitable learning opportunities for all.

9.8 RECOMMENDATIONS AND POLICY DEVELOPMENT IN DIGITAL EDUCATION

This research chapter provides insights into the digitalization of education in the postpandemic Indian context. By examining the opportunities, challenges, and impact of digital technologies on education quality, access, equity, and pedagogical practices, this study aims to inform policymakers, educators, and stakeholders in shaping effective strategies and policies for inclusive and sustainable digital education in India. When considering future research and policy development in digital education in the Indian context, here are some recommendations to explore in the chapter on the digitalization of education:

- Impact assessment: Conduct comprehensive research to assess the impact of digital education initiatives implemented during the pandemic. Evaluate the effectiveness of various digital tools, platforms, and teaching methodologies in improving learning outcomes and student engagement. The implementation of technology, particularly team-based technology and instructor-led learning options, can offer students an engaging and diverse learning environment (ClearTouch, 2020). This research can inform future policy decisions and help identify best practices in digital education.

- Pedagogical approaches: Investigate innovative pedagogical approaches that integrate technology effectively in the teaching–learning process. Explore strategies for promoting critical thinking, problem-solving, collaboration, and creativity in digital education. Research on learner-centric approaches and personalized learning models in the digital realm can provide insights into effective instructional practices.
- Teacher training and professional development: Focus on research that examines the needs and challenges of teachers in the digital education landscape. Identify effective methods for training teachers in digital literacy, digital content creation, and online teaching techniques. Research on professional development programs and their impact on teacher effectiveness in digital education can contribute to policy development in this area.
- Equity and inclusion: Conduct research on strategies to ensure equitable access to digital education for all students, particularly those from disadvantaged backgrounds and marginalized communities. Investigate ways to bridge the digital divide, address language barriers, and promote inclusive digital education practices. Explore the potential of assistive technologies and accessibility features to cater to diverse learning needs.
- Infrastructure development: Study the infrastructure requirements for effective digital education implementation in different settings, including rural areas and underserved regions. Examine the challenges and opportunities associated with improving internet connectivity, power supply, and access to digital devices. Research on cost-effective solutions, alternative energy sources, and infrastructure models can inform policy decisions in infrastructure development.
- Data privacy and security: Explore the ethical and legal aspects of data privacy and security in digital education. Investigate the

measures required to protect student data, ensure compliance with data protection regulations, and establish robust cybersecurity practices. Research on privacy-enhancing technologies, data governance frameworks, and policies related to data handling in digital education is essential.

- Sociocultural context: Investigate the sociocultural factors influencing the adoption and effectiveness of digital education in the Indian context. Examine the impact of cultural norms, social beliefs, and community engagement on digital education practices. Research on culturally responsive digital content, inclusive pedagogies, and strategies to engage parents and local communities can inform policy development.
- Policy framework: Analyze existing policies and frameworks related to digital education in India and identify areas for improvement. Investigate policy implementation challenges and explore policy recommendations to foster the sustainable integration of digital education into the education system. Research on international best practices and comparative studies can provide insights for policy development in India.
- Long-term sustainability: Study the long-term sustainability of digital education initiatives beyond the immediate postpandemic period. Analyze the financial, technical, and institutional requirements for scaling up and sustaining digital education practices. Research on funding models, public–private partnerships, and governance structures can contribute to the development of sustainable policies in digital education.

These recommendations can guide future research and policy development in the digitalization of education in postpandemic India. By addressing these areas, policymakers and researchers can contribute to the growth and effectiveness of digital education, ultimately enhancing access to quality education for all learners.

9.9 CONCLUSION

In conclusion, future research and policy development in digital education, with a specific focus on rural areas and girls, are of paramount importance in shaping an inclusive and equitable educational landscape in postpandemic India. The research conducted by Kamarianos et al.

(2020) additionally validated that online classes were more beneficial for contemporary generations compared to earlier ones. The study revealed that students perceived online classes as fostering a more active learning approach. The recommendations put forward provide a roadmap for exploring key areas that require attention and further investigation. The research delves into the specific challenges faced by rural areas in terms of limited internet connectivity, availability of digital devices, and infrastructure constraints. By understanding these challenges, policymakers can develop targeted policies and initiatives to bridge the digital divide, ensuring that students in rural areas have equal access to digital education resources and opportunities.

Similarly, research also addresses the unique barriers faced by girls in accessing digital education. Cultural norms, societal expectations, and gender biases can impact girls' participation and engagement in digital learning. Investigating these barriers and identifying strategies to overcome them will contribute to the development of policies that promote gender equality in digital education. Even though recent developments in educational technologies and digital platforms provided a strong foundation for adapting to the situation, educational institutions ran into several logistical, technical, financial, and social challenges when adopting online education on a large scale during the pandemic (Oyedotun, 2020). Moreover, research also focuses on the impact of digital education initiatives in rural areas and among girls. Assessing the effectiveness of these initiatives, their impact on learning outcomes, and their ability to address educational disparities will provide valuable insights for policy development. Additionally, understanding the pedagogical approaches and teaching methodologies that work best for rural students and girls in the digital realm will help enhance educational practices and ensure their inclusivity.

Policy development in digital education for rural areas and girls is guided by research findings and best practices. It also highlights the infrastructural needs of rural areas, including improving internet connectivity and power supply, providing affordable and accessible digital devices, and strengthening digital literacy training for teachers and students. Gender-sensitive policies also promote equal access, encourage girls' enrolment and retention in digital education programs, and foster an inclusive and supportive learning environment. Government programs like the "Aakash tablet project" and similar regional initiatives that give students laptops and tablets play a significant role in closing the digital divide, especially for students from underserved communities (Bapna et al., 2020).

By placing a specific emphasis on rural areas and girls in future research and policy development, India can create an educational ecosystem that leaves no one behind. Through sustained efforts and evidence-based policies, digital education can become a powerful tool for empowering rural students and girls, breaking down barriers, and fostering inclusive and quality learning opportunities for all. Platforms such as YouTube, blogs, websites, Twitter, Facebook, Instagram, and similar channels are indispensable (Cinelli et al., 2020). Social media has now evolved into an educational tool employed within institutions or classrooms to facilitate efficient learning and teaching practices (Hamadi et al., 2021). Ultimately, this will contribute to the holistic development and empowerment of rural communities and girls, paving the way for a more equitable and prosperous society.

KEYWORDS

- **development**
- **education**
- **E-learning**
- **technology**
- **vocational**

REFERENCES

Abbasi, S., Ayoob, T., Malik, A. & Memon, S. I. (2020). Perceptions of students regarding E-learning during COVID-19 at a private medical college. *Pakistan Journal of Medical Sciences, 36*, 57–64.

Al-Adwan, A. S. (2020). Investigating the drivers and barriers to MOOCs adoption. The perspective of TAM. *Education and Information Technologies*, 25(6), 5771–5779. https://doi.org/10.100710639-020-10250-2.

Bapna, A., Garg, K. & Mehra, A. (2020). Digital divide and the Aakash tablet technology intervention in education. *Economic and Political Weekly*, 55(10), 27–34.

Burgess, S., Henrik, H., April, S., Burgess, S. & Sievertsen, H. H. (2021). Schools, skills, and learning: The impact of COVID-19 on education. Voxeu.Org. https://cepr.org/voxeu.

Cao, W., Fang, Z., Hou, G., Han, M., Xu, X., Dong, J. & Zheng, J. (2020). The psychological impact of the COVID-19 epidemic on college students in China. *Psychiatry Research.* https://doi.org/10.1016/j.psychres.2020.112934.

Cinelli, M., Quattrociocchi, W., Galeazzi, A., Valensise, C. M., Brugnoli, E. & Schmidt, A. L. (2020). The COVID-19 social media infodemic. *Scientific Reports, 10*(1), 1–10.

ClearTouch (2020). Technology in the classroom: Advantages and disadvantages. https://www.getcleartouch.com/technology-in-the-classroom-advantages-anddisadvantages.

Debre, M. J. & Dijkstra, H. (2021). COVID-19 and policy responses by international organizations: Crisis of liberal international order or window of opportunity?. *Global Policy*, 12(4), 443–454. https://doi.org/10.1111/1758-5899.12975.

Donaghy, D. (2021). Defining digital capital and digital poverty. *Oxford Academic ITNOW*, 63(1), 54–55.

Hamadi, M., El-Den, J., Narumon Sriratanaviriyakul, C. & Azam, S. (2021). A social media adoption framework as pedagogical instruments in higher education classrooms. *E-Learning and Digital Media, 18*(1), 55–85.

Harwell, D. (2020). Mass school closures in the wake of the coronavirus are driving a new wave of student surveillance. Washington. https://www.washingtonpost.com/technology/2020/04/01/online-proctoring-college-exams-coronavirus/.

Illavarasan, P. V. (2013). The digital divide in India, Inferences from the ICT workforce. In Ragnedda, M. & Muschert, G. W. (Eds.), The Digital Divide. The Internet and Social Inequality in International Perspective, Routledge, pp. 134–146.

Jena, P. K. (2020). Challenges and opportunities created by Covid-19 for ODL: Case study of challenges and opportunities created by Covid-19 for the novel COVID-19. The *Human Rights*, 8(2), 92–107.

Kadam, S. A. (2021). Flipped classroom-based framework to repurpose online collaboration tool as a learning management system for online education. *The Online Journal of Distance Education and e-Learning, 9*(1), 84–91.

Kamarianos, I., Adamopoulou, A., Lambropoulos, H. & Stamelos, G. (2020). Towards an understanding of university students' response in times of pandemic crisis (COVID-19). *European Journal of Education Studies*, 7(7), 20–40.

Khan, M. A., Kamal, T., Illiyan, A. & Asif, M. (2021). School students' perception and challenges towards online classes during COVID-19 pandemic in India: An econometric analysis. *Sustainability*. https://doi: org/10.3390/su13094786.

Khan, S., Al-Dmour, A., Bali, V., Rabbani, M. R. & Thirunavukkarasu, K. (2021). Cloud computing based futuristic e4ducational model for virtual learning. *Journal of Statistics and Management Systems*, 6(2), 1–29.

Khokhar, A. S. (2016). Digital literacy. *International Journal of Digital Literacy and Digital Competence*, 7(3), 1–12. https://doi.org/10.4018/IJDLDC.2016070101.

Lepp, L., Aaviku T., Leijen Ä., Pedaste M. & Saks, K. (2021). Teaching during COVID-19: The decisions made in teaching. *Education Sciences*, 11(2), 47.

Li, C. & Lalani, F. (2020). The COVID-19 Pandemic has Changed Education Forever. World Economic Forum. https://www.weforum.org/agenda/2020/04/coronavirus-education-global-covid19-online-digital-learning/.

Makosa, P. (2014). Advantages and Disadvantages of Digital Education. https://www.researchgate.net/publication/264419797.

Matulessy, A., Saragih, S., Nawafil, N., Perdana, H. & Pandin, M. (2021). Social support and emotional maturity to reduce students' online learning anxiety during the Covid-19 pandemic. *International Journal of Environmental Research and Public Health*. https:// doi: org/10.20944/preprints202101.0013.v1.

McDougall, L. (2000). Gender gap in literacy in Uttar Pradesh: Questions for decentralised educational planning, *Economic and Political Weekly*, 35(19), 1649–1658.

McKibbin, W. J. & Roshen, J. (2020). The Global Macroeconomic Impacts of COVID-19: Seven Scenarios. CAMA Working Paper. http://dx.doi.org/10.2139/ssrn.354 7729.

Nambiar, D. (2020). The impact of online learning during COVID-19: students' and teachers' perspective. *The International Journal of Indian Psychology*, 8(2), 783–793.

Oyedotun, T. D. (2020). A sudden change of pedagogy in education driven by COVID-19: Perspectives and evaluation from a developing country. *Research Global*. https://doi. org/10.1016/j.resglo.2020.100029.

Sansa, N. A. (2020). Analysis of the Impact of the COVID-19 on the Petrol Price in China. https://ssrn.com/abstract=3547413.

Selwyn, N. (2020). After COVID-19: The Longer-Term Impacts of the Coronavirus Crisis on Education. Monash University, Melbourne. https://educationfutures.monash.edu/ all%2D-present/after-covid-19.

Sharma, B. (2020). Educational technology-mitigating Covid-19 impact on learning. *International Journal of Advanced Research in Engineering and Technology*, 11(4), 500–508.

Siemens, G. (2020). Research pundits. A Google Scholar search of prominent voices quickly reveals those who have earned the right to provide [tweet]. Twitter. https:// twitter.com/ gsiemens/status/1246920826282110976.

St. Amour, M. (2020). Privacy and the online pivot. Inside Higher Ed, 25 March. https://www. insidehighered.com/news/2020/03/25/pivot-online-raises-concerns-ferpa-surveillance.

Telecom Regulatory Authority of India (2019). Annual Report. https://www.trai.gov.in/ sites/default/files/Annaul_Report_02032021_0.pdf.

UNESCO (2015). Education for All Global Monitoring Report. https://en.unesco.org/ gem-report/taxonomy/term/199.

UNESCO (2020). Global Education Meeting Extraordinary Session on Education post-COVID-19 Background document. https://unesdoc.unesco.org/ark:/48223/ pf0000375301.

Upadhyay, A. K. (2021). Information literacy: An overview. *Elementary Education Online*, 20(1), 4227–4234. https://www.ilkogretim-online.org/fulltext/218-1639838295.pdf.

Wenham, C., Smith, J. & Morgan, R. (2020). COVID-19: The gendered impacts of the outbreak. *The Lancet*, 395(10227), 846–848.

CHAPTER 10

Fintech Usage and Sustainable Organizational Performance: A Conceptual Framework for Malaysian Manufacturing Small- and Medium-Sized Enterprises (SMEs)

ARSALAN HUSSAIN

College of Business Management, Institute of Business Management, Karachi, Pakistan

ABSTRACT

This research focuses on the use of fintech by Malaysian small- and medium-sized enterprises (SMEs) for sustainable organizational performance, with an international mindset as a moderating role. Most previous publications describe the failure rate of Malaysian SMEs as alarming, with 60% of new SMEs going bankrupt within five years of start-up. Moreover, only 4 out of 10 SMEs are able to meet the challenges of growth. Barriers to SME growth have long been an unresolved issue in Malaysia. A few researchers have studied the use of fintech by SMEs. However, little is known about the underlying factors in the technological, organizational and environmental (TOE) context that do not explain the use of fintech for sustainable organizational performance in SMEs. The framework of this study uses dynamic capability theory and the TOE model. The researcher will collect data from Malaysian SMEs that use fintech in their business activities. This study is beneficial for fintech practitioners and policy

Corporate Governance, Digitalization, and Energy Transition: Imen Baccouche and Afef Khalil. (Eds.)

DOI: 10.1201/9781779643407-12

makers to improve the financial situation and social and environmental performance of SMEs. Meanwhile, from the theoretical perspective, this research's outcome can introduce the international mindset to the current literature that impacts the view of risk in the global outreach of Malaysian SMEs.

10.1 INTRODUCTION

Small- and medium-enterprises (SMEs) are a crucial pillar of Malaysia's economy, forming 98.5% of its total establishments. According to the latest mid-term review of the 11th Malaysia Plan 2016–2020 report, SMEs are expected to contribute up to 41% of the country's GDP by 2020, and approximately 32 initiatives will be intensified to develop resilient and sustainable SMEs. However, SMEs' failure rate in Malaysia is shocking, whereby 60% of the new SMEs fail within five years of establishment very high compared to other developed countries. Moreover, only 4 out of 10 SMEs can meet the challenges associated with growth successfully. A recent Chief Executive Officer (CEO) also acknowledged that SMEs cannot survive without digitalizing their businesses (Wong et al., 2020). Thus, SMEs need to view technology adoption as an investment rather than a cost to sustainable growth. However, the challenging goal to achieve SMEs in Malaysia is currently facing a few problems, such as a shortage of skills for foreign workers and being slow to adopt new technologies toward sustainable performance (Ambad et al., 2020).

Malaysian SMEs are gradually moving toward digital transformation with the vision to improve SMEs' performance through technology usage such as financial technology. In this regard, SMEs' sustainable performance can be increased by using fintech with an international mindset. In realizing this digital transformation, the Malaysian government has demonstrated a huge effort in preparing the digital environment to guide the SMEs to prepare them for the transformation. Unfortunately, such efforts toward digitalization have seemed to be unfruitful; Malaysian SMEs still lack the full digital capability to use matured fintech resources and organizational transformation (Büyüközkan & Göçer, 2018), which subsequently improve their performance (Agyapong et al., 2021).

The use of fintech as a concept has a recent history and results in drastic change, particularly for SMEs. Further, fintech usage by the business owner was seriously underused. The Department of Statistics indicates that "nine out of 10 business establishments in Malaysia are SMEs. Only twenty-eight (28%) percent of these have an online presence and surprisingly only 15% are using that for export purposes" (Digitalnews, 2018). According to the Masterplan Implementation 2012–2020 report of Malaysian SMEs, among the key goals, the first goal is innovation and technology adoption. Thus, there is a desperate need to understand the determinants of fintech use and how this usage can enhance Malaysian SMEs' overall global outreach. Hence, this research also attempts to incorporate the international mindset as a moderating variable to examine the actual causes and problems of not reaching the global marketplace.

Previous scholars have also demonstrated that an international mindset can reveal global strategies to meet the local market by introducing process innovation to reach opportunities globally (Agyapong et al., 2021). Based on the study, it is necessary to introduce an international mindset into the scope of the study lacking in previous research. Introducing a new factor is expected to provide more effective guidance in understanding the factors of financial technology as proposed in this study. Hence, to fill up the gap, a certain modification and extension of the dynamic capability theory (DCT) integrate it with the technological, organizational, and environmental (TOE) model in this research where the adoption-performance model could provide more guidance to industry and policy-makers to promote fintech usage in Malaysia.

Besides, previous studies have investigated Enterprise resource planning adoption (Aremu et al., 2020), social media adoption (Ahmad et al., 2019), adoption-related to big data (Ardito et al., 2019), and the use of e-marketing influence on firm performance (Sheikh et al., 2018). However, the use of fintech influence on sustainable organizational performance is still a missing link in the literature. Thus, the present study will identify the relationship between the use of fintech with the financial, social, and environmental dimensions of sustainable organizational performance. This study will examine the relationship between relative advantage, IT infrastructure, organizational readiness, top management support, competitive orientation, and government support on fintech use toward the sustainable performance of Malaysian SMEs. Thus, this study uses the moderating effect of the international mindset between the fintech and sustainable performance of SMEs.

The remainder of this chapter is organized as follows. Section 10.2 introduces the theoretical foundations along with the detailed literature review, while Section 10.3 describes the methodology and research design for the current conceptual chapter. Section 10.4 provides the implications and limitations of the research with a remarkable conclusion.

10.2 LITERATURE REVIEW

Dynamic capabilities (DCs) are considered the competencies that identify new opportunities for internal and external resources to address rapidly changing business environments. As explained by Teece et al. (1997) "dynamic capabilities refer to the firm's ability to integrate, build and reconfigure internal and external competences to address rapidly changing environments." Moreover, DCT has been applied in technology adoption studies and describes how the firm functions, operates, and gains competitive advantage by using technology innovation to dynamically influence organizational performance (Nasution et al., 2021). Before DCT, Venkatesh et al. (2003) highlighted that most of the researchers formulated their research framework by selecting constructs across models, e.g., Theory of Reasoned Action, Technology Acceptance Model (Najib & Fahma, 2020), Theory of Planned Behavior. However, there is no empirical study that integrated DCT with the TOE model for fintech usage and sustainable organizational performance in the previous literature.

The literature also reveals that the measurement of an organization's performance should be multidimensional indicators (Cheah et al., 2019). It should consolidate financial, social, and environmental dimensions as essential criteria in the rapidly changing global business environment (Fernando et al., 2019). Performance measurement by combining the financial, social, and environmental dimensions is known as sustainable organizational performance. Further, SMEs' current technologies and industry dynamics are synergized to gain a competitive advantage (Ch'ng et al., 2021), which eventually leads to sustainable organizational performance. Thus, this study anticipates the use of fintech as a core mediating DC that raises the sustainability of manufacturing SMEs in Malaysia.

Moreover, the international mindset of having the ability to view globally to acquire knowledge related to suppliers, customers, and other market players enables firms to acquire the local market needs (Kyvik, 2018). Further, the study discusses that the international mindset has become a precondition to evaluating global market trends and future competitive positions (Agyapong et al., 2021). Thus, the study contributes to the existing literature gap by introducing the international mindset's moderating role between the use of fintech and sustainable organizational performance. The study uses the DCT to explain the TOE factors and the moderating role of the international mindset relationship.

TOE model is considered the most relevant framework to investigate technology usage, such as financial technology (Depietro et al., 1990). Scholars have concluded this model as a comprehensive model because it explains intrafirm level issues and problems of particular technology adoption (Oliveira & Martins, 2010). To explain the underlying issues related to the use of fintech for Malaysian sustainable performance of SMEs, this study used technological factors (relative advantage, IT infrastructure), organizational factors (organizational readiness, top management support), and environmental (competitive orientation, government support), which eventually lead to sustainable organizational performance.

Considering the aforementioned use of fintech issues related to the TOE model, the technological context, which is one of the three constructs of the TOE model, mainly focuses on internal and external IT infrastructure. This factor is essential for specific organizations' hardware, software, and operational processes such as payment process systems, computers, and the Internet (Mkansi, 2022). Thus, the possession of the required IT infrastructure is an essential factor to implement fintech innovation in a firm. Likewise, the anticipated advantages of implementing fintech, which is known as a relative advantage of particular technology use (Ahmad et al., 2019). The literature also depicts two categories of expected advantages: direct and indirect advantages that focus on internal efficiency and service quality improvement (Ilin et al., 2017).

Alongside the technological factor, the scope of organizational context covers the organization's size, scope, and managerial structure. Yoon and George (2013) describe organizational readiness as a vital element that covers information system knowledge, IT skills, technical competencies, and financial resources of the firm. Moreover, the successful implementation of technological innovation (such as fintech) has been adopted with top management support (Hussein et al., 2019).

In the environmental context, previous studies have identified how a firm can compete with competitors and industry, and deal with the government Further, the environmental factors include the regulatory environment, a service provider of technology, and industry structure

(Baker, 2012). In the present study, the competitive orientation serves as an analytical tool to acquire relevant information related to buyers and competitors in the target market through financial technology. Likewise, the scholars have used government support in innovation usage like e-marketing, e-procurement, e-banking, and e-government (Kazungu et al., 2015; Mohtaramzadeh et al., 2018; Sánchez et al., 2018). However, there are very rare researches available that identified government support concerning the use of fintech. To fill up the existing gap, this study will examine the relationship between relative advantage, IT infrastructure, organizational readiness, top management support, competitive orientation, and government support on fintech usage toward Malaysian structural equation model (SEM)'s sustainable performance. This study will also investigate the effect of international mindset as moderate between SME's fintech adoption and sustainable performance (Figure 10.1).

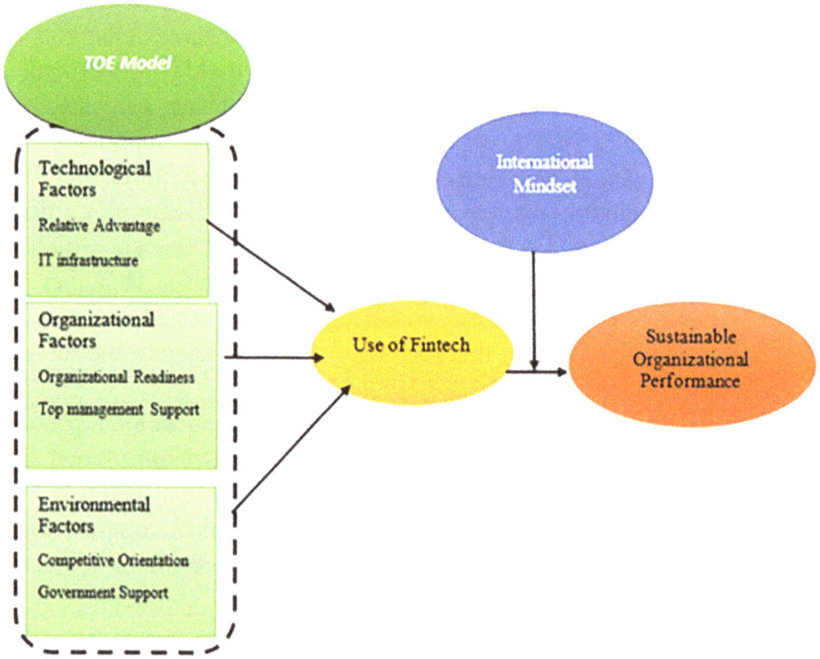

FIGURE 10.1 The effect of the TOE model on sustainable organizational performance through the mediation of the use of fintech.

Source: Author

10.3 PROPOSED METHODOLOGY

10.3.1 SAMPLE AND DATA COLLECTION

The study focuses on the sustainable organizational performance of SMEs existing in Malaysia by using a quantitative method of data collection. A structural questionnaire is designed by using a seven-point Likert scale, which was anchored by "strongly disagree" (1) to "strongly agree" (7). The questions were designed to probe the constructs that would determine the SME's sustainable organizational performance and use of fintech. Quantitative questionnaires will be delivered to the prospective respondents which are top-level managers/CEO of the targeted SMEs. The current study will employ a simple random sampling technique for each industry covered under the heading of SME in Malaysia. According to the Department of Statistics Malaysia, the industry-wise percentage contribution shows that agriculture (52.8%), construction (46.4%), services (42.2%), manufacturing (34.4%), and minning & quaring (2.4%). The SMEs that have officially registered their profiles in the Malaysian e-marketplaces from the aforementioned industries will be the unit of analysis of the present study. The data collection activity is planned for three months to collect data.

10.3.2 THE INSTRUMENT DEVELOPMENT

This quantitative study employed a questionnaire survey. Sustainable organizational performance will be measured by three dimensions, namely, financial, social, and environmental. The financial performance will be measured by using the scale (Choi & Yu, 2014), while social and environmental performance will be measured by using the scale of (Eccles et al., 2014). Likewise, to measure the study's independent variables, the study adopted the following scales from the previous studies to suit the scope of research in Malaysia. The survey questionnaire of relative advantage is adapted from Premkumar et al. (1994), IT infrastructure from Premkumar and Ramamurthy (1995), Organizational readiness from Claiborne et al. (2013), Top management support from Soliman and Janz (2004), competitive orientation Jaworski and Kohli (1993) and Han et al. (1998), government support from Looi (2005), use of fintech from Mainardes et al. (2023), and finally International mindset scale is adapted from Nummela et al. (2004) and Ciszewska-Mlinarič (2015).

10.3.3 DATA ANALYSIS PROCESS

This research will use an SEM with a partial least squares (PLS) approach using the SmartPLS software version 4. Further, Reinartz et al. (2009) mentioned that "PLS is the preferable approach when researchers focus on prediction and theory development," especially for a model that involves formative and reflective latent variables. To assess the measurement and structural model, specifically, SmartPLS and bootstrap resampling (5000 resamples) were used. Furthermore, all other necessary criteria suggested by Hair et al. (2017) will be tested, that is, convergent validity, discriminant validity, and measurement invariance.

This chapter's novelty is on the research framework model of sustainability for the SMEs' performance. It will be developed based on two theories—DC and the TOE model, which is enhanced and tested empirically via the study's outcome on managers and owners of SMEs. However, sustainable organizational performance consists of three dimensions which are financial, social, and environmental.

10.4 CONCLUSION

The present research applied the TOE-based framework to conceptually analyze the usage of fintech to sustain organizational performance for Malaysian SMEs. For this purpose, the researcher has developed a comprehensive framework to ascertain the association between TOE factors and sustainable organizational performance. Since the use of fintech is growing rapidly across the globe, the international mindset can play a significant moderating role between the use of fintech and sustainable organizational performance. To the best of research knowledge, this research is the first to place the moderating linkage of international mindset between fintech use and sustainable organizational performance. Specifically, this study examined the relationship between relative advantage, IT infrastructure, organizational readiness, top management support, competitive orientation, and government support on fintech use toward Malaysian SMEs' sustainable performance. This chapter contributed to the body of knowledge to test the fintech usage relationship with SMEs' sustainable performance and also the effect of international mindset on the literature for sustainable growth of SMEs.

This chapter contributes to the National policy of sustainable growth of SMEs to increase Malaysia's economic growth. This study could act as a guideline for SMEs in influencing fintech usage on their sustainable business performances. In particular, the researchers have addressed the critical findings concerning the international mindset's role as moderating through an empirical analysis that the previous researchers do not broadly cover. From the practical perspective, this would consequently enhance the adoption of fintech in Malaysian SMEs which would indirectly boost the economy. Meanwhile, from a theoretical standpoint, this study's outcome contributes to the literature as one of the essential factors in measuring the successful use of fintech toward sustainable performance with an international mindset. Further, the research implies that massive investment in fintech usage alone will not bring benefits to SMEs. Instead, the top management should understand the international mindset to improve sustainable performance and remain competitive in the manufacturing industry of Malaysia.

KEYWORDS

- **digitalization**
- **fintech**
- **Malaysia**
- **performance**

REFERENCES

Agyapong, A., Maaledidong, P. D. & Mensah, H. K. (2021). Performance outcome of entrepreneurial behavior of SMEs in a developing economy: The role of international mindset. *Journal of Strategy and Management*, 14(2), 227–245.

Ahmad, S. Z., Abu Bakar, A. R. & Ahmad, N. (2019). Social media adoption and its impact on firm performance: The case of the UAE. *International Journal of Entrepreneurial Behavior & Research*, 25(1), 84–111.

Ardito, L., Scuotto, V., Del Giudice, M. & Petruzzelli, A. M. (2019). A bibliometric analysis of research on Big Data analytics for business and management. *Management Decision*, 57(8), 1993–2009.

Aremu, A. Y., Shahzad, A. & Hassan, S. (2020). The impacts of enterprise resource planning system adoption on firm's performance among medium-sized enterprises. *International Journal of Information Systems and Social Change*, 11(1), 24–42.

Baker, J. (2012). The technology-organization-environment framework. *Information Systems Theory: Explaining and Predicting Our Digital Society*, 1, 231–245.

Büyüközkan, G. & Göçer, F. (2018). Digital Supply Chain: Literature review and a proposed framework for future research. *Computers in Industry*, 97, 157–177.

Ch'ng, P. C., Cheah, J. & Amran, A. (2021). Eco-innovation practices and sustainable business performance: The moderating effect of market turbulence in the Malaysian technology industry. *Journal of Cleaner Production*, 283, 45–56.

Cheah, J., Amran, A. & Yahya, S. (2019). Internal-oriented resources and social enterprises' performance: How can social enterprises help themselves before helping others? *Journal of Cleaner Production*, 211, 607–619.

Choi, Y. & Yu, Y. (2014). The influence of perceived corporate sustainability practices on employees and organizational performance. *Sustainability*, 6(1), 348–364.

Ciszewska-Mlinarič, M. (2015). Global mindset and internationalization of Polish SMEs: Antecedents and outcomes. *Problemy Zarządzania*, 13(1), 22–35.

Claiborne, N., Auerbach, C., Lawrence, C. & Schudrich, W. Z. (2013). Organizational change: The role of climate and job satisfaction in child welfare workers' perception of readiness for change. *Children and Youth Services Review*, 35(12), 1–10.

Depietro, R., Wiarda, E. & Fleischer, M. (1990). The context for change: Organization, technology and environment. *The Processes of Technological Innovation*, 199(0), 151–175.

Digitalnews, S. (2018). Malaysia is on track to achieve 21% e-commerce growth by 2020. https://www.digitalnewsasia.com/digital-economy/malaysia-track-achieve-21-e-commerce-growth-2020.

Eccles, R. G., Ioannou, I. & Serafeim, G. (2014). The impact of corporate sustainability on organizational processes and performance. *Management Science*, 60(11), 2835–2857.

Fernando, Y., Jabbour, C. J. C. & Wah, W. X. (2019). Pursuing green growth in technology firms through the connections between environmental innovation and sustainable business performance: Does service capability matter? *Resources, Conservation and Recycling*, 141, 8–20.

Han, J. K., Kim, N. & Srivastava, R. K. (1998). Market orientation and organizational performance: Is innovation a missing link? *Journal of Marketing*, 62(4), 30–45.

Hussein, L. A., Baharudin, A. S., Jayaraman, K. & Kiumarsi, S. H. A. I. A. N. (2019). B2B e-commerce technology factors with mediating effect perceived usefulness in Jordanian manufacturing SMEs. *Journal of Engineering Science and Technology*, 14(1), 411–429.

Ilin, V., Ivetić, J. & Simić, D. (2017). Understanding the determinants of e-business adoption in ERP-enabled firms and non-ERP-enabled firms: A case study of the Western Balkan Peninsula. *Technological Forecasting and Social Change*, 125, 206–223.

Jaworski, B. J. & Kohli, A. K. (1993). Market orientation: Antecedents and consequences. *Journal of Marketing*, 57(3), 53–70.

Kazungu, I., Panga, F. P. & Mchopa, A. (2015). Impediments to the adoption of e-marketing by Tanzanian small and medium-sized enterprises: An explanatory model. *International Journal of Economics, Commerce and Management*, 3(6), 587–597.

Kyvik, O. (2018). The global mindset: A must for international innovation and entrepreneurship. *International Entrepreneurship and Management Journal*, 14(2), 309–327.

Looi, H. C. (2005). E-commerce adoption in Brunei Darussalam: A quantitative analysis of factors influencing its adoption. *Communications of the Association for Information Systems*, 15(1), 3.

Mkansi, M. (2022). E-business adoption costs and strategies for retail micro businesses. *Electronic Commerce Research*, 22(4), 1153–1193.

Mohtaramzadeh, M., Ramayah, T. & Jun-Hwa, C. (2018). B2B E-commerce adoption in Iranian manufacturing companies: Analyzing the moderating role of organizational culture. *International Journal of Human-Computer Interaction*, 34(7), 621–639.

Najib, M. & Fahma, F. (2020). Investigating the adoption of digital payment system through an extended technology acceptance model: An insight from the Indonesian small and medium enterprises. *International Journal on Advanced Science, Engineering and Information Technology*, 10(4), 1702–1708.

Nasution, M. D. T. P., Rafiki, A., Lubis, A. & Rossanty, Y. (2021). Entrepreneurial orientation, knowledge management, dynamic capabilities towards e-commerce adoption of SMEs in Indonesia. *Journal of Science and Technology Policy Management*, 12(2), 256–282.

Nummela, N., Saarenketo, S. & Puumalainen, K. (2004). Is a global mindset a prerequisite for successful internationalization? *Canadian Journal of Administrative Sciences*, 21(1), 51–64.

Oliveira, T. & Martins, M. F. (2010). Understanding e-business adoption across industries in European countries. *Industrial Management & Data Systems*, 110(9), 1337–1354.

Premkumar, G. & Ramamurthy, K. (1995). The role of inter-organizational and organizational factors on the decision mode for adoption of inter-organizational systems. *Decision Sciences*, 26(3), 303–336.

Premkumar, G., Ramamurthy, K. & Nilakanta, S. (1994). Implementation of electronic data interchange: An innovation diffusion perspective. *Journal of Management Information Systems*, 11(2), 157–186.

Reinartz, W., Krafft, M., & Hoyer, W. D. (2004). The customer relationship management process: Its measurement and impact on performance. *Journal of Marketing Research*, 41(3), 293–305.

Soliman, K. S., & Janz, B. D. (2004). A conceptual model for knowledge management systems implementation in small business organizations. *Information Resources Management Journal*, 17(4), 1–12.

Teece, D. J., Pisano, G., & Shuen, A. (1997). Dynamic capabilities and strategic management. *Strategic Management Journal*, 18(7), 509–533.

Yoon, S., & George, J. F. (2013). The effects of trust and risk on the acceptance of electronic commerce. *Information & Management*, 50(7), 415–426.

PART III

Energy Transition and Environmental Dynamics

DOI: 10.1201/9781779643407-13

CHAPTER 11

Energizing Governance During Energy Transition: The Potential Role of Blockchain Technology

RANIA MAKNI

Esprit School of Business, and Laboratory of Economics and Applied Finance (LEFA, LR05ES07), IHEC, Carthage University, Tunisia

ABSTRACT

The severe impact of global climate change requires rapid political and social transitions toward more sustainable, resilient, and environmentally friendly energy resources. Digital transformation and sustainable development are two closely interlinked global trends that impact many aspects of global economic activities and our daily lives. In particular, digital innovations are major catalysts in the transition to sustainable, low-carbon energy systems. At the same time, energy transitions raise several governance-related challenges whose solutions remain little explored. Recent studies have shown that blockchain-based energy transition solutions offer advantages in terms of better coordination, reduced transaction costs, elimination of intermediation, improved transparency, immutability, traceability, operational efficiency, and enhanced security and privacy. Blockchain can also meet certain institutional constraints linked to the establishment of a climate of trust. This chapter explores the potential role that blockchain technology can play in addressing the governance challenges associated with decentralized, low-carbon energy transitions. It provides a comprehensive review of blockchain's role in addressing some governance challenges associated with green energy transition projects.

Corporate Governance, Digitalization, and Energy Transition: Imen Baccouche and Afef Khalil. (Eds.)

DOI: 10.1201/9781779643407-14

11.1 INTRODUCTION

Energy transition is vital for limiting the risks and effects of climate change and for meeting the Paris Agreement to limit temperature rise to 1.5°C above preindustrial levels. According to IRENA (2023), the energy industry needs to invest around 150 trillion USD to realize the 1.5°C target by 2050. Adoption of clean technology, digitalization, an effective regulatory environment, and establishing synergies across sectors are some essential requisites for an effective transition toward a low-carbon energy ecosystem. Although renewable energy use has grown considerably in the past few years thanks to stimulating energy policy measures and fiscal/financial incentives, there is a lot to be done to meet the desired objectives.

Bulkeley (2005) suggested that renewable energies must have a new environmental governance model that goes beyond traditional models of politics of scale where environmental choices are made by networking and new forms of regulation that cut with traditional models which tend to be organized around geographic limits. Renewable governance should circumvent obstacles associated with organized hierarchies, separation of decision-making levels, and the distinctions between territorial governments and other actors. In this regard, many researchers have emphasized the importance of decentralization and community engagement during energy transition. Beauchampet and Walsh (2021) suggested that energy transition requires a greater interaction between citizens and the energy system. The energy community (Renewable Energy Community (REC) and Citizen Energy Community[1] (CEC)) was introduced by the European Commission in its legislation in 2019[2] to encourage the active participation of citizens and micro-, small-, and medium-sized enterprises in renewable energy implementation through consuming, producing, selling, storing energy.

The remainder of this chapter is organized as follows: In Section 11.2, we describe the governance mechanisms driving technology transitions to distributed and decentralized energy systems. In Section 11.3, we present the characteristics of blockchain-enabled innovations during the green energy transition. In Section 11.4, we discuss the role of blockchain technology in tackling the governance constraints of decentralized energy transitions. Finally, in Section 11.5, we provide a synthesis of the key merits of blockchain technology when it comes to boosting governance during green energy transition.

---

1. Lennon et al. (2023) analyze the key obstacles and drivers of CEC in Europe.
2. Energy communities (europa.eu)

11.2 TRANSITION TO DECENTRALIZED ENERGY SYSTEMS

In conventional energy systems, stakeholders that engage in system governance are confined to a limited number of elite engineers and government officials. This constraint creates an impression that energy systems are complex technologies that are difficult to assimilate by an ordinary citizen and hence they remain disconnected from people's lives. However, renewable energies can make considerable societal change since their use could result in a large decentralization of the energy system and a rethinking of its proper governance model.

In comparison to large-scale energy projects, decentralized energy systems have several benefits, including environmental responsibility, reduced capital costs, greater affordability and efficiency, minimizing risk, and a simpler ability to deal with operational issues. Despite these benefits, the style of governance adopted while designing these systems can have a significant impact on whether green energies will have a positive impact on local communities.

According to Geels et al. (2017), the transition from centralized nonrenewable energy systems toward more sustainable, decentralized, and flexible renewable-energy systems is characterized by socio-technical dynamics involving social, political, and cultural processes, in addition to changes in consumer behavior.

According to Di Silvestre et al. (2018), there are three main forces exerting pressure on the energy sector. The first one is decarbonization by reducing emissions and encouraging the usage of renewable energy sources (RES). The second force is decentralization by substituting historically centralized energy systems with smaller production units located closer to consumers. The third force is the digitalization of energy systems which reengineered how conventional centralized energy systems have operated in the past, leading to more transparent and effective transactions.

11.3 BLOCKCHAIN TECHNOLOGY'S ROLE IN THE ENERGY SECTOR

Blockchain technology, also known as Distributed Ledger Technology, is well known for its association with the cryptocurrency market, and it has attracted the interests of governments, researchers, energy supply companies, startups, technology developers, and financial institutions for its potential use in supporting energy transition. Blockchain provides the greatest synergy between many financial infrastructures. According to the Organisation for Economic Co-operation and Development, blockchain through peer-to-peer (P2P) transactions allows for the reduction of transaction costs and regulatory costs of intermediary entities that regulate contracts, which could result in increased competition and a larger range of options for customers. Blockchain could help accelerate the implementation of decentralized and green power by reducing the difficulty of managing networks with a large number of small-scale renewable and distributed energy resources.

Andoni et al. (2019) suggested that blockchain technologies have the potential to significantly improve energy system operations, markets, and consumers. It allows the elimination of intermediaries, enhances transparency, and secures transactions. The authors highlighted that above all, blockchain provides unique opportunities for encouraging consumers and small renewable generators to participate more actively in the energy market and monetize the assets they generate. The transition toward this vision requires new business models and provides new market models.

Mccarthy et al. (2018) advocated the importance of blockchain technology in fostering sustainable energy usage as well as in establishing a circular economy by providing a distributed trading system. In line with this, Pee et al. (2019) and Mylrea and Gourisetti (2017) underlined the role of blockchain-based energy trading platforms in offering a P2P trading system that can freely transact the produced energy, where prosumers and consumers could buy and sell renewable energy surplus on a P2P basis offering.

Other authors suggest that blockchain application in energy transitions requires a holistic multidimensional approach. The major constraints for blockchain development in the energy sector cited in the literature (apart from technical constraints) are principally regulation, cost, and pricing. Ahl et al. (2019) developed a five-dimensional framework for analyzing blockchain-based P2P microgrids. The first dimension is technological and covers the energy management system, the power grid, and the P2P network. The second dimension is economical and covers the energy market processes, the prosumer business models, and the smart contracts. The third dimension is social, and it embeds socioeconomic incentives, stakeholder interest management, and community engagement. The fourth dimension is environmental and covers self-sufficiency and life-cycle impact. The fifth dimension is institutional and covers market regulations, grid programs, P2P regulations, and institutional innovation tools.

Hooper and Holtbrügge (2020) demonstrated how blockchain applications in international business offer better protection for property rights and decreased transaction costs. Moreover, since data do not need to be given to or coordinated by centralized organisms, the risks associated with fraud and data breaches are reduced. Blockchain has also the potential to improve societal welfare by increasing consumer transparency and satisfaction across all investigated industries. However, the authors suggested that restrictions and supervision must be exerted to avoid the exploitation of user anonymity for criminal activities such as corruption and tax evasion. Furthermore, since the decentralized nature of blockchain technology limits direct government action, coregulation between formal institutions and informal players becomes essential.

11.4 BLOCKCHAIN'S ROLE IN THE GOVERNANCE OF THE ENERGY TRANSITION

Blockchain has been reported in the literature as an innovative method to revive governance that is rivaling established traditional economic entities such as corporations, financial markets, networks, relational contracts, and governments by proposing an alternative form of organizational governance, whereby decentralization differentiates blockchain-based corporate governance from conventional hierarchical models (Davidson et al., 2016; Narayanan et al., 2016). According to Lumineau et al. (2021), blockchain may change the way transactions are governed by offering a new method of orchestrating partnerships. The authors illustrated how blockchain governance differs in several aspects from traditional contractual and relational governance. In the same line for the banking sector, MacDonald et al. (2016) stated that blockchain is not only a new technology, but it also plays the same role as banks. The authors stated that the development of blockchain technology could lead to a major rethinking of the nature of governance in banking services.

In the renewable energy transition, blockchain governance can play an important role by enabling decentralized decision-making, improving transparency, and ensuring accountability. Recent studies have shown that blockchain-based governance offers several advantages such as greater coordination for energy transformations, reduced transaction costs, removal of intermediation, enhanced transparency, immutability, traceability, and efficiency of operations, and better security and privacy. Blockchain can also overcome institutional constraints linked to confidence building. It allows better governance during energy transitions by improving transparency and accountability of renewable energy markets. As blockchain-based energy trading platforms can enable P2P energy trading, they can leverage blockchain to track the origin of RECs, ensuring that the energy being purchased is from renewable sources and not from nonrenewable sources that have been "greenwashed." Saxena et al. (2019) suggested that in the energy sector, blockchain can ensure transaction transparency and confidentiality in the absence of trusted brokers in P2P energy trading situations that involve untrusted entities.

11.4.1 THE BLOCKCHAIN TECHNOLOGY AND SMART CONTRACTS

Decentralized autonomous organizations (DAOs) that operate through smart contracts on a blockchain platform benefit from transparent decision-making and governance without the need for centralized intermediaries. Smart contracts can be exploited to govern renewable energy projects, such as community-owned solar or wind farms, by allowing stakeholders to vote on decisions related to the project. Mylrea and Gourisetti (2017) suggested that smart contracts based on blockchain can reduce the need for intermediation with P2P trading, enabling the implementation and monetization of decentralized energy trading and exchanges while benefiting from the inherent benefits of blockchain in terms of speed, scale, and security of transactions. According to Davidson et al. (2018), smart contracts enable structuring of the relationship among the various players thanks to their intrinsic "self-enforcing" mechanisms.

According to Zachariadis et al. (2019), smart contracts have the potential to minimize opportunism by challenging the "economic efficiency of hierarchies (which exploits incomplete contracts) and relational contracting over markets (based on trust between parties)" as stated by Davidson et al. (2018).

11.4.2 ENERGY TRADING USING CRYPTOCURRENCIES ENERGY COINS

Many authors, including Akasiadis and Chalkiadakis (2016) and Mihaylov et al. (2014), advocated the use of cryptocurrencies or energy coins for P2P energy trading. According to them, using cryptocurrencies offers a distributed, secured, and transparent way for renewable energy trading. Akasiadis and Chalkiadakis (2016) offer a cryptocurrency method that allows prosumer groups to regulate offer and demand in the market. In this model, the energy that goes into the grid is converted to a virtual currency that allows prosumers and consumers to trade in a cooperative approach. The value of the coins is then determined by the supply–demand situation at the moment of injection so that the true cost of energy is reflected in the pricing. These coins can be used to trade in exchange markets or to purchase electricity from the grid.

11.4.3 BLOCKCHAIN GOVERNANCE CHALLENGES

Several studies have explored some governance challenges[3] associated with blockchain as well as some underlying technical issues about operations speed, data volume, and energy consumption,[4] in addition to nontechnical factors about policies and regulation setup. Ahl et al. (2022) suggested that blockchain energy applications require multidimensional evolution, especially in terms of regulation. The authors identified the key challenges and opportunities in applying blockchain in the energy market. In the same line, Burger and Weinmann (2022) observed that although the role of blockchain solutions in energy markets expands, as does its recognition from participants and stakeholders in the energy ecosystem, a major barrier to innovation remains the regulation of energy markets to allow for P2P trading, usage-driven network cost distribution, and bottom-up pricing markets.

11.5 DISCUSSION AND CONCLUSION

This chapter aimed to provide a comprehensive review of the potential role of blockchain technology in reshaping governance in today's green energy

3. Zachariadis et al. (2019) and Rikken et al. (2019) examine the governance issues encountered by blockchain technology.
4. OECD 2023

transitions. Our synthesis of earlier contributions revealed that blockchain-based energy trading platforms can help alleviate some of the governance constraints reported in the scientific literature on green energy transition. Among the key governance constraints that are impeding the adoption and diffusion of blockchain technology in green energy transitions, we can cite (1) the lack of accurate information for coordination and cooperation among participants in the energy system, (2) the lack of operational control and rule enforcement, and (3) the lack of adequate regulations and policies. Zhang et al. (2017) highlighted that in China, there is a gap between the technological advancements made in energy transitions and the laws that hamper the transition toward low-carbon energy usage. In summary, the main benefits of blockchain adoption in support of better governance during the green energy transition, as reported in the literature, are the following.

11.5.1 TRANSPARENCY VIA P2P ENERGY TRADING

Blockchain can ensure that each participant in the energy supply network has access to the same information by providing a transparent and secure record of energy financial transactions. This may help in reducing information asymmetry, which is a major issue in the energy trade. Blockchain also enhances transparency and reduces information asymmetry thanks to the deliverance of the RECs.[5] Blockchain technology can be utilized to build a safe and transparent system for tracking renewable energy usage in the power grid. It can deliver marketable certificates that indicate the environmental features of renewable energy generation. This can assist in ensuring that energy users receive the energy for which they have paid and that the energy supplied is from renewable sources.

11.5.2 FLEXIBILITY

RECs provide official confirmation of the usage of renewable energy from the grid without having to set up renewable energy installations in personal residences or company premises, thus allowing carbon flexible footprint reduction.

5. According to the United States Environmental Protection Agency, "RECs are market-based instruments that represent attributes of 1 MWh renewable electricity generation."

11.5.3 TRACEABILITY

Blockchain can be used to track the generation, use, and delivery of energy. This can provide some guarantee that energy is generated from RESs and distributed sustainably and efficiently. It can also help to limit the risk of corruption and guarantee the validity of energy certificates.

11.5.4 BOOST CONFIDENCE

Blockchain technology has the potential to enable the creation of a more efficient and decentralized electricity system. Energy producers can securely record data linked to energy production and consumption utilizing blockchain-based systems, enabling better tracking and verification of renewable energy generation. This can help to guarantee that energy is distributed and used in the most efficient and possible sustainable way.

11.5.5 ACCOUNTABILITY

Smart contracts enabled by blockchain technology are automatic agreements that have been designed to execute the conditions of the contract automatically. This eliminates the need for intermediaries during energy operations, thus lowering the possibility of conflicts and increasing accountability.

11.5.6 DEMOCRATIZATION

Blockchain favors the democratization of energy systems by reducing the authority of centralized energy providers while increasing customer engagement in the energy market. This can contribute toward a more environmentally friendly democratic and distributed energy sector.

11.5.7 DECENTRALIZATION

DAOs are decentralized organizations functioning on a blockchain using smart contracts, enabling transparent decision-making and governance without the use of centralized intermediaries. DAOs can be used to govern renewable energy projects like community-owned solar or wind farms by enabling stakeholders to vote on project decisions.

11.5.8 FINANCING

In terms of asset ownership, there is evidence that blockchain-based platforms redirect microinvestments from individuals as well as companies all over the world to finance transformative energy projects in the poorest regions of the world. Overall, blockchain governance has the potential to improve the efficiency and effectiveness of renewable energy transitions by enabling decentralized decision-making, improving transparency, reducing corruption, boosting trust by reducing information asymmetry, and ensuring accountability. For these systems to become widespread shortly, technical development and inclusive regulatory frameworks will need to be addressed. In addition, future research can focus on addressing important related topics about stakeholder engagement mechanisms, accountability and transparency mechanisms, and public education and awareness of green energy transitions.

KEYWORDS

- **climate change**
- **energizing governance**
- **energy transition**
- **transition**

REFERENCES

Ahl, A., Goto, M., Yarime, M., Tanaka, K. & Sagawa, D. (2022). Challenges and opportunities of blockchain energy applications: Interrelatedness among technological, economic, social, environmental, and institutional dimensions. *Renewable and Sustainable Energy Reviews*, 166, 11–26.

Ahl, A., Yarime, M., Tanaka, K. & Sagawa, D. (2019). Review of blockchain-based distributed energy: Implications for institutional development. *Renewable and Sustainable Energy Reviews*, 107, 200–211.

Akasiadis, C. & Chalkiadakis, G. (2016). Decentralized large-scale electricity consumption shifting by prosumer cooperatives. In *ECAI*, pp. 175–183.

Andoni, M., Robu, V., Flynn, D., Abram, S., Geach, D., Jenkins, D. & Peacock, A. (2019). Blockchain technology in the energy sector: A systematic review of challenges and opportunities. *Renewable and Sustainable Energy Reviews*, 100, 143–174.

Beauchampet, I. & Walsh, B. (2021). Energy citizenship in the Netherlands: The complexities of public engagement in a large-scale energy transition. *Energy Research & Social Science*, 76, 10–20.

Bulkeley, H. (2005). Reconfiguring environmental governance: Towards a politics of scales and networks. *Political Geography*, 24(8), 875–902.

Burger, C. & Weinmann, J. (2022). Blockchain platforms in energy markets—A critical assessment. *Journal of Risk and Financial Management*, 15(11), 5–16.

Davidson, S., De Filippi, P. & Potts, J. (2016). Disrupting governance: The new institutional economics of distributed ledger technology. SSRN 2811995.

Davidson, S., De Filippi, P. & Potts, J. (2018). Blockchains and the economic institutions of capitalism. *Journal of Institutional Economics*, *14*(4), 639–658.

Di Silvestre, M. L., Favuzza, S., Sanseverino, E. R. & Zizzo, G. (2018). How decarbonization, digitalization, and decentralization are changing key power infrastructures. *Renewable and Sustainable Energy Reviews*, 93, 483–498.

Geels, F. W., Sovacool, B. K., Schwanen, T. & Sorrell, S. (2017). The socio-technical dynamics of low-carbon transitions. *Joule*, 1(3), 463–479.

Hooper, A. & Holtbrügge, D. (2020). Blockchain technology in international business: changing the agenda for global governance. *Review of International Business and Strategy*, 30(2), 183–200.

IRENA (2023). World Energy Transitions Outlook 2023: 1.5°C Pathway. International Renewable Energy Agency, Abu Dhabi.

Lennon, B., Velasco-Herrejón, P. & Dunphy, N. P. (2023). Operationalizing participation: Key obstacles and drivers to citizen energy community formation in Europe's energy transition. *Science Talks*, 5, 10–18.

Lumineau, F., Wang, W. & Schilke, O. (2021). Blockchain governance—A new way of organizing collaborations?. *Organization Science*, 32(2), 500–521.

MacDonald, T. J., Allen, D. W. & Potts, J. (2016). Blockchains and the Boundaries of Self-Organized Economies: Predictions for the Future of Banking. Springer International Publishing.

McCarthy, J., Rainer, G., & O'Neill, P. (2018). Exploring the role of digital transformation in the retail sector. *Journal of Business Research*, 88, 392-399.

Mihaylov, M., Jurado, S., Avellana, N., Van Moffaert, K., de Abril, I. M. & Nowe, A. (2014). Nrgcoin: Virtual currency for the trading of renewable energy in smart grids. In *Proceedings of the 11th International Conference European Energy Market (EEM)*, IEEE, 1–6.

Mylrea, M. & Gourisetti, S. N. G. (2017). Blockchain for smart grid resilience: Exchanging distributed energy at speed, scale and security. In *2017 Resilience Week (RWS)*. IEEE, 18–23.

Narayanan, A., Bonneau, J., Felten, E., Miller, A. & Goldfeder, S. (2016). Bitcoin and cryptocurrency technologies: A comprehensive introduction. Princeton University Press, Princeton, NJ.

OECD (2023). Renewable Energy (Indicator). https://doi.org/10.1787/aac7c3f1-en.

Pee, L. G., Kankanhalli, A., & Tan, B. C. (2019). The influence of organizational factors on business intelligence systems success: A multi-method study. *Information & Management*, 56(3), 366–379.

Rikken, O., Janssen, M. & Kwee, Z. (2019). Governance challenges of blockchain and decentralized autonomous organizations. *Information Polity*, 24(4), 397–417.

Saxena, S., Farag, H., Brookson, A., Turesson, H. & Kim, H. (2019). Design and field implementation of blockchain-based renewable energy trading in residential communities. In *2019 2nd International Conference on Smart Grid and Renewable Energy (SGRE)*. IEEE, 1–6.

Zachariadis, M., Hileman, G. & Scott, S. V. (2019). Governance and control in distributed ledgers: Understanding the challenges facing blockchain technology in financial services. *Information and Organization*. https://dl.acm.org/doi/abs/10.1016/j.infoandorg.2019.03.001

Zhang, H., Xie, X., & Wei, K. K. (2017). Exploring the impact of IT infrastructure on knowledge management and organizational performance. *Information & Management*, 54(4), 473–481.

CHAPTER 12

Does Climate Risk Affect Liquidity Risk? A System Generalized Method of Moments (SGMM) Analysis for Middle East North Africa (MENA) Banks

MOHAMED ALI KHEMIRI

VPNC Lab, Faculty of Law, Economics and Management of Jendouba, University of Jendouba, Jendouba, Tunisia

ABSTRACT

The physical risks of climate change can affect banks. There are plenty of ways in which climate risk could reduce the financial sector's liquidity, including the possibility that withdrawals of deposits due to physical risks (such as wildfires and floods) could exceed predictions. This chapter aims to investigate the interaction between climate risk and liquidity risk in the Middle East North Africa (MENA) region. It uses a sample of 68 MENA banks during the period 2005–2020 and performs the System Generalized Method of Moments. Due to several economic, financial, and regulatory differences, the sample as a whole has been divided into two subsamples. The first covers 50 banks located in the Middle East region and the second is relative to 18 banks located in the North Africa region. The empirical findings support a negative correlation between climate risk and liquidity risk for the whole sample. An improvement in the climate risk index significantly decreases liquidity risk for MENA banks. However, the disaggregate analysis shows that the results differ across regions. We found that any improvement in the climate risk index increases liquidity

Corporate Governance, Digitalization, and Energy Transition: Imen Baccouche and Afef Khalil. (Eds.)

DOI: 10.1201/9781779643407-15

risk for banks in the Middle East, while there is no significant effect for banks located in the North Africa region.

12.1 INTRODUCTION

The physical risks of climate change can affect banks. There are several ways that climate risk could decrease the liquidity of the financial industry, including the potential for deposit withdrawals as a result of physical risks (such as wildfires and floods) to exceed predictions. Potentially, the direct effects of climate risk on bank loan portfolios could have an impact on bank liquidity. Investing in sectors like agriculture, which are susceptible to the impacts of climate change, must be considered by banks. Droughts, storms, and sea level rise are just a few examples of climate-related events that could increase defaults and losses for the energy and tourism sectors. This asset reduction may make it more difficult for the bank to fulfill its obligations in a short time as a result of a possible decline in liquidity (Su et al., 2022). Similar to that, there may be an economic impact on a larger scale. Events brought on by climate change may cause supply chains to break down, business expenses to rise, and consumer spending to drop, all of which might lead to a decline in economic activity and lower company profits (Yu et al., 2022). As a result, the bank's loan portfolio might depreciate, which would decrease its liquidity (Mirza et al., 2023).

The literature makes use of three different liquidity constructs. These include the ratio of loans to deposits (Mili et al., 2019; Fallanca et al., 2020; Afzal and Firdousi, 2022), the liquidity coverage ratio (G'omez-Ortega et al., 2022; Nguyen et al., 2022), and the ratio of market funds to tangible banking assets (Khemakhem and Boujelbene, 2018; Chipalkatti et al., 2020; Abdelsalam et al., 2022). Few studies specifically addressed the connection between climate risk and bank liquidity risk in the Middle East North Africa (MENA) region. Moreover, there is a lack of research on this topic in the Middle East and North Africa region. By examining the correlation between climate risk and liquidity risk in the two sets of countries, this study seeks to fill this gap.

To capture the relationship between climate change and liquidity risk, the dependent variable is the liquidity risk measured by the loan-to-deposit (LTD) ratio. Our independent variable is the climate risk index (CRI) of Resource Watch. The index aims to demonstrate the adverse effects that climate change has had on many different countries. These include climatological events like wildfires, hydrological events like floods, and meteorological happenings like storms. Low climatic risk is indicated by a high index score, and a lower score on the index is an indication of a higher climate risk. The financial sector's ability to provide liquidity will regress as climate risk rises and banks in nations with higher climate risk will have less liquidity (Hughes, 2022).

The chapter is organized as follows: Section 12.2 provides a review of the literature. Section 12.3 details the sample and empirical methods. The discussion of the empirical results is presented in Section 12.4, and the chapter concludes in Section 12.5.

12.2 LITERATURE REVIEW AND HYPOTHESIS

Given the importance of banks in the financial system and their effect on economic development, many studies have been conducted to explore factors that drive banking liquidity and some other studies have been focused on the link between climate risk and banking liquidity.

Lang et al. (2023) studied the interaction of climate risk and banking liquidity. To this end, they used a sample of banks from 23 emerging markets. The main empirical findings indicate that liquidity is sensitive to climate risk and that banks based in countries with higher climate risk feel greater pressure on their liquidity. Additionally, Li and Wu (2023) examined a sample of 403 commercial banks from China during the period of 2008–2018. Findings suggest that the availability of bank loans is significantly impacted negatively by climate risk. Nevertheless, the government's performance in climate protection and its increased financial resources can counteract this adverse effect. The study also discovered that banks with lower deposit levels and banks situated in coastal areas are more severely impacted negatively by climate risk.

Lee et al. (2022), using data from 56 countries over the period 1995–2012, examined whether bank and country characteristics affected the link between climate risk and bank liquidity generation. The primary empirical results show that while climate adaptation has good effects, climate sensitivity and exposure have negative consequences on total liquidity production. These consequences are more severe for larger banks with less capital, banks situated in low-GDP (gross domestic product) countries, and banks, respectively. We hypothesize that:

H1. Climate risk is negatively associated with liquidity risk.

12.3 RESEARCH METHODOLOGY

12.3.1 SAMPLE AND DATA COLLECTION

To explore the relationship between climate risk and liquidity risk, we used an initial sample of 109 banks located in 10 MENA countries over the period 2005–2020. However, due to the availability and the continuity of bank information, several banks have been excluded. Hence, the final sample contains only 68 conventional banks.

To get a better understanding and reliable results on the impact of CRI on liquidity risk we split the MENA region into two subregions. The first bloc contains the Middle East countries with a sample of 50 banks and the second involves the North African countries with a sample of 18 banks (see Table 12.1).

TABLE 12.1 Number of Banks by Country

Middle East Countries		North African Countries	
Countries	**Number of Banks**	**Countries**	**Number of Banks**
Jordan	13	Egypt	4
Kuwait	5	Morocco	4
Oman	3	Tunisia	10
Lebanon	4		
Qatar	4		
Saudi Arabia	8		
United Arab Emirates	13		
Number of banks	**50**	Number of banks	**18**
Total		**68 banks**	

12.3.2 VARIABLES MEASUREMENT

The current study uses the LTD ratio to measure the liquidity risk as a dependent variable. As explanatory variables, we introduced four categories of variables in the econometric model. The first category is relative to climate risk measured by the CRI. The second category is relative to bank specifics; we included bank size (BS) to explain changes in bank performance. The nonperforming loans (NPLs) are measured by bank nonperforming loans to gross loans (%). The return on assets (ROA) reflects profitability. Capital adequacy ratio (CAR) considered as a key determinant of bank performance is also included. The third category of variables is relative to industry specifics. Bank concentration (CONC) and bank competition (LERN) are recognized as drivers for bank profitability and bank stability. The fourth category is relative to the macroeconomic conditions proxied by the growth rate of GDP (GDPG) and the inflation rate (INF).

Data related to bank-level data, which concern financial and accounting variables, are obtained from the Thomson Reuters database and annual reports of each bank. However, country-level data that reflect industry specifics and macroeconomic conditions are collected from two main sources. The first one is the Global Financial Indicators Database and the World Bank Indicators Database. Data on the CRI are obtained from German Resource Watch. All variables' definitions are given in Table 12.2.

TABLE 12.2 Definition of Variables

Variables	Definitions	Measures
	Dependent variables (LTD)	
LTD	Liquidity risk	Loans to deposits ratio (%)
	Climate risk	
CRI	Climate risk index	CRI of Resource Watch
	Bank specifics	
NPLs	Nonperforming loans	Bank nonperforming loans to gross loans (%)
BS	Bank size	Natural logarithm of total assets
CAR	Capital adequacy ratio	Bank capital to total assets (%)
ROA	Return on assets	Net income after tax to total assets
	Industry specifics	
CONC	Bank concentration	Bank concentration (%)
LERN	Bank competition	The Lerner index
	Macroeconomic conditions	
GDPG	The growth rate of GDP	Annual growth rate of GDP (%)
INF	The inflation rate	Consumer price index (%)

12.3.3 MODEL SPECIFICATION

To investigate the correlation between climate change and liquidity risk, the econometric model can be presented as follows:

$$\text{LTD}_{i,t} = \beta_0 + \beta_1\text{CRI}_{i,t} + \beta_2\text{ROA}_{i,t} + \beta_3\text{BS}_{i,t} + \beta_4\text{CAR}_{i,t} + \beta_5\text{NPLs}_{i,t} + \beta_6\text{CONC}_{i,t} + \beta_7\text{LERN}_{i,t} + \beta_8\text{GDPG}_{i,t} + \beta_9\text{INF}_{i,t} + \varepsilon_{i,t} \quad (12.1)$$

12.3.4 METHODOLOGY

This chapter uses the system-generalized method of moment (SGMM)'s estimators as an empirical strategy. Using the SGMM method helps solve the problem of endogeneity which is considered one of the most serious problems in corporate and banking finance. Additionally, the OLS and the fixed- and random-effect models always face several problems like omitted variables bias and measurement errors. To overcome this problem, in this chapter, we use the SGMM method proposed by Blundell and Bond (1998). Finally, the SGMM method provides robust results and consistent parameter estimates (Zhou et al., 2014; Teixeira & Queirós, 2016; Danisman & Tarazi, 2020; Hakimi et al., 2020).

12.4 EMPIRICAL FINDINGS

12.4.1 DESCRIPTIVE STATISTICS

Table 12.3 presents descriptive statistics which inform about climate change, bank specifics, industry specifics, and macroeconomic conditions in the MENA region. The average value of liquidity risk (LTD) is equal to 82.676 with a maximum value of 215.322 and a minimum value of 1.438. The average CRI of conventional banks is 100.830 with a maximum value of 173.670. The average value of bank profitability (PROF) measured by (ROA) is equal to 1.954 with a maximum value of 101.432 and a minimum value of −10.304. The size of banks (BS) which is equal on average to 9.887 is small. It has a maximum value of 18.080 and a minimum value of 2.660. The average value of the CAR is 14.869 with minimum and maximum values of 1.256 and 40.350, respectively. The average value of credit risk (credit risk) measured by NPLs is equal to 8.267 with a maximum value of 58.130 and a minimum value of 0.010. As for the industry specifics bank concentration (CONC) and bank competition (LERN), results recorded in Table 12.3 indicate that the average value of bank concentration (CONC) is equal to 67.906 with a maximum value of 100.000 and a minimum value of 40.218. The average value of bank competition (LERN) is equal to 0.423 with a maximum value of 0.615 and a minimum value of 0.098.

TABLE 12.3 Descriptive Statistics

Variables	Mean	Std. Dev.	Min	Max
LTD	82.676	27.869	1.438	215.322
CRI	100.830	31.404	12.250	173.670
ROA	1.954	3.505	−10. 304	101.432
BS	9.887	2.660	5.045	18.080
CAR	14.869	4.941	1.256	40.350
NPLs	8.267	7.692	0.010	58.130
CONC	67.906	19.267	40.218	100.000
LERN	0.423	0.109	0.098	0.615
GDPG	3.225	4.465	−21.464	26.170
INF	3.955	6.403	−4.863	84.864

Concerning the macroeconomic conditions variables, Table 12.3 shows that the average value of the growth rate of GDP (GDPG) is equal to 3.225 with a maximum value of 26.170 and a minimum value of −21.464. The average value of the inflation rate (INF) is 3.955 with minimum and maximum values of −4.863 and 84.864, respectively.

12.4.2 CROSS-CORRELATION MATRIX

The cross-correlation matrix gives information on the level and the nature of linkages between variables by determining the coefficients of their linear correlations. Table 12.4 presents the cross-correlation matrix of all variables used in this study.

12.4.3 DISCUSSION RESULTS

12.4.3.1 DISCUSSION RESULTS OF THE AGGREGATE ANALYSIS

The first step of the empirical strategy followed in this chapter consists of testing the impact of climate change measured by the CRI on the bank liquidity risk in the MENA region measured by the LTD. According to Table 12.5, the empirical findings support a negative relationship between climate risk and liquidity for the whole sample. An improvement in the CRI significantly decreases liquidity risk for MENA banks. This finding is in line with different studies (Lee et al., 2022; Lang et al., 2023; Li and Wu, 2023). Results also indicate that bank profitability measured by ROA significantly decreases bank liquidity risk. A 1% decrease in the ROA increases liquidity

TABLE 12.4 Cross-Correlation Matrix

	CRI	ROA	BS	CAR	NPLs	CONC	LERN	GDPG	INF
CRI	1.0000								
ROA	−0.0008	1.0000							
	0.9777								
BS	−0.0112	−0.0398	1.0000						
	0.7110	0.1902							
CAR	0.1654*	0.2447*	0.0073	1.0000					
	0.0000	0.0000	0.8091						
NPLs	0.0443	−0.0349	−0.2635*	−0.2331*	1.0000				
	0.2395	0.3536	0.0000	0.0000					
CONC	0.0684*	0.0659*	−0.1930*	0.0556	−0.0205	1.0000			
	0.0240	0.0297	0.0000	0.0668	0.5862				
LERN	0.0127	0.1091	−0.2379*	0.2359*	−0.2673*	0.1586*	1.0000		
	0.7457	0.0054	0.0000	0.0000	0.0000	0.0000			
GDPG	0.1114*	0.1135*	−0.0843*	0.0304	−0.0590	0.0101	−0.0022	1.0000	
	0.0002	0.0002	0.0054	0.3168	0.1178	0.7398	0.9562		
INF	0.0602	0.0068	0.0820*	−0.0904*	0.1552*	0.1356	−0.2422*	−0.1157*	1.0000
	0.0529	0.8270	0.0083	0.0037	0.0000	0.0000	0.0000	0.0002	

risk by 172.7%. Moreover, empirical results show that a rise in bank competition is associated with a greater sensitivity of the bank's liquidity risk in the MENA region. Bank liquidity risk rises with increased bank competition. Findings also indicate that growth economic negatively and significantly affects the level of liquidity risk, while the inflation rate has a positive but not significant impact on liquidity risk. The level of growth economic plays a crucial role in driving bank profitability. In a stable macroeconomic environment marked by an improvement in economic conditions, the level of growth economic positively affects the profitability of banks. Unlike the effect of GDP, we found that any increase in the inflation rate significantly decreases bank profitability. A higher level of inflation increases the operating costs and the financial expenses and consequently, it results in a decrease in bank profitability. Additionally, due to an increase in financial expenses, any increase in the inflation rate reduces the ability of borrowers to repay their loans. In this case, the quality of loans deteriorated and the level of NPLs increased which decreased the profitability of banks.

TABLE 12.5 Results of the Aggregate Analysis

	LTD			
	Coef.	**Std. Err.**	**Z**	**P > z**
LTD(−1)	0.511	0.006	76.55	0.000***
CRI	−0.030	0.004	−6.38	0.000***
ROA	−1.728	0.126	−13.61	0.000***
BS	−3.731	0.575	−6.48	0.000***
CAR	−0.254	0.054	−4.72	0.000***
NPLs	−0.140	0.057	−2.45	0.014**
CONC	−1.089	0.041	−26.13	0.000***
LERN	84.341	3.461	24.37	0.000***
GDPG	−0.409	0.030	−13.52	0.000***
INF	0.071	0.104	0.68	0.495*
_cons	124.124	5.003	24.81	0.000***
AR(1)			−2.044	
Prob			0.0410	
AR(2)			0.920	
Prob			0.3575	
Sargan test			52.043	
Prob			0.1623	

* significant at 10%; ** significant at 5%; *** significant at 1%

12.4.3.2 DISCUSSION RESULTS OF THE DISAGGREGATE ANALYSIS: MIDDLE EASTERN COUNTRIES VS. NORTH AFRICAN COUNTRIES

According to Table 12.6, the disaggregate analysis shows that the results differ across regions. We found that any improvement in the CRI increases liquidity risk for banks in the Middle East, while there is no significant effect for banks located in the North Africa region. This finding is consistent with various studies (Lee et al., 2022; Lang et al., 2023; Li and Wu, 2023). Before delving into the analysis, it is worth mentioning that there exists a macroeconomic heterogeneity between MENA countries despite belonging to the same bloc. Therefore, to get a better understanding and reliable results on the impact of CRI on bank liquidity risk, we split the MENA region into two subregions. The first bloc contains the Middle Eastern countries and the second involves the North African countries. We follow the same empirical strategy for the disaggregate analysis based on the Middle Eastern and North African countries. The output of the model has provided two different. Indeed, unlike the results of the whole sample that confirm the negative effect of both climate risk on liquidity risk, the results of the disaggregate analysis indicate that the effect of CRI differs across the two regions of Middle Eastern and North African countries. Findings displayed in Table 12.6 show that for the Middle Eastern countries, climate risk does not exert any significant effect on bank liquidity risk measured by LTD. However, we found the opposite results for the North African countries.

12.5 CONCLUSION

This chapter aims to investigate the interaction between climate risk and liquidity risk in the MENA region. It uses a sample of 68 MENA banks during the period 2005–2020 and performs the SGMM. Due to several economic, financial, and regulatory differences, two subsamples were created from the whole sample. The first covers 50 banks located in the Middle East region and the second is relative to 18 banks located in the North Africa region. Overall, the empirical findings support a negative relationship between climate risk and liquidity for the whole sample. An improvement in the CRI significantly decreases liquidity risk for MENA banks. However, the disaggregate analysis shows that the results differ

TABLE 12.6 Results of the Effect of CRI on Liquidity Risk (*Middle Eastern vs. North African Countries)*

	Middle East				**North Africa**			
	LTD				**LTD**			
	Coef.	**Std. Err.**	**Z**	**P>z**	**Coef.**	**Std. Err.**	**Z**	**P>z**
LTD(−1)	0.559	0.032	17.37	0.000***	0.142	0.083	1.69	0.091*
CRI	0.041	0.007	5.50	0.000***	−0.033	0.075	−0.44	0.660
ROA	−0.233	0.498	−0.45	0.653	−11.690	6.259	-1.87	0.062*
BS	−1.255	0.388	−3.24	0.001***	27.651	13.674	2.02	0.043**
CAR	−0.354	0.065	−5.24	0.000***	−7.112	5.260	−1.35	0.176
NPLs	−0.174	0.084	−2.08	0.038**	0.426	1.389	0.31	0.759
CONC	−0.265	0.064	−4.14	0.000***	−4.338	1.326	−3.27	0.001***
LERN	34.761	6.459	5.38	0.000***	20.737	319.889	0.06	0.948
GDPG	−0.004	0.033	−0.13	0.894	−3.372	0.809	−4.17	0.000***
INF	0.705	0.131	5.37	0.000***	−17.192	6.747	−2.55	0.011**
_cons	51.282	4.839	10.60	0.000***	233.405	236.858	0.99	0.324
AR(1)			−2.923					
Prob			0.004					
AR(2)			0.9509				1.5352	
Prob			0.3416				0.1247	
Sargan test			25.344				9.4861	
Prob			0.9853				1.0000	

* significant at 10%; ** significant at 5%; *** significant at 1%

across regions. We found that any improvement in the CRI increases liquidity risk for banks in the Middle East, while there is no significant effect for banks located in the North Africa region.

The results of this chapter could have important policy implications for both policymakers and bankers. First, the findings imply that policymakers should proceed with prudence when developing and putting into practice climate-related measures because these can have an impact on the production of liquidity, which in turn can have an impact on macroeconomic stability. Second, bankers must use sustainable financial practices to advance sustainable development goals and guard against environmental harm. Third, in climate-risky nations, banks may face greater liquidity demands. Finally, commercial banks should modify the structure of their credit business and develop new lending products. The limitation of this study is the use of the LTD ratio as the only measure of liquidity risk. Other measures can be used as robustness checks for the relationship between climate risk and bank liquidity risk.

KEYWORDS

- **climate risk**
- **liquidity risk**
- **MENA banks**
- **SGMM**

REFERENCES

Abdelsalam, O., Elnahass, M., Ahmed, H. & Williams, J. (2022). Asset securitizations and bank stability: Evidence from different banking systems. *Global Financial Journal*. https://doi.org/10.1016/J.GFJ.2020.100551.

Afzal, A. & Firdousi, S. F. (2022). Does the market discipline banks? Evidence from Balkan states. *Journal of Risk Finance*, 23, 418–436. https://doi.org/10.1108/JRF-01-2022-0024/ FULL/XML.

Chipalkatti, N., DiPierro, M., Luft, C. & Plamondon, J. (2020). Loan fair values and the financial crisis. *Journal of Risk Finance*, 21, 559–576. https://doi.org/10.1108/ JRF-04-2020- 0081/FULL/XML.

Fallanca, M. G., Forgione, A. F. & Otranto, E. (2020). Forecasting the macro determinants of bank credit quality: A non-linear perspective. *Journal of Risk Finance*, 21, 423–443. https:// doi.org/10.1108/JRF-10-2019-0202/FULL/PDF.

G´omez-Ortega, A., Gelashvili, V., Delgado Jal´on, M. L. & Rivero Men´endez, J. A. (2022). Impact of the application of IFRS 9 on listed Spanish credit institutions: Implications from the regulatory, supervisory and auditing point of view. *Journal of Risk Finance*, 23, 437–455. https://doi.org/10.1108/JRF-01-2022-0023/FULL/XML.

Hakimi, A., Boussaada, R. & Hamdi, H. (2020). The interactional relationships between credit risk, liquidity risk and bank profitability in MENA region. *Global Business Review*, 16, 20–33.

Hughes, A. (2022). Commentary: Thinking about climate risk as a supply-side shock. *Journal of Risk Finance*, 23, 324–325. -.

Khemakhem, S. & Boujelbene, Y. (2018). Predicting credit risk based on financial and non-financial variables and data mining. *Review of Accounting and Finance*, 17, 316–340. https://doi. org/10.1108/RAF-07-2017-0143/FULL/XML.

Lee,C. C., Wang, C. W., Thinh, B. T. & Xu, Z. T. (2022). Climate risk and bank liquidity creation: International evidence. *International Review of Financial*, 17, 205–216.

Mili, M., Khayati, A. & Khouaja, A. (2019). Do bank independence and diversification affect bank failures in Europe? *Review of Accounting and Finance*, 18, 366–398. https://doi.org/10.1108/ RAF-09-2017-0181/FULL/XML.

Mirza, N., Afzal, A., Umar, M. & Skare, M. (2023). The impact of green lending on banking performance: Evidence from SME credit portfolios in the BRIC. *Economic Analysis Policy,* 77, 843–850. https://doi.org/10.1016/J.EAP.2022.12.024.

Nguyen, T., Nguyen, V. H. & Hong, T. V. (2022). How do banks price liquidity? The role of market power. *Global Financial Journal,* 53, 10–36. https://doi.org/10.1016/J.GFJ.2022.100736.

Lang, Q., Ma, F., Mirza, N. & Umar, M. (2023). The interaction of climate risk and bank liquidity: An emerging market perspective for transitions to low carbon energy.*Technological Forecasting and Social Change*. https://doi.org/10.1016/j.techfore.2023.122480.

Li, S. & Wu, X. (2023). How does climate risk affect bank loan supply? Empirical evidence from China. *Economic Change and Restructuring*. https://doi.org/10.1007/s10644–023-09505–9.

Su, C. W., Mirza, N., Umar, M., Chang, T. & Albu, L. L. (2022). Resource extraction, greenhouse emissions, and banking performance. *Resource Policy*, 79, 10–22. https://doi.org/10.1016/J.RESOURPOL.2022.103122.

Yu, B., Li, C., Mirza, N. & Umar, M. (2022). Forecasting credit ratings of decarbonized firms: Comparative assessment of machine learning models. *Technological Forecasting and Social Change*. https://doi.org/10.1016/J.TECHFORE.2021.121255.

CHAPTER 13

Environment Social Governance (ESG) Criteria and Socially Responsible Investment: The Impact on the Energy Sector and Opportunities for Sustainable Investment Practices

BINCY BABURAJ KALUVILLA

Emirates Academy of Hospitality Management, Dubai, UAE

ABSTRACT

As the global shift toward sustainability gains traction, the significance of integrating Environmental, Social, and Governance (ESG) criteria in investment decisions is underscored. This chapter emphasizes the profound impact of ESG criteria on the energy sector. The objective is to understand the role of Socially Responsible Investment (SRI) in championing sustainable investment practices and enhancing the energy sector's performance. Various ESG metrics, such as carbon emissions, water management, human rights, diversity, equity, and inclusion, are scrutinized for their bearing on investment choices. Methodologically, the research presents a case study of a renewable energy project, thoroughly evaluating its ESG performance. This encompasses an analysis of the project's financial outcomes, social ramifications, and ecological sustainability. Results demonstrate the pivotal importance of ESG considerations in investment evaluations. Key challenges and prospects for the application of ESG criteria in investments are dissected, with a particular focus on the transformative role of

Corporate Governance, Digitalization, and Energy Transition: Imen Baccouche and Afef Khalil. (Eds.)

DOI: 10.1201/9781779643407-16

technology and digitalization in refining ESG data collection and analysis. The chapter concludes with an affirmation of the necessity to embed ESG criteria in investment judgments to foster sustainable procedures and positively influence the energy sector's comprehensive performance. This work serves as a clarion call for investors to give precedence to ESG components in their decision-making processes, underscoring the manifold advantages of SRI.

13.1 INTRODUCTION

In the realm of investment analysis, lies a fascinating domain known as Environmental, Social, and Governance (ESG) criteria—a collection of nonfinancial facets that pique the interest of investors when contemplating potential ventures. This novel concept emerged as a potent response to the mounting apprehensions surrounding the adverse environmental and societal impacts of corporate undertakings. Moreover, it also addresses the pressing need for ethical and responsible governance. The principal aim that underpins the integration of ESG criteria into investment decisions extends far beyond the confines of financial gains (Bassen & Kovacheva, 2018). Instead, it seeks to forge a path toward generating positive impacts that resonate with wider societal and environmental objectives. By judiciously incorporating ESG factors, investors endeavor to bolster companies that exemplify sustainable practices, exhibit ethical behavior, and showcase an unwavering commitment to social responsibility.

Numerous empirical investigations have indisputably demonstrated that weaving ESG criteria into investment strategies bestows a myriad of benefits upon stakeholders. These benefits encompass enhanced long-term performance, mitigated risk exposure, and heightened portfolio resilience (Scholtens & Sievänen, 2018; Hassan et al., 2020). As a natural consequence of these findings, institutional investors, asset managers, and even individual investors have taken a momentous stride toward embracing sustainable investment practices. The underlying aspiration goes beyond the mere fulfillment of financial goals; it seeks to contribute meaningfully to the cultivation of a more sustainable and equitable world.

In this illuminating journey through the labyrinth of investment wisdom, we shall unravel the enigmatic nature of ESG criteria, shedding light on the hidden gems that often elude the gaze of conventional analyses. Join us as we delve into the depths of this fascinating realm, where the convergence of financial acumen and societal consciousness creates an altogether new paradigm for investing—a realm where prosperity and benevolence intertwine in unprecedented harmony. At the very heart of the grand tapestry of global sustainability lies the energy sector, an indispensable catalyst propelling economic growth and progress. This formidable industry casts its influential reach across various sectors, leaving a profound impact on the environment and society at large. Historically, traditional energy sources, such as fossil fuels, have regrettably been linked to ecological degradation, entailing a trail of greenhouse gas emissions, air pollution, and the lamentable destruction of precious habitats. As the pendulum of environmental consciousness swings, the energy sector now stands amid mounting pressure to transition toward sustainable and renewable energy sources (Friede et al., 2015; Dowling et al., 2019).

Enter the realm of renewable energy technologies—an enchanting array encompassing solar, wind, hydroelectric, and geothermal power. Within these wondrous alternatives lie promising solutions to alleviate the environmental burdens of energy production and consumption. With each dawn, renewable energy beckons the energy sector to embark on a transformative journey—a journey that leads toward a future adorned with a low-carbon, sustainable grace.

Beyond its profound dedication to environmental stewardship, the energy sector has assumed a mantle of responsibility that transcends the bounds of ecology. This noble commitment encompasses the very fabric of ESG principles. Herein, the spotlight extends to the social tapestry, weaving together threads of labor rights, community engagement, and workforce diversity. Simultaneously, the governance realm reflects a radiant commitment to transparency in decision-making and the embodiment of unwavering ethical business practices (Nguyen & El-Mansi, 2020).

As we traverse the horizon of possibilities in the energy sector's unwavering pursuit of sustainability, let us pause to marvel at the grandeur of this metamorphosis. Through the fusion of technological innovation and ethical principles, the energy sector emerges as a shining beacon—illuminating the path toward a harmonious coexistence of human progress and planetary preservation. Together, we embark on an expedition that promises a brighter and more promising world for generations yet to come.

In this chapter, we delve into the profound implications of integrating ESG variables into the fabric of financial decision-making, with a specific focus on their impact within the energy industry. Our mission is to illuminate the potential of sustainable investing practices in driving positive transformation within this critical sector by meticulously examining the salience of ESG considerations.

Central to our exploration is the profound influence wielded by ESG factors on the strategic allocation of capital in the domain of energy investments. Through meticulous analysis, we traverse the multifaceted dimensions of ESG concerns, encompassing environmental issues like the intricacies of carbon emissions and the judicious management of water resources. Additionally, we venture into the labyrinth of social considerations, embracing the ethos of diversity, justice, and inclusion, while also shedding light on the governance aspects of accountability and transparency.

Within the pages of this chapter, we scrutinize the potential of Socially Responsible Investment (SRI) as a catalyst for fostering sustainable business practices within the energy industry. In our relentless pursuit of knowledge, we dedicate ourselves to comprehensively assessing the financial returns, social impacts, and environmental sustainability entailed in investments aligned with ESG principles. This endeavor leads us to conduct an in-depth analysis of a renewable energy project, unraveling its intricacies to discern the impact of ESG-conscious decision-making.

As we embark on this intellectual voyage, we grapple with the challenges and opportunities inherent in integrating ESG elements into the tapestry of investment choices. Embracing technological advancements, we explore novel ways of gathering and analyzing data to drive more informed judgments. Ultimately, our overarching objective is to underscore the profound influence of ESG factors on sustainable investment practices within the energy sector. By inspiring investors to accord priority to ESG concerns in their decision-making processes, the energy industry assumes a pivotal role in advancing global sustainability objectives, fostering positive social change, and heralding a future of environmental prosperity.

In the context of the energy sector, consider the case of SolarTech Inc., a burgeoning solar energy firm that ardently adopted ESG criteria. The company not only invested heavily in environmentally friendly technologies but also prioritized community engagement, ensuring the local populace benefitted from its operations. They cultivated a diverse workforce, maintained transparent governance, and established partnerships with local nongovernment organizations (NGOs) to bolster community welfare. As a result, not only did SolarTech Inc. witness a surge in investments from sustainability-conscious investors, but it also ingrained itself deeply within the community, ensuring its long-term viability and growth. This case serves as a testament to the profound impact of integrating ESG criteria into the operational and investment strategies of firms in the energy sector.

This chapter unfolds in a structured manner, beginning with a deep dive into the theoretical foundations of ESG criteria and their significance in the modern investment landscape. Following this, we will explore the unique challenges and opportunities the energy sector faces in the wake of rising ESG considerations. Through a series of case studies, including the aforementioned SolarTech Inc., we aim to provide tangible insights into the real-world applications and outcomes of ESG-driven investment strategies. The concluding sections will encapsulate the broader implications for stakeholders and offer recommendations for firms and investors alike, looking to navigate this evolving landscape.

13.2 LITERATURE REVIEW

13.2.1 ESG CRITERIA AND SRI

In the realm of corporate evaluation, we encounter the multifaceted ESG criteria, which form a comprehensive set of nonfinancial metrics exercised by discerning investors. These profound considerations delve into a company's plausible impact on both society and the environment (Berg et al., 2020). Within this discerning ESG framework, we encounter three primary dimensions demanding our profound contemplation:

Environmental Factors: Encompassing the very essence of ecological prowess, these meticulous criteria earnestly scrutinize a company's environmental performance and its adept approach to prudently managing environmental perils. Paramount elements constituting this domain include the company's carbon emissions, its unwavering dedication to energy efficiency, adroit waste management practices, judicious water utilization, and resolute endeavors to assuage the tempestuous ripples of climate change (Sachs et al., 2019). At its core, the company's environmental stance assumes a position of profound significance, unriddling the enigma of its relentless dedication to sustainable practices and the profound impact it may wield upon the environment.

Social Factors: Venturing into the labyrinth of human interactions and noble camaraderie, these discerning criteria meticulously assess a company's intricate relationships with its esteemed workforce, esteemed clientele, esteemed suppliers, cherished communities, and an array of other stakeholders etched in the tapestry of its existence. Among the quintessential aspects under contemplation, we uncover the labyrinthine labor practices, the delightful embrace of employee diversity and inclusion, the laudable safeguarding of human rights, the vigilant guardianship of customer data privacy, the fervent engagement with the community, and the praiseworthy contributions to the amelioration of social welfare (Khan et al., 2018). Within this profound exploration, we unfurl the company's profound commitment to ethical comportment and its unwavering allegiance to social responsibility.

Governance Factors: Peering into the sanctum of organizational orchestration, these astute criteria train their discerning gaze on a company's internal management and the meticulous oversight mechanisms set in motion. Capturing crucial elements such as the tapestry of board structure, the discerning remuneration bestowed upon the esteemed executives, the resolute upholding of shareholder rights, the praiseworthy transparency meticulously interwoven into financial reporting, and the unwavering adherence to ethical business practices (Hassan et al., 2021), this realm ensures the emergence of a corporate ethos characterized by accountability, judicious decision-making, and the unwavering guardianship of the shareholders' prized interests.

Integrating ESG criteria into investment decisions holds escalating significance due to several pivotal reasons:

Risk Management: ESG factors offer valuable insights into a company's susceptibility to diverse risks, encompassing environmental liabilities, legal disputes, reputational hazards, and social contentions. By judiciously considering these factors, investors attain heightened discernment, enabling them to make well-informed decisions aimed at mitigating potential risks (Bassen & Kovacheva, 2018).

Long-Term Performance: Research attests that companies exhibiting robust ESG performance are apt to outshine their counterparts over the long haul. Firms that prioritize sustainability and uphold responsible business practices stand poised to adapt adeptly to shifting market landscapes and societal exigencies, amplifying their enduring viability and profitability (Friede et al., 2015).

Stakeholder Expectations: Investors, consumers, employees, and regulators increasingly expect companies to address ESG issues responsibly. Companies that fail to meet these expectations risk facing reputational damage, legal challenges, and loss of investor confidence (Scholtens & Sievänen, 2018).

Regulatory Landscape: Many jurisdictions are imposing stricter regulations related to ESG disclosures and responsible investment practices. Incorporating ESG criteria in investment decisions helps ensure compliance with evolving regulatory requirements (Grewal & Wang, 2020).

SRI, also known as sustainable or ethical investing, refers to an investment approach that considers not only financial returns but also the social and environmental impacts of investments. SRI is guided by several principles:

Positive Impact: SRI seeks to invest in companies and projects that actively contribute to positive social and environmental outcomes. It focuses on enterprises involved in renewable energy, clean technology, healthcare, education, and other sectors that address societal challenges (Clark et al., 2019).

Ethical Screening: SRI employs ethical screens to bar companies involved in activities deemed harmful, such as weapons production, tobacco, or human rights violations. This screening process harmonizes investment choices with investors' deeply held values and convictions (Barth et al., 2021).

Engagement and Advocacy: SRI investors frequently collaborate with companies to champion responsible practices and foster enhancements in their ESG performance. Shareholder advocacy and proxy voting stand as indispensable tools, propelling affirmative changes within these corporations (Hassan et al., 2020).

Transparency and Reporting: Transparency embodies a fundamental tenet of SRI. Investors actively seek companies that proffer comprehensive and accurate ESG disclosures, thereby empowering them to effectively appraise the company's dedicated endeavors toward sustainability (Viganò et al., 2021).

In conclusion, comprehending ESG criteria and embracing SRI practices constitute pivotal strides toward sustainable and responsible investing. Integrating ESG factors into investment decisions not only bolsters risk management but also aligns investments with societal and environmental objectives, thus contributing to a more sustainable and just world.

13.2.2 THE IMPACT OF ESG CRITERIA ON THE ENERGY SECTOR

ESG factors shape the energy sector's sustainability and responsibility. Crucial role in responsible practices. Several key ESG criteria are particularly relevant to the industry:

Carbon Emissions: The energy sector is a significant contributor to greenhouse gas emissions, primarily through the combustion of fossil fuels. As the world seeks to address climate change, companies' efforts to reduce their carbon footprint are under increased scrutiny (IPCC, 2018). Renewable energy projects and energy efficiency measures are examples of strategies adopted to mitigate carbon emissions.

Water Management: Energy production and extraction processes often have substantial water requirements. Proper water management is critical to ensure sustainable water usage and avoid environmental impacts, especially in regions facing water scarcity (UNEP, 2019).

Human Rights: The energy sector's activities can have direct and indirect impacts on human rights, including labor rights and community rights (Business & Human Rights Resource Centre, 2021). Respect for human rights is essential in fostering sustainable and ethical practices within the industry.

Diversity, Equity, and Inclusion: Promoting diversity and inclusion within the energy sector is vital for a fair and equitable workforce (Dowling et al., 2019). Ensuring equal opportunities for individuals of diverse backgrounds helps build a sustainable and socially responsible industry.

13.2.3 THE INFLUENCE OF ESG CRITERIA ON INVESTMENT DECISIONS IN THE ENERGY SECTOR

ESG criteria have a significant influence on investment decisions within the energy industry. Investors are increasingly considering the environmental and social performance of energy companies to make informed investment choices (Di Guilio et al., 2020). Several factors contribute to the growing importance of ESG in the sector:

Financial Performance: Research indicates that energy companies with strong ESG performance are more likely to attract investments and achieve better financial performance over the long term (Hoepner et al.,

2019). Investors recognize that sustainable business practices can lead to enhanced shareholder value.

Regulatory Compliance: With the rise of sustainability-focused regulations, energy companies must demonstrate compliance with ESG standards to access certain markets and funding opportunities (PricewaterhouseCoopers (PwC), 2021). Investors consider a company's ability to meet regulatory requirements as an indicator of its long-term viability.

Social License to Operate: The energy sector, under Kapoor & Kulshrestha's (2019) scrutiny, grapples with environmental and social repercussions. Adhering to ESG principles is vital for social acceptance and averting reputational hazards.

13.2.4 SRI AND SUSTAINABLE PRACTICES

13.2.4.1 ADVANTAGES AND BENEFITS OF SRI FOR THE ENERGY SECTOR

SRI presents an array of advantages for the energy sector, offering a pathway for companies to harmonize their business methodologies with the tenets of ESG principles (Linnenluecke et al., 2017). Key benefits encompass:

Reputation and Brand Value Enhancement: Embracing SRI practices empowers energy enterprises to cultivate a positive standing and elevate their brand worth. With a burgeoning awareness among investors and consumers regarding sustainability, SRI beckons a broader community of socially conscious stakeholders.

Access to Capital: Prioritizing sustainability and social responsibility fosters an inviting landscape for responsible investors (Hawn & DuBois, 2019). SRI funds and institutional investors seek companies displaying robust ESG performance, becoming a potential source of capital for sustainable energy ventures.

Risk Mitigation: SRI strategies entail a comprehensive evaluation of ESG risks and opportunities. By tackling environmental and social risks head-on, energy companies can prudently counter potential financial and reputational hazards (Bassen & Giese, 2019).

Long-Term Value Creation: At the heart of SRI lies an unwavering focus on sustainable business practices that engender long-term value creation. Enterprises amalgamating ESG factors into their decision-making processes gain the fortitude to navigate shifting market dynamics and stakeholder expectations effectively.

In essence, SRI bolsters the energy sector's alignment with responsible and sustainable paradigms, entailing far-reaching benefits in terms of market perception, financial resilience, and the fulfillment of broader societal obligations.

13.2.4.2 EVALUATING THE FINANCIAL PERFORMANCE OF SOCIALLY RESPONSIBLE ENERGY INVESTMENTS

Assessing the financial performance of socially responsible energy investments is a critical aspect of SRI. Research has shown that SRI can deliver competitive financial returns while aligning investments with sustainability goals (Friede et al., 2015).

Financial Metrics: Investors evaluate the financial performance of SRI energy investments using traditional metrics like return on investment (ROI), net present value, and cash flow analysis.

ESG Metrics: In addition to financial metrics, investors consider ESG-related metrics to assess the social and environmental impact of their investments. These metrics may include carbon emissions reduction, water consumption efficiency, and community development initiatives.

Comparative Analysis: Comparative analysis against non-SRI energy investments helps investors understand the potential financial advantages of responsible investments in the energy sector (Maddox & Siedlok, 2019).

13.2.4.3 EXAMINING THE SOCIAL AND ENVIRONMENTAL IMPACTS OF SUSTAINABLE INVESTMENTS

Sustainable energy investments in the energy sector necessitate a comprehensive assessment of their social and environmental impacts. On the social front, such investments manifest positive outcomes by generating employment opportunities, bolstering local communities, and promoting inclusivity. The evaluation process involves scrutinizing aspects like job creation, workforce diversity, and community engagement (Khan & Serafeim, 2020).

From an environmental perspective, sustainable energy investments play a pivotal role in curbing carbon emissions, enhancing air and water quality, and safeguarding precious natural resources. Evaluating these impacts entails gauging the reduction in greenhouse gas emissions, improvements in energy efficiency, and the preservation of biodiversity (Nguyen & El-Mansi, 2020).

By diligently examining the social and environmental implications of these investments, investors can glean valuable insights into their contributions toward larger sustainability objectives.

13.3 RESEARCH METHODOLOGY

Two case studies are used in our chapter. Ørsted: Formerly known as DONG Energy, Ørsted underwent a significant transition from fossil fuels to renewable energy, establishing itself as a global leader in the process. With a keen focus on ESG principles, Ørsted's investments in offshore wind farms, ambitious carbon-neutral targets, sustainable supply chain initiatives, and active community engagement have made it an exemplary model in the energy sector. Its commitment to sustainability not only influenced the energy industry but also demonstrated that profitability and sustainability can coexist harmoniously.

Enel: As an Italian multinational energy powerhouse, Enel stands out for its deep-rooted commitment to ESG principles and sustainability. Recognized globally for its relentless dedication to renewable energy, Enel has made significant strides in solar, wind, and hydroelectric power investments. With staunch decarbonization commitments, innovative technology pursuits, and robust social impact practices, Enel is not only pushing the boundaries of green technology adoption but also setting commendable standards of responsible operations in the energy sector.

13.3.1 CASE STUDY: ØRSTED—A LEADING RENEWABLE ENERGY COMPANY

Ørsted, once DONG Energy, shifted from fossil fuels to renewable energy, becoming a global leader (Jones et al., 2019). ESG principles played a pivotal role in this triumphant transformation.

- **Renewable Energy Investments:** Ørsted has invested heavily in renewable energy projects, particularly offshore wind farms. It has become a major player in the offshore wind industry, contributing significantly to reducing carbon emissions.

- **Carbon Reduction Targets:** The company set ambitious targets to become carbon-neutral by 2025. It focuses on reducing its carbon emissions and those generated from its value chain.
- **Sustainable Supply Chain:** Ørsted actively works with its suppliers to ensure adherence to sustainability standards. It considers ESG factors when selecting partners and requires them to meet strict environmental and social criteria.
- **Community Engagement:** The company engages with local communities in the regions where it operates to foster positive relationships and ensure socioeconomic benefits for the communities.

Ørsted's ESG commitment significantly influences the energy sector. Its shift to renewables inspires other firms, fueling global renewable energy market growth (Ivanova et al., 2021). Ørsted's ESG initiatives prove profitable business can align with sustainability, setting a model for the energy industry.

13.3.2 CASE STUDY: ENEL—PROMOTING SUSTAINABILITY THROUGH INNOVATION

Enel, the Italian multinational energy firm, deeply integrates ESG principles into its business strategy (Dominguez-Faus et al., 2017). Esteemed as a top renewable energy company globally, it garners acclaim for its relentless pursuit of sustainability.

- **Renewable Energy Investments:** Enel has made substantial investments in renewable energy ventures, encompassing solar, wind, and hydroelectric power. Their primary objective revolves around augmenting renewable energy capacity and curtailing carbon intensity.
- **Decarbonization Commitments:** Enel harbors resolute ambitions in the domain of decarbonization, striving to derive 70% of its generation mix from renewable sources by 2030.
- **Innovation and Technology:** Pioneering the realm of innovation and technology, the company actively explores cutting-edge technologies to enhance energy efficiency and seamlessly integrate renewable energy into the grid.

- **Social Impact:** Enel fosters meaningful engagement with local communities and stakeholders, attuned to comprehending their requisites and apprehensions, ultimately ensuring positive social impacts arising from its projects.

Enel's strong focus on ESG principles makes it a leading force in energy sector sustainability. Their dedication to renewable energy and innovation drives the industry's green technology adoption (Tran et al., 2018). Additionally, Enel's stakeholder engagement and social impact practices set a responsible benchmark in the sector.

13.3.3 VARIABLES MEASUREMENT

13.3.3.1 FINANCIAL ASPECT EVALUATION

To assess the financial aspect of the renewable energy project, a comprehensive financial analysis was conducted. The following key metrics were considered:

- **ROI:** Calculated based on the projected revenue from energy sales and the initial investment cost, considering factors such as operation and maintenance expenses, and the projected lifespan of the solar panels.
- **Payback Period:** Determined by dividing the initial investment cost by the annual net cash flows generated by the project until the investment is recovered.
- **Levelized Cost of Energy (LCOE):** Evaluated to compare the cost of electricity generated by the solar project with the prevailing market rates.

13.3.3.2 SOCIAL ASPECT EVALUATION

The social impact of the renewable energy project was assessed through a combination of qualitative and quantitative methods:

- **Job Creation:** The project's job impact, encompassing both construction and operation, was assessed, including local workforce involvement analysis for direct and indirect employment.

- **Community Engagement:** Stakeholder consultations and community engagement initiatives were examined to gauge the project's efforts to address local concerns and foster positive relationships with nearby communities.
- **Social Welfare Programs:** The project's contributions to social welfare programs, such as supporting local schools, healthcare facilities, and community development projects, were assessed.

13.3.3.3 ENVIRONMENTAL ASPECT EVALUATION

Assessing renewable energy projects' eco-performance through specific criteria.

- **Carbon Emissions Reduction:** The project's estimated carbon dioxide (CO_2) emission reduction over its lifespan was calculated by comparing it with an equivalent capacity of fossil fuel-based energy generation.
- **Land Use Impact:** The project's land footprint and its potential impact on local biodiversity and ecosystems were examined.
- **Water Usage:** The project's water requirements and its potential impact on local water resources were analyzed.

13.4 DISCUSSION RESULTS

13.4.1 THE PROJECT'S ESG PERFORMANCE AND ITS IMPLICATIONS FOR THE ENERGY SECTOR

The renewable energy project demonstrated strong ESG performance across various dimensions:

- **Financial Performance:** The renewable energy project displayed robust ESG performance, embracing financial prowess with a competitive ROI and quick payback period. LCOE analysis further affirmed its economic appeal, with solar energy generation costs rivaling traditional sources. Implications for the energy sector are profound.

- **Social Impact:** The project significantly contributed to job creation in the region during its construction and operation phases. Community engagement efforts were successful in addressing local concerns and promoting positive social outcomes.
- **Environmental Impact:** The renewable energy project showcased a notable reduction in carbon emissions compared to fossil fuel-based energy sources. It had a minimal land footprint and water consumption, leading to limited environmental impacts.

We argue that the renewable energy project's exemplary ESG performance showcases the merits of investing in sustainable energy solutions, setting a precedent for similar projects. By embracing ESG principles, energy firms can allure conscientious investors, boost their reputation, and advance global sustainability objectives. Moreover, policymakers can utilize this case study to promote renewable energy initiatives that prioritize economic, social, and environmental sustainability.

Despite the growing recognition of the importance of ESG criteria in investment decisions, the energy sector faces several challenges in fully integrating sustainability considerations:

Limited Data Availability: Access to comprehensive and reliable ESG data remains a challenge. Many energy companies may not have standardized reporting practices, hindering the assessment of their ESG performance (Vidal & Marques, 2019).

Short-Term Focus: The energy sector is often driven by short-term financial goals, which can overshadow long-term sustainability considerations. ESG investments may have longer payback periods, leading to reluctance in some cases (Flammer, 2018).

Complexity of ESG Metrics: Assessing ESG factors involves a wide range of qualitative and quantitative metrics. Determining the materiality of these metrics and their relevance to specific energy projects can be challenging (Grewal & Salimath, 2021).

Regulatory Uncertainty: Inconsistent or evolving ESG regulations can create uncertainty for energy investors, impacting their decision-making process (Dudley et al., 2018).

To overcome the challenges, the energy sector can adopt innovative solutions and strategies:

Standardized Reporting: Encouraging energy companies to adopt standardized ESG reporting frameworks, such as the Global Reporting

Initiative or the Sustainability Accounting Standards Board, can enhance the transparency and comparability of ESG data (Harris & Crane, 2018).

Integrated Decision-Making: Integrating ESG considerations into the overall decision-making process of energy companies can help align short-term financial goals with long-term sustainability objectives (Bertels & Papania, 2020).

Engagement and Collaboration: Engaging with stakeholders, including investors, regulators, communities, and NGOs, can foster a collaborative approach to addressing ESG challenges collectively (Venghaus et al., 2021).

Risk Assessment: Conducting robust ESG risk assessments can help energy companies identify potential environmental and social risks and develop mitigation strategies (Kumar & Prasad, 2020).

Leveraging advancements in technology and data analysis has emerged as a cornerstone in the seamless integration of ESG criteria within the energy sector. From harnessing the capabilities of artificial intelligence (AI) to utilizing blockchain for transparent data management, these tools offer a revolutionary approach to informed and sustainable investment decisions. Technology and data analysis are pivotal in integrating ESG criteria into energy sector investment decisions:

ESG Data Analytics: Advanced tools process vast ESG data, identifying patterns and extracting insights for informed choices (Viganò et al., 2021).

AI: AI-powered algorithms enhance ESG analysis by automating data collection, detecting trends, and predicting risks (Desmoulins-Lebeault & Seaman, 2022).

Blockchain Technology: Blockchain improves ESG data transparency, reliability, and immutability (Heras-Saizarbitoria et al., 2021).

Remote Sensing and Internet of Things (IoT): Utilizing remote sensing and the IoT enables real-time monitoring of environmental impacts and sustainability performance tracking (Ermolaeva & Lobova, 2019).

13.4.2 BEST PRACTICES AND GUIDELINES FOR ESG INTEGRATION IN ENERGY INVESTMENTS

For investors and stakeholders venturing into the energy sector, it is imperative to recognize and implement strategic measures that align with sustainable and responsible practices. From conducting thorough ESG assessments to fostering collaborations, these recommendations serve as a roadmap to navigate the complex landscape of energy investments with a sustainability lens.

Comprehensive ESG Assessment: To make informed energy investments, investors and stakeholders must conduct a comprehensive ESG assessment, incorporating financial, social, and environmental factors. This ensures a holistic grasp of the investment's impact (Pietz, 2021).

Long-Term Perspective: Prioritize a long-term outlook while making energy investment decisions, carefully considering potential risks and opportunities tied to sustainability challenges, regulatory shifts, and societal expectations (Kneip, 2019).

Engagement with Energy Companies: Actively engage with energy companies, urging them to adopt and reveal robust ESG practices. Engaged investors can wield influence, pushing companies to prioritize sustainability and transparency in their operations (Epstein, 2019).

Collaboration with Peers: Collaborate with other investors and stakeholders to share best practices, experiences, and insights on ESG integration. Joint efforts can enhance the collective impact of sustainability initiatives (Hauck, 2020).

To foster a more sustainable future, it is crucial to establish robust standards for sustainable investment practices within the energy sector. By championing transparency, materiality assessments, and regulatory collaborations, the industry can pave the way for a more responsible and consistent approach to ESG integration and corporate governance.

Standardization of ESG Reporting: Advocate for the standardization of ESG reporting practices across the energy sector. The establishment of industry-wide reporting standards would improve the comparability and transparency of ESG data (Ismail & Goos, 2019).

Incorporate Materiality Assessments: Encourage energy companies to conduct materiality assessments to identify ESG factors that are most relevant and impactful to their business and stakeholders (Erwin & Pagell, 2021).

Engagement with Regulatory Bodies: Collaborate with regulatory bodies to develop and enforce sustainability regulations and guidelines for the energy industry. This would create a level playing field and incentivize companies to integrate ESG practices (Rudolph & Dierkes, 2022).

ESG Integration in Corporate Governance: Promote the integration of ESG criteria in the governance structures of energy companies.

Board-level oversight and accountability for ESG performance can drive sustainable practices (Todorovic, 2021).

Harnessing the power of collaboration stands as a pivotal strategy for embedding ESG principles within the energy industry. By fostering partnerships, championing green finance, and promoting knowledge sharing, stakeholders can collectively drive the industry toward a more sustainable and responsible future.

Multistakeholder Partnerships: Facilitate multistakeholder partnerships involving investors, energy companies, NGOs, governments, and local communities. These partnerships can drive collective action on sustainability challenges (Park, 2020).

Green Finance Initiatives: Support and participate in green finance initiatives that promote sustainable investments in the energy sector. These initiatives can direct capital toward environmentally and socially responsible projects (Lubin, 2019).

Knowledge Sharing and Capacity Building: Foster knowledge-sharing and capacity-building programs to educate investors, energy professionals, and stakeholders on ESG integration best practices (Kendrick & Warr, 2018).

Impact Investing: Explore impact investing opportunities that prioritize investments in projects with measurable positive social and environmental impacts. Impact investors can play a transformative role in promoting sustainability in the energy sector (Sorrell, 2021).

13.5 CONCLUSION

This chapter explored the vital role of ESG criteria in energy sector investments. The analysis highlighted the value of ESG integration for fostering sustainability and responsible practices, illuminating key insights that underscore its significance in the energy industry. This chapter has shed light on the profound influence of ESG criteria on investment decisions, particularly within the energy sector.

13.5.1 THEORETICAL IMPLICATIONS

The integration of ESG criteria in investment decisions underscores a paradigm shift in traditional investment theories. It challenges the conventional wisdom of profit maximization, proposing that sustainable and responsible practices can coexist with, and even enhance, financial performance. The case studies of Ørsted and Enel further enrich academic discourse, exemplifying the real-world application of ESG theories in corporate strategies.

13.5.2 PRACTICAL IMPLICATIONS

For practitioners, especially those in the energy sector, the findings provide a roadmap for aligning business strategies with global sustainability goals. Companies like Ørsted and Enel serve as benchmarks, illustrating that a genuine commitment to ESG principles can lead to competitive advantage, brand enhancement, and stakeholder trust. Investors, too, can derive insights on how ESG factors can be pivotal in risk mitigation and long-term value creation.

13.5.3 LIMITATIONS OF THE STUDY AND FUTURE RESEARCH

While this chapter offers valuable insights, it predominantly focuses on the energy sector, which may not be directly translatable to other industries. Moreover, the reliance on select case studies may not capture the entire spectrum of ESG implementation challenges and successes across diverse corporate landscapes. There is a pressing need for comparative studies that assess ESG criteria's impact across different sectors. Additionally, with the dynamic nature of ESG metrics, continuous research on evolving best practices, technological advancements in ESG data collection, and the intersection of ESG with emerging global challenges will be invaluable. In essence, as the world grapples with pressing environmental and social challenges, the integration of ESG criteria in investment decisions emerges not as a mere trend but as an imperative for sustainable future growth.

KEYWORDS

- **energy sector**
- **ESG**
- **investment practices**
- **sustainability**

REFERENCES

Barth, E., Cebula, R. & Jun, C. (2021). Ethical screening in socially responsible mutual funds. *Journal of Business Ethics,* 174(3), 711–727.

Bassen, A., & Giese, S. (2019). Socially responsible investment and fiduciary duty: Putting the 's' in ESG. *Journal of Business Ethics,* 156(2), 321–347.

Bassen, A., & Kovacheva, S. (2018). Why do firms invest in corporate social responsibility? *Journal of Business Ethics,* 152(1), 203–219.

Berg, S., Kölbel, J. F. & Rigobon, R. (2020). Aggregate confusion: The divergence of ESG ratings. *Journal of Financial Economics,* 136(2), 330–352.

Bertels, S. & Papania, L. (2020). The business case for sustainability-driven innovation in the oil and gas sector. *Journal of Cleaner Production,* 260, 12–18.

Business & Human Rights Resource Centre. (2021). Human rights in the oil, gas, and coal industry. https://www.business-humanrights.org/en/latest-news/oil-gas-coal/.

Clark, G. L., Feiner, A. & Viehs, M. (2019). From the stockholder to the stakeholder: How sustainability can drive financial outperformance. *Journal of Corporate Finance,* 52, 72–93.

Desmoulins-Lebeault, F. & Seaman, C. (2022). The artificial intelligence of things for sustainable energy: A research agenda. *Journal of Cleaner Production,* 340, 13–25.

Di Guilio, L., McHale, M. & Siemiatycki, M. (2020). Green energy investments in the oil and gas sector: The role of the carbon disclosure project. *Energy Policy,* 144, 11–16.

Dominguez-Faus, R., Bressers, N., Nijssen, E. J. & Turnhout, E. (2017). Greening the grid: The case of Enel and the gradual transformation of the Italian electricity system. *Energy Policy,* 107, 225–239.

Dowling, M., Azevedo, I. M. L. & Botterill, L. C. (2019). Transformative capacity for diversity, equity, and inclusion in the oil and gas industry. *Journal of Business Ethics,* 159(2), 369–382.

Dudley, L., Wengel, J. & Wijermars, M. (2018). Corporate social responsibility in the oil and gas sector. *Journal of Cleaner Production,* 178, 880–896.

Epstein, M. J. (2019). Making a case for integrating environmental, social, and governance (ESG) factors into investment processes. *Financial Analysts Journal,* 75(4), 11–20.

Ermolaeva, O. & Lobova, O. (2019). Application of remote sensing and IoT technologies for the environmental monitoring of oil and gas facilities. *IOP Conference Series: Earth and Environmental Science,* 231(1), 12–19.

Erwin, R. S. & Pagell, M. (2021). Using materiality assessments to define and prioritize ESG issues for business practitioners. *Business & Society,* 60(4), 799–830.

Flammer, C. (2018). Corporate social responsibility and shareholder reaction: The environmental awareness of investors. *Academy of Management Journal,* 61(2), 639–659.

Friede, G., Busch, T. & Bassen, A. (2015). ESG and financial performance: aggregated evidence from more than 2000 empirical studies. *Journal of Sustainable Finance & Investment,* 5(4), 210–233.

Grewal, R. & Salimath, M. S. (2021). Socially responsible investing and investment performance: An empirical study. *International Journal of Finance and Economics,* 26(2), 2428–2444.

Grewal, R. & Wang, S. (2020). The impact of mandatory corporate social responsibility (CSR) reporting on firm performance: Evidence from a quasi-experiment. *Journal of Marketing Research,* 57(6), 1071–1090.

Harris, J. D. & Crane, A. (2018). ESG for long-term value: Best practices for CIOs and investment teams. *Journal of Asset Management,* 19(6), 381–392.

Hassan, K. M., Rahman, M. M., Khanam, R. & Farhana, D. F. (2021). ESG performance and corporate financial performance: The moderating role of board independence. *Journal of Business Ethics,* 170(1), 53–70.

Hassan, K. M., Rahman, M. M., Khanam, R. & Rahman, M. M. (2020). The impact of environmental, social, and governance (ESG) performance on firm value: Evidence from global top 50 firms. *Journal of Business Ethics,* 163(2), 283–316.

Hauck, J. (2020). The effect of sustainability collaboration on corporate value: A meta-analysis. *Journal of Cleaner Production,* 255, 12–22.

Hawn, O. & DuBois, C. (2019). The CSR bottom line: Preventing corporate social irresponsibility. *Journal of Business Ethics,* 156(4), 939–953.

Heras-Saizarbitoria, I., Garaizar, P. & Maiz, J. (2021). Blockchain technology for sustainable development: A scoping review. *Sustainability,* 13(8), 15–22.

Hoepner, A. G., Oikonomou, I. & Scholtens, B. (2019). The effects of corporate and country sustainability characteristics on the cost of debt: An international investigation. *Journal of Business Finance & Accounting,* 46(5–6), 733–766.

Intergovernmental Panel on Climate Change (IPCC). (2018). Global warming of 1.5°C. https://www.ipcc.ch/sr15/.

Ismail, N. & Goos, M. (2019). Measuring sustainability performance in the energy sector: A critical review of current practices and their limitations. *Renewable and Sustainable Energy Reviews,* 105, 299–313.

Ivanova, A., Stauffer, A. W. & Koppell, J. G. (2021). Toward a new orthodoxy? Insights from the Danish green growth model. *Global Environmental Politics,* 21(2), 99–122.

Jones, M. L., Mitchell, C. & Wiese, K. (2019). The development of Ørsted's business model from oil and gas to offshore wind energy. *Energy Policy,* 134, 11–26.

Kapoor, A., & Kulshrestha, N. (2019). Social license to operate in the energy sector: A systematic review of the literature. *Energy Policy,* 132, 1370–1382.

Kendrick, T. & Warr, B. (2018). Capacity development in renewable energy projects: Insights from international experience. *Renewable and Sustainable Energy Reviews,* 91, 168–178.

Khan, M. S. & Serafeim, G. (2020). Corporate environmental management and credit risk. *Journal of Financial Economics,* 135(3), 704–724.

Khan, M. S., Serafeim, G. & Yoon, A. (2018). Corporate sustainability: First evidence on materiality. *The Accounting Review,* 93(3), 323–351.

Kneip, A. (2019). The role of ESG rating agencies in responsible investing: An exploration. *Journal of Sustainable Finance & Investment,* 9(1), 1–19.

Kumar, N. & Prasad, D. (2020). A framework for assessing corporate environmental, social, and governance (ESG) risks in the oil and gas industry. *Sustainable Production and Consumption,* 24, 270–283.

Linnenluecke, M. K., Verreynne, M. L. & Williams, A. (2017). Corporate sustainability and organizational culture. *Journal of World Business,* 52(6), 842–857.

Lubin, D. A. (2019). Green bonds and environmental sustainability: An exploratory study. *Journal of Cleaner Production,* 228, 1559–1569.

Maddox, L. M. & Siedlok, F. (2019). Social finance as a strategic choice for sustainability-focused firms: A paradox perspective. *Journal of Business Ethics,* 156(2), 437–450.

Nguyen, D. T. & El-Mansi, M. (2020). Do environmental, social, and governance investments impact the financial performance of public utilities? Empirical evidence from the UK. *Business Strategy and the Environment,* 29(7), 3083–3096.

Park, J. H. (2020). Exploring the role of multi-stakeholder partnerships in sustainable urban development. *Sustainable Cities and Society,* 54, 10–19.

Pietz, M. (2021). Introducing a framework for ESG integration in private equity investment. *Journal of Sustainable Finance & Investment,* 11(1), 44–63.

PricewaterhouseCoopers (PwC). (2021). Sustainability and the transformation of the oil and gas industry. https://www.pwc.com/us/en/industries/oil-gas/library/sustainability-oil-gas.html.

Rudolph, T. & Dierkes, M. (2022). Sustainability-oriented corporate governance: Conceptualization and empirical evidence. *Journal of Business Ethics,* 177(3), 695–715.

Sachs, S., Rühli, E. & Schmidt, P. (2019). Determinants of corporate social responsibility disclosure: An application of stakeholder theory. *Journal of Business Ethics,* 158(1), 109–126.

Scholtens, B. & Sievänen, R. (2018). Drivers of socially responsible investing: A case study of four Nordic countries. *Journal of Business Ethics,* 151(1), 163–181.

Sorrell, S. (2021). Addressing the challenges of energy and climate governance: Insights from a global survey. *Energy Policy,* 148, 11–19.

Todorovic, N. (2021). Corporate governance in the oil and gas industry: A review of the literature and a research agenda. *Journal of World Business,* 56(3), 10–19.

Tran, T. N., Kizilcec, R. & Gunther, R. (2018). Enel and the New Utility: From traditional electricity to renewable energy. *Stanford Graduate School of Business Case GS-82.* https://www.sbs.ox.ac.uk/sites/default/files/2021–04/Enel-Case-Study.pdf.

UN Environment Programme (UNEP). (2019). Water for sustainable development. https://www.unep.org/resources/report/water-sustainable-development.

Venghaus, J., Maciejewski, M. & Roithmayr, F. (2021). Institutional perspectives on overcoming sustainable energy development dilemmas in different regions. *Energy Policy,* 153, 112–118.

Vidal, M. A. & Marques, A. (2019). Environmental, social, and governance integration in energy investment decision-making. *Energy,* 176, 1147–1157.

Viganò, L., Tschopp, D. & Andrikopoulos, A. (2021). Big data and ESG investing: A systematic review of the literature. *Finance Research Letters,* 41, 10–18.

Viganò, L., Tschopp, D. & Andrikopoulos, A. (2021). In the eye of the beholder: How socially responsible investing affects asset allocation. *Journal of Financial Markets,* 57, 10–15.

Index

D

E

V

W

Z

For Product Safety Concerns and Information please contact our EU representative GPSR@taylorandfrancis.com
Taylor & Francis Verlag GmbH, Kaufingerstraße 24, 80331 München, Germany

www.ingramcontent.com/pod-product-compliance
Lightning Source LLC
LaVergne TN
LVHW020627300926
849161LV00004B/628
9781779643391